THE ART OF
COMPELLING
FICTION

THE ART OF
COMPELLING
FICTION

CHRISTOPHER T. LELAND

STORY PRESS
CINCINNATI, OHIO

The Art of Compelling Fiction. Copyright © 1998 by Christopher T. Leland. Printed and bound in the United States of America. All rights reserved. No part of this book may be reproduced in any form or by any electronic or mechanical means including information storage and retrieval systems without permission in writing from the publisher, except by a reviewer, who may quote brief passages in a review. Published by Story Press, an imprint of F&W Publications, Inc., 1507 Dana Avenue, Cincinnati, Ohio 45207. (800) 289-0963. First edition.

Story Press Books are available from your local bookstore or direct from the publisher.

02 01 00 99 98   5 4 3 2 1

Library of Congress Cataloging-in-Publication Data

Leland, Christopher T.
    The art of compelling fiction / Christopher T. Leland.
        p.   cm.
    Includes index.
    ISBN 1-884910-30-0 (alk. paper)
    1. Fiction—Authorship. 2. Fiction—Technique. I. Title.
PN3355.L376   1998
808.3—dc21   97-45986
                                                                    CIP

Designed by Clare Finney
Cover illustration copyright © Celia Johnson/SIS

For Diana and Milly

ACKNOWLEDGMENTS

Special thanks to those from whom I have learned, as both student and colleague: Darcy and Dick; my fellows at the Warren College Writing Program; Monroe, Mary, Jonathan and Michael; Anne, Chris, Mike, Anca, Bill and Steve.

I owe a great debt to those who have studied fiction with me over the years. Teaching is reciprocal, and I have learned at least as much from them as they have from me. What is most useful in this volume is the result of their insights and labors, not mine.

And as always, for Osvaldo, whose love and patience make anything possible.

CONTENTS

INTRODUCTION

Literature is an act of collusion. Reader and writer engage in a conspiracy, and through the imperfect system of language, the two cooperate to make a world. Thus, we can accompany Dante as he enters the frozen heart of hell, or drift idyllically with Huck and Jim down the Mississippi, momentarily free of the ugliness of race and class and history, joined to some deeper truth of love.

As our title indicates, we are especially interested in what makes a story or novel compelling. All of us know texts that seem perfectly adequate, ones with solid plots, realized characters, competent writing, that still somehow fail to grab us. Many's the time I have been reading a book when something came up: a visit from an old friend, a plumbing emergency, a nasty assault by the flu. In some cases, I've fought myself out of a feverish haze to keep reading or spent the weekend hoping the unexpected guest would decide on a nice, hot bath or call it quits early one evening so I could squeeze in another chapter. In other instances, however, I've never picked up the book again. Whatever its virtues, it did not *compel* me to finish it.

Part of this may be individual. There's no explaining taste, after all. Readers look for different things in the books they take from the shelves, as I'll discuss in chapter one. Nonetheless, by playing with the way a story is structured or a character presented, a writer can transform an able story into a compelling one, a story that a wide (or wider) range of readers will find both intriguing and unforgettable.

In what follows, I talk about relatively traditional elements in the writer's bag of tricks—style, diction, plot, character. I present selections from various published texts to exemplify issues while also making considerable reference to certain "prototexts," stories that don't really exist, but serve to illustrate particular principles or methodologies. I deal mostly with fiction that broadly fits within the traditions of realism and romance. What is not much discussed is the experimental or avant garde, though bear in mind that what seemed wildly innovative writing fifty or a hundred years ago has become commonplace today. I do not investigate radical variants in form—in part because of my belief that it is wise to first master the conventional modes of any art before one goes about breaking those modes apart.

This book is intended as an adventure. It is not intended to be "right." What is praised here may not work for you. What your story or novel ought to do may be exactly opposite what is set forth on these pages. But that, as you probably already know, can be valuable. We learn by both positive and negative example.

This is a loose-limbed text: anecdotal, sometimes chatty and determined to be open and friendly. When things are not going your way, writing can be a pretty glum business, so it's worth remembering that this is supposed to be pleasurable exercise, not a catechism class. Creating fiction—and learning to create more compelling fiction—should be a source of enjoyment, not a chore.

I want to help you, as writer, develop a consciousness of audience without betraying your artistic standards and principles. You want to write the text that will make the reader read—through lunch, on the subway, in the parking lot, at every spare moment, breathless to discover what happens, who is the villain or hero, why this comedy or catastrophe has befallen these people whom your readers are helping you create in their own heads.

In the end, your goal is not to write like me or John Irving or T. Coraghessan Boyle or anyone else. It is, rather, to write like yourself. You can learn from Irving and Boyle, not to mention Shakespeare and Milton and Virginia Woolf and Mario Vargas Llosa. But the work will ultimately be your own. It will succeed or fail on the basis of what you bring to it.

Above all else, your fiction must be true, meaning that it must be "honest." Then, whether you sell a thousand copies or a million, you know you have done what you intended: to touch the lives of your readers, make some infinitesimal difference. There is no greater reward for a writer than receiving the unsolicited letter from Oshkosh or Amarillo that tells you: "You moved me," "You told me exactly what it was like," "I knew precisely what you were talking about, and thank you."

Remember that. We who write all want to be rich and famous and featured in *People* or *The New York Times Book Review*. Most of us won't achieve these, but we can achieve connection with those individual readers into whose lives our stories have integrated themselves, and so attain new life among those we will never meet.

ONE

WRITERS AND READERS

The act of creation is a mysterious thing.

This holds as true for writing as for any other art or invention. Ever since humanity settled down and got comfy in caves, the species has been leaving tracks, footprints of its presence, to fulfill functions not immediately practical. The drawings of the hunt at *le grotte de Lascaux* in France, the outlines of hands that cover the rocky walls of Altamira in Spain may have had some magical significance, but they were also a way for our primitive ancestors to say, "We were here."

Our notions of where storytelling began are vague. Before written language, the legends and myths that sustained civilizations were passed down orally, and what is transmitted orally is by definition ephemeral and mutable. Think of the game "telephone" you might have played when you were in junior high school, in which six or eight people sit in a circle and whisper a piece of information ear to ear. The words spoken aloud by the eighth person are different—sometimes subtly, sometimes radically—from those the first person transmitted to the second. In the retelling, inevitably, there are mis-cues, misunderstandings, deformations, just as there are in the gossip you picked up yesterday about someone at the office.

Beyond that, of course, a culture's values and ideas change, so its stories may be transmuted to serve new ends. It was only long after people began to settle in cities that the Egyptians came up with their hieroglyphics, the Sumerians their cuneiform, the Chinese their ideo-graphs, and that finally the Phoenicians invented and the Greeks per-fected the alphabet, and so we were able to read *The Book of the Dead* or *Gilgamesh* or Plato's philosophy or, for that matter, the Bible. Even then, the same tale might be set down one way by one generation and in quite a different way by its great-great-grandchildren. You need look no further than the first two chapters of Genesis to see this. There, God seems to create the universe not once but twice. The first version in Genesis 1:1 to 2:4a probably dates from the seventh century B.C., while 2:4b to 2:24 represent an older tradition from some three hundred years earlier. These differ radically in tone, in sequence of events, in ideology, in the characterization not only of man, but of God.

Anthropologists have observed cultures in South American jungles, Africa and the islands of the Pacific that are not so different from those of our preliterate forebears. Among these peoples in our own century, we find that, virtually without exception, bards or shamans or priests tell stories that try to answer the same three questions: Where did we come from? Where are we going? What is happening to us now?

The contemporary reader may seem sophisticated, but the distance between her and the Melanesian woman squatting beside a fire with a baby at her breast, listening to an elder repeat the tribal tale of human origins, is not as great as we might believe. Even in a country as large and diverse as the United States, writers strive to tell us who we are, how we came to be that way, what this means, how we are changing and what this will mean tomorrow or the next day. If you doubt this, look to Russell Banks' novel *Continental Drift*. Its parallel stories of immigrants to Florida from New Hampshire and from Haiti finally end in catastrophic collision, but in so doing they help us understand the dialectic nature of American history itself, its eddies and currents, the rise and fall of its peoples and the world of the mid-1980s.

As a writer, always remember that this is the task you have taken on. Even in an age of dwindling readership, when we seriously discuss whether the novel is dead, the writer is or should strive to be the bard of the tribe, vast though that tribe may be. The writer is the one who explains the present, taps the past and dreams the future.

WHAT DO READERS WANT?

That's all very nice, you say, but I don't know that I'm quite ready to take on the role of Homer, and it's not entirely clear to me how Stephen King or Elmore Leonard or Barbara Cartland (to name but three exceedingly popular authors of the end of the twentieth century) are explaining to the American tribe its origins and destinies. Such reservations are fair enough, though, as we'll see, even these more committedly commercial authors may be saying more than they appear to.

Given the large and overlapping reading publics that exist today, a legitimate question from a writer is, What do readers want? This may ring a little desperate, as did Sigmund Freud's famous and frustrated "What does woman want," but, in very broad terms, we can delineate some of the motivations readers have to read books. What makes a book a page-turner for one person and not another? What compels me to stay up till 4 A.M. to finish a novel that you're perfectly content to peruse for forty minutes each day on your commute? Part, but only part, of the answer lies in what your audience is seeking in the act of reading.

But Enough About You

Perhaps the most obvious demand a reader can make is "Tell me about me." People like to see themselves in fiction. They want to encounter situations that parallel those they are familiar with; and, at best, find ways to deal with their own problems through the resolutions characters achieve. Writers are not therapists, but in their delvings into the human heart they often reveal certain truths or insights that bring comfort to a reader or provide, for lack of a better term, a new "angle" on a situation the reader finds himself confronted with. Certainly, writers of adolescent fiction—such as Judy Blume or S.E. Hinton—consciously undertake this in their explorations of growing up and its endless worries and challenges: pregnancy, peer pressure, gangs, uncomprehending (and incomprehensible) parents. Their stories allow readers to get a clearer picture of themselves by providing the context of a recognizable world—populated with figures similar to those they know, but different—in which the readers can see familiar problems resolved.

In the mid-1990s, Terry McMillan's novel *Waiting to Exhale* enjoyed tremendous success, first as a book and later as a film, to the happy surprise of both publishers and filmmakers. In retrospect, the story's popularity is not so difficult to explain. The novel focuses on the friendship and the various tribulations of four African-American professional women in their thirties. If you review fiction of the last decade or so, it's not easy to find another novel centered on that group of people and their particular experiences. In describing the joys and difficulties of her characters' lives, McMillan told her readers about themselves—a phenomenon that rippled out in ever wider circles. If the obvious, initial audience was African-American women in their thirties, the book also appealed to women in their thirties, women in general, African-Americans in general and so on.

To take another example, it's argued that the explosion over the last decade and a half of novels and stories directed primarily at gay and Lesbian readers is explicable, in part, by the fact that this subset of the population so rarely sees its stories represented in any other medium. For a variety of reasons—economic, political and social—television and film shy away from the presentation of multifaceted homosexual characters, and so this audience must seek its reflection in fiction. A number of major publishing houses in New York City now have some sort of "gay imprint" (Stonewall Inn Editions, Plume), and many smaller houses (Alyson, Gay Sunshine Press) thrive by specializing in this market.

That said, remember that while individual authors may direct their work at very specific markets, a fiction should, at best, transcend its particular niche and appeal more broadly, humanly, to a larger audience. This is what happened with McMillan's novel, and with Edmund White's *A Boy's Own Story* of 1982. The latter was, on the one hand, consciously a portrait of the upper-middle-class adolescence of a gay teenage boy in the 1950s. However, White's novel is not merely about being gay. It is about being a teenager, about being a child of divorced and competing parents, about the peaks and valleys he experiences in trying to figure out the manifold complexities of the universe of adults.

In sum, it is a bildungsroman, as the literary critics say, a novel of growing up, a staple of fiction since the eighteenth century. If it is distinctive because its protagonist is homosexual, it is as well part of a long tradition. Decades after first publication, readers still lose themselves in *Little Women, Huckleberry Finn*, Thomas Wolfe's *Look Homeward, Angel* and J.D. Salinger's *The Catcher in the Rye*. Despite the fact that a contemporary sixteen-year-old is unlikely to find himself floating down the mighty Mississippi or holed up in a Manhattan hotel, the desire for freedom, the angst of confronting that mysterious realm of adults or the dream of a complex but still comforting and peaceful family and society speak as powerfully to him as they did to readers in 1870 or 1930 or 1957. Though he may not come from as wild and woolly a family as Wolfe's Eugene Gant, our reader can identify with the character's feelings of frustration and loneliness. Though, we hope, he will avoid the madness that finally consumes Holden Caulfield, he can feel Holden's pain and dreams viscerally. They may be different in the details from his own, but Salinger, like Wolfe, Alcott and White, has captured the emotions of adolescence in such a way that the reader can identify them, be they the reader's present feelings or those of a man recollecting them as he sits now, at fifty, to reread these texts once again.

Why would he do so? Perhaps because those texts help tell him "where he came from." The experience of the new reading will doubtless be different from his first, motivated by different desires. But it can indeed be as intense, as *compelled*, as it was thirty-five years before.

Escape

Just as a reader may say to an author, "Tell me about myself," so she may say, "Help me escape myself." One of literature's great and traditional functions is to conjure up glittering people and faraway places that help us momentarily put aside the drudgery of the everyday world. As far back as the Romans, we have examples of romances—tales of love and adventure that come to a happy ending—laboriously copied by hand on papyrus. This kind of story weaves its way through history up to the present day. Modern fiction owes its existence to these narratives. What many define as the first novel as we know it is Miguel de Cervantes' *Don Quijote*, whose hero is hopelessly addicted to, and hopelessly addled by, the tales of chivalrous derring-do that were immensely popular throughout Europe in the fifteenth and sixteenth centuries.

It may seem quite a ways from Cervantes to Danielle Steel and Barbara Cartland, to Tom Clancy and Stephen King. Yet, once again, the distance is not quite so great as it seems. Melville's earliest and most successful novels—*Typee, Omoo, White Jacket*—were stories of the sea, of raging storms, narrow escapes and idyllic South Sea islands. Robert Louis Stevenson, H. Rider Haggard and Jack London all strove to be (and often were) the best-sellers of their days. Louisa May Alcott wrote some surprisingly lurid mysteries and love stories along with her better-known novels of New England family life, and even William Faulkner quite self-consciously set out to write a truly sensationalist (some would argue quasi-pornographic) book when, after the disappointing sales of *The Sound and the Fury*, he put pen to paper to create *Sanctuary*.

Escapist fiction can, on the surface, differ wildly. It may be hard to see how a Horatio Alger "boy's book" of "luck and pluck" (which was actually an Alger title), a horror story by Stephen King, a mystery by Agatha Christie, a tale of deception and adultery among the rich and famous by Judith Krantz and a semigothic romance such as Victoria Holt's *The Mistress of Mellyn* can have anything in common. Yet all involve stories of adversity overcome. They almost inevitably end heroically. These are, in the classical sense, comedies, not in that they are funny, but in that they end with the world set right again. A romance novel by Cartland and her endless cohorts closes with marriage, the feast scene that Greeks, Romans and Elizabethans saw as the sign of a harmonious universe. Mysteries show us situations in which the legitimate order of things is disrupted and solving the case implies the restoration of that order: God's back in his heaven, all's right with the world.

Even the horror story, born of legend and fairy tale, of religious faith and fear of the devil, follows this pattern, though the contemporary writer of such stories oftentimes leaves the door slightly ajar at the conclusion. This is not only because it provides the happy option of a sequel should the book be a success, but it relates too to our bloody century's suspicion that evil is not something so easily dispensed with. King, with his demons bursting forth in a recognizable America of high school proms and fast cars and Cokes and fries at McDonald's, is a master of leaving his reader with the threat that what has been loosed upon suburbia is only in temporary abeyance.

Getting to Know the Other

The kind of fiction just discussed is closely related to a third variety, one that often, in its general outline, is not easily distinguished from its more popular comic kin. We might call this the fiction of otherness: It appeals to the reader not primarily because it allows him to escape his own reality, but because it explains to him other realities, or creates them of the whole cloth. This category is broad indeed, for otherness may be found in a person, a place, a time, a geography. It can be self-consciously informative or educational. The obvious examples are most of the novels of James Michener, including *Hawaii*, *Texas*, *Poland*, which combine epic events with a great deal of data regarding history, ethnography, customs, sociology and so on. If, on the one hand, this author's model is *War and Peace*, the other is the fictionalized biography of Davy Crockett or Queen Liliuokalani of his youth.

Many more consciously literary fictions, however, employ historical settings to tell us about other times and places, but at the same time they make us recognize ourselves, one way or another, in a world that seems so vastly different. The South African Mary Renault wrote highly literate novels set in ancient Greece or in the courts of Alexander the Great and his Hellenistic successors, stories that not only evoke for us an exotic and lost world of privilege and luxury, but also demonstrate how those peoples of long ago—in their lusts and loves and enmities—were often remarkably like our modern selves. The great writers of the American South—Faulkner, Eudora Welty, Robert Penn Warren—return again and again to the antebellum world of slavery, the bloodbath of the Civil War and the chaos of Reconstruction not only to find out where Southerners came from, but also to attempt to explain and comprehend the great and ever-present conundrum of American society, that of racial conflict.

Otherness can be established not only by a different time, but also by a different place. Certainly, no American seriously interested in the realities of contemporary Colombia or of Latin America in general can escape reading Gabriel García Márquez's *One Hundred Years of Solitude*, nor can she get a better grip on the difference of the world of North Africa—and our ultimate Western incomprehension of it—than in the novels and stories of the American expatriate Paul Bowles. Such writers, perhaps, are all related to the Joseph Conrad of *Heart of Darkness*. Their fictions, rather than reassuring us as escapist novels do, discomfit us, teach us not that the world is pretty much the same, but that it is a diverse and sometimes incomprehensible place, one that is often beautiful, one we can sometimes recognize, but one that is often frightening and dangerous.

Such difference is not limited to locale. Yet another manifestation of reader interest in otherness may be found in characters. Victor Hugo brings us the deformed but ultimately heroic Quasimodo in *The*

Hunchback of Notre Dame; Forrest Gump—simple-minded but sound of heart—became a kind of folk hero of the early '90s. Beyond this, in the last couple of decades, we have seen a plethora of true crime books, which attempt, one way or another, to explain the apparently inexplicable: serial killers, infanticides and so on. We should remember, however, that many of these books can trace their origins, first of all, to books defined by their own authors as nonfiction novels: Truman Capote's *In Cold Blood* and Norman Mailer's *The Executioner's Song*. Both these men made their reputations as writers of fiction, and both employed in these real stories of senseless violence all the tools of the novelist's trade. The cases they were dealing with actually occurred, but the psychological insight they brought to the living individuals they were writing about were, I would suggest, precisely the kind that the fiction writer brings to bear when he sets out to create any character who is not overtly the persona—the autobiographical image—of the author.

Readers often want to understand the minds of murderers, of politicians, of soldiers, of saints, of all those people they are not and will never be. And you, as writer, with research and the will and, most of all, the imagination, can bring this to them. Fyodor Dostoevsky did not have to kill someone to create his Raskolnikov in *Crime and Punishment*, nor did Gustave Flaubert have to be an adulterous Frenchwoman of the middle orders to give us Madame Bovary. The latter, however, did say, *"Madame Bovary, c'est moi"*—"I *am* Madame Bovary." Her psychology, her moral blindness, her personality were, indeed, there somewhere inside the French writer, and out of himself, he gave her life and then gave her to us.

There are genres, of course, where otherness is all, or at least apparently so. These are science fiction and fantasy. In these fictions, the author is free to invent everything, not just characters and situations, but even customs, flora and fauna and systems of time. It has been my experience in workshops that those who write science fiction or fantasy, certainly among the most imaginative of genres, don't trust their imaginations enough. There is too little new about the worlds created. Often, we end up reading about various technologies, about machines, rather than about people and the lives they lead in brave new worlds.

For an example of just how other a fictional world can be, have a look at Samuel Delany's *Stars in My Pocket Like Grains of Sand*. There is a point where it appears that the inhabitants of a particular planet to which we have just been introduced are continually changing gender. A person referred to as "she" by three others is suddenly referred to as "he" by a fourth. What is soon explained to us, however, is that, in this world, pronouns indicate not gender, but the degree of emotional involvement one character has with another. Hence, the beloved, whether man or woman, is always "he," while all other people are "she." Delany does not limit himself to taking us to "warp 4." Rather, he imagines a world in which something we take for granted—that pronouns are gender specific—cannot be assumed. He shows us that in another world, in another system of thinking or language, pronouns might be determined by something very different from what we're used to.

It's the Same Old Story

Some readers want to be taken out of this world to hear of people and places never thought of. Others simply want to hear an old, familiar tale. Remember how as a child you often preferred the same bedtime story again and again? You could make the argument that those addicted to a particular genre—romance readers or thriller readers or mystery readers—are simply consuming the same work again: different in its particulars but essentially identical in its broad outline. Cinderella's prince arrives; the plot to blow up the world is foiled; the murderer is revealed. As I'll discuss in upcoming chapters, there are certain plots that seem to emerge repeatedly in literary fiction. The prodigal son; the patient wife; the apprenticeship of a youth to an older, wiser man; tales of journey and quest—we see these over and over in literature from around the world. Arthur Laurents' script for the musical *West Side Story* was self-consciously derived from Shakespeare's *Romeo and Juliet*, but it was hardly the first work to play a variation on feuding families and lovers who get together against all odds, and it will certainly not be the last. The image of the bumpkin just arrived in the metropolis has provided equal inspiration for Elizabethans, Victorians and contemporary Americans. The journey to exotic lands goes back at least as far as *The Odyssey*, is found again in *The Seven Voyages of Sinbad* and is with us still in as modern a novel as Paul Theroux's *The Mosquito Coast*.

I could continue indefinitely here, inventing and refining new categories of literary endeavor, but for the present, this should suffice. What you need to consider is the tremendous variety of purposes fiction can serve, and then, before your own work, ask where yours fits in, what it does to give readers of a particular type what they seek.

WHAT CAN WRITERS DO?

So, if we now know at least some of the things readers *want* in a text, what can writers—and you specifically—do about it? First, ask yourself a couple of basic questions: Why do you read? and Why do you write?

Why Do You Read?

As regards the first question, the answer may not be the key in understanding precisely what kind of fictions you ought to create, but it will give you an idea of where your interests lie. For example, you may be a great fan of mysteries but find you are not a capable practitioner of the genre. Fine mystery writing is a complicated skill, one that requires considerable practice. Beyond this, it may presume a certain kind of intelligence, a mind that possesses an almost mathematical precision, which many of us are not endowed with. Still, your taste for mysteries may indicate something else about you as writer—an interest in the problem of evil, or in conflict resolved, or in the simple discovery of truth—that you can put to good use in stories that themselves do not center on murder and mayhem, but on the complexities of everyday life. We often casually remark that somebody's behavior in a particular situation is peculiar. Certainly you've heard your mother say, "Why Martha ever married Frank is a mystery to me." Quotidian experience can be quite as tantalizingly complicated and rife with apparently inexplicable motives as anything you find on the police blotter.

Still, your own tastes in reading are likely to indicate the direction your own fiction should go. Raymond Chandler or Margaret Atwood or Bret Easton Ellis *speaks* to your imagination in a particular way, and hence it is likely, though not certain, that your imagination itself wishes to speak in a similar manner. Imitation remains the sincerest form of flattery, and there is no writer, even the greatest of them, who has not been influenced—often consciously so—by those who came before her. Shakespeare, after all, was building on the foundations of English drama laid by his near contemporaries Thomas Kyd and Christopher Marlowe, who themselves were combining influences of Roman theater on the one hand and that which had arisen from church pageants on the other. Likewise, there is a line that runs from Marlowe's play *Dr. Faustus* to our first great novel of science gone awry, Mary Shelley's *Frankenstein*, to Michael Crichton's *Jurassic Park*. The disillusion of the novelists of World War I—Erich Maria Remarque, Ernest Hemingway—paved the way for the dark fiction to emerge from the next great war, that of Norman Mailer and James Jones, which in turn provided models for the bleak evocations of Vietnam in the work of Tim O'Brien and John Del Vecchio.

This issue is one to which I will return in the next chapter, as I discuss where we find our material when writing. For the moment, simply consider that what you feel compelled to read may be a good guide to the kind of fiction you can produce that will compel another reader to pick up your text.

Why Do You Write?

Even more basic is that second question: Why do you write? Against all odds, why do some of us feel compelled to put pen to paper, fingers to keyboard, and try to communicate feelings and characters and situations to others? The choice of the verb there was not accidental, for, after twenty years of workshops, I have pretty much concluded—and this is certainly not an original notion—that writing *is* a compulsion. The way you *know* you're a writer is that you cannot *not* write. You may take breaks, that is, you may not type out a new story for a year or two, but inevitably you sit down and do it, again and again.

This does not necessarily mean, sad to say, you're a good writer. I have known many cases of people of obvious talent who, when it came down to it, walked away from writing fiction with perhaps a shiver of regret, but little more, and found their personal realization elsewhere. Likewise, I have had those who really did have that "fire in the belly," but who were, frankly, not very able or imaginative. They wrote and wrote, and yet what they had to say was not especially interesting or compelling. With these, I continue to hope that something will change in their lives that will free up their creativity and allow them to tap the real stories they have to tell.

For example, some years back, I had a man in a workshop who obviously had a fine family novel in him. However, despite my proddings, he wrote in just about every genre you can think of but avoided absolutely anything associated with his own experience. I came to believe that, with the passage of time, perhaps only after the death of his parents, he would actually be able to write the book it seemed so apparent he needed to, but there was nothing particular that could be done to extract that text from him till then.

In considering your own experience, you should try to determine what is both unique and universal about it. More than ten years ago, I was teaching at a university in the Ivy League where entrance into the creative writing workshops was competitive. Each September and January, another novelist and I would confront a stack of 150 to 350 stories and try, in three or four days, to winnow from those the sixty students we would admit to the workshops. For three terms in a row, there was a submission from one young man about "The Old West." The story was awful: stilted in language, clumsy in plot, devoid of characterization. To this day, I still remember the name of the protagonist (though I won't mention it here)—one of the most cartoonish heroes ever to grace any pages I've read.

After having failed three times to get into the course, the author of the piece came to see me. He wasn't sullen or angry, but perplexed and hurt. I tried to be gentler than I was in the preceding paragraph and eventually nursed the conversation in the direction of where he was from, what he liked to do, who he was. He was the son of immigrants and had grown up in a once flourishing, now crumbling industrial town of the East. As we talked, he told of a trip back to the Old Country to see his grandmother, mentioned something about a pair of her earrings she had given him as a present and described a lush, tropical world that contrasted starkly with the drab, seaside town whence he came. I finally said, "But why don't you write about that?"

He looked at me, genuinely bewildered, and said, "But nobody would be interested in that!"

This is not an uncommon response. What sounded to me exotic and intriguing and moving—a boy discovering his roots, as it were; discovering a world he might have been part of but was not and could not be; that gift so inappropriate and yet so right—seemed to the student common and unexceptional. For most of us, what we actually live strikes us as, simply, life, our own dull little existence that nobody else would particularly want to hear about.

What this student needed to do, and what might also be useful for you, is to try to defamiliarize yourself a bit with your own experience. Take a step back and reconsider your growing up, for example. Was yours quite the big, happy family you imagined it to be? How was it like and different from the big, happy families next door or across the street? Try to recollect what made your family distinctive. This can sometimes be a little painful, as we come to recognize the failings of those we love or of our own selves, or remember traumas or disappointments we put behind us long ago. Mom did have a tendency to tipple in the afternoons; Dad was kind of cool and distant. Big brother, Will, really was the family favorite, and you yourself were a perfect pill of an adolescent. In this process, you may come to the conclusion your family was somehow dysfunctional. Don't be too concerned. Does anybody talk about functional families? Leo Tolstoy, the Russian novelist, probably had it right over a hundred years ago in the first line of his *Anna Karenina*: "All happy families resemble one other. Each unhappy family is unhappy in its own way." That distinctiveness of unhappiness, I might assert, is what makes a family interesting.

What goes for your childhood goes for the rest of your experience, including your present-day life. Look around yourself with analytical eyes, as if you were viewing not your own world, but that of someone else. You will—inevitably, I would say—discover that there are elements that are truly universal and truly unique. There will be certain aspects, if only you can get the perspective, that you will recognize as both—universal in general outline but obviously unique in the details and nuances.

With that student just mentioned, the return to the world of his past, of his ancestors, was certainly a common experience or dream for virtually all Americans, most all of us finally the children of immigrants and a people, in any case, in almost constant motion—moving here, moving there, relocating for reasons of school or job or simple desire. We're all from someplace else. But the specific details of my student's specific journey to a specific old country were distinctive. His own trip to a foreign land, his meeting with his grandmother, her gift to him of a pair of earrings she had been given by his long-dead grandfather (pretty impractical in those days before such jewelry on men was common as it is now)—these were details that made his story different from all other stories about such explorations of our roots.

The following term he submitted a story about that trip and those earrings.

He made the cut.

EVALUATING YOUR OWN WORK

One of the most difficult things for any writer, for any artist, perhaps for any individual, is to be objective about her own work. Obviously, with something we have devoted real effort to, something we've created, something we've given not only our time and labor but (we often feel) our hearts and souls, making judgments (especially negative ones) can be difficult. Your stories are a bit like children, and we know how difficult it can be for parents to admit some failing in their offspring.

Though it's hard, getting some distance on your work is extraordinarily important. One of the easiest ways to do this is simply with time. In workshops, I generally ask that writers *not* revise stories they've already presented to the group and use them for later presentations. The reason is simple. I do not think that in three months the author is far enough away from the original, grueling creation of a piece to go back and make judgments about its revision. In critique, he has probably received a dozen worthy, often contradictory suggestions as to how the story might be improved. Only with time will he be able to evaluate which of those suggestions is truly useful to him, which jibe with his particular, perhaps unconscious, concept of the story and what it is to do.

The Inventory

There are, in addition, exercises that may be useful to you here at the beginning of your career that involve your entire corpus, of which the inventory is perhaps the most important. Take out all the fiction you've written, read through it in a relatively short period of time, and then, as objectively as you can, make a list evaluating each story's particular strengths and weaknesses. What you're likely to find is that you're consistently strong in certain areas and less so in others.

It's not unusual, for example, for men to discover that their male characters have dimension and faceted personalities and their female characters seem flat and predictable. This comes as no particular surprise. We all likely feel more confident of our comprehension of our own gender than of the other, and we live in a culture in which, despite changes in the last couple of decades, it is still men who wield most of the power and influence. Hence, understanding male psychology is something both men and women strive to accomplish.

To take another more stylistic example: Is there dialogue? A lot? None? With any given story, it's hard to say if the dialogue is too much, too little or just right, but do you note, for example, that you *never* employ dialogue or do so only in a real pinch? Read the verbal exchanges aloud (or perhaps even better, have a friend or two read them back and forth while you just listen). Do the words have the feel of real speech? Writing is both an art and a skill, and though it may be true that the sparkling repartee of a writer such as Oscar Wilde is simply the product of genius, you can, with attention and effort, develop a capacity to reproduce the rhythms and quirks of speech.

Invent as many areas of critique as you can that relate to plot, characterization, style and so on. Make your inventory, let it sit for a few days, then read your work again and make a separate inventory. Compare the new one with the earlier one. Stepping back from your own texts is no easy feat. You may want to repeat this process a third time, say, in the course of a month. Often, you'll find your lists don't entirely correlate, meaning you failed to notice in your first reading that, for example, you have an addiction (this is true in my case, at least) to adjectives in triads ("cold and depthless and still," "beaten, bloodied, hopeless"). In addition, something may have bothered you on your first read-through that on the third no longer seemed a problem. It may not be, though you should ask yourself if your initial impression was, in fact, correct.

By the time this process is finished (and note that you *do* have to repeat it at least once), you should have some notion of where your fiction is working and where it needs a little help. Though we like to think of ourselves as possessed by demons of creativity, plunging forward on wings of inspiration, there is a great deal in the act of writing that is entirely self-conscious. While many great and enduring texts remain in some inexplicable, mystical way "gifts" to their authors, much of what we do is craft, and craft, by definition, is something you can improve on.

Phil's Case

Let's take an imaginary writer, Phil, who has written six or seven stories and has spent the last month or so "taking inventory." I realize this sounds like one of those driver's education films you saw in high school, but bear with me. Phil is twenty-eight, single, a bit of a swinger in a lower executive position at one of the major banks in the Miami suburb where he lives. His prospects in his job are bright, and he's generally content, though he does think back a bit nostalgically to his days in high school and junior college when he was something of a hellion, did some surfing, hung out with his buddies and worked irregularly at the local convenience store.

Those experiences tend to be the ones from which he's derived those stories he's written. Now, having reviewed them, he's come up with the following list of twelve elements, these having been winnowed from twenty-five or thirty queries he made to himself after rereading his work. These aren't the only ups and downs he found in his fiction, but rather, those that seem most notable. He'll keep the inventories filed away for future reference so when he repeats this process in a year or so, he can see if there are other areas he might consider polishing.

This is a good strategy. We can all, in paroxysms of self-criticism, come up with so many things "wrong" that we ultimately paralyze ourselves. In Edward Gorey's *The Unstrung Harp: or, Mr. Earbrass Writes a Novel*, our poor protagonist, deep into his new opus, makes the mistake of rereading it and finds it "Dreadful. Dreadful. Dreadful." Certainly, any author has had the experience of writing that key scene at 2 A.M. and finding it breathtaking, reading it at 2 P.M. the next day and finding it absolutely shallow and stupid, and reading it a week later and seeing that it has its obvious virtues but could use a little buffing here and there.

Allow for the fact that most of us are not geniuses. It may be that Gioacchino Rossini, the composer, was so brilliant (and so lazy) that when he was writing operas in bed, if an unfinished page accidentally fell to the floor, he would simply write a new one rather than retrieve the one he had been working on. But neither you nor I, I suspect, is quite that clever. Be hard on yourself, but also take into account that learning to do anything is a process, that a chess master becomes one by playing a lot of chess, that a fashion designer throws away a lot more sketches than he keeps. In reviewing an inventory, select a half dozen elements you feel confident about, and a half dozen you feel are in need of some attention.

Here is Phil's list.

Strengths	Problems
• Powerful action sequences	• "Busy" stories with too much happening too fast
• Vivid descriptions	• Too much description? Does this slow the story needlessly?
• Complex protagonists	• Are all my heroes the same guy?
• Good dialogue	• A lack of female characters; and those present too vague
• Good pacing (though see note re: description)	• Stories tend to be pretty long
• I like the "feel" of these pieces; their view of the world as difficult but finally one a person can, if not conquer, adjust to while still keeping his integrity.	• Is the adjustment pretty much identical in all the stories?

You can see that Phil has found six pluses and six minuses regarding the six stories he's written. Yet it is a bit more involved than that. Phil feels he writes good dialogue. He admires his protagonists and likes the ideology of his stories, the way the world is perceived. He's not entirely convinced by his female characters, however, and he senses that the stories may be a bit long-winded, which he ought to recognize as both a market problem (it's pretty difficult to place a story of more than 5,000 words anyplace) and one that indicates he may need to tighten up the prose.

This relates, obviously, to one of those ambivalent judgments he makes about his work. His descriptive passages are "vivid," and yet he wonders if he doesn't, for lack of a better term, blather on, get a bit too discursive in those paragraphs. He thinks the pacing of the stories is good, the rate at which they develop and resolve, but wonders if that might not be even better if those descriptions were a shade less elaborated, sharper and leaner.

Too, though he writes action well, he wonders if he's not in some ways giving himself a break, doing what he knows he's capable of, and so, in the end, cluttering up his pieces with too much event, undermining their impact by throwing so much activity into the fiction that the reader never gets to quite appreciate the significance of what's going on. The same holds true when he considers his protagonists. He likes his heroes and thinks they ring true, but is he writing the same individual over and over again, in a sense writing the same story again and again?

So what is to be done?

Phil's an apprentice, and he knows and accepts it. This is an important understanding. It is rare that a writer is an Arthur Rimbaud, a monster of nature who wrote his masterpiece, *A Season in Hell*, when he was still a teenager. On the basis of his inventory, Phil might well jot down the following as his next project.

> A sixty-year-old widow, Gloria, lives in an apartment in a small industrial city in New Hampshire. She goes to the market, where she bumps into Tom Frankel, who was her late husband, Mikey's, best friend. Back at the apartment, she unpacks her groceries and thinks of Tom, especially of his hands. She remembers that Mikey told her Tom was a minor league baseball pitcher, but when his father died he came home from the Toledo Mud Hens and went to work in the local mill. She thinks about Mikey back then, when both they and Tom were young, and of her forty years with her husband. She remembers how Tom's wife left him years ago. She starts cooking some Rice-a-Roni, and says to herself she really ought to have the kitchen repainted.

Hello? you say. Why should our twenty-eight-year-old, swinging ex-surfer, rising-banking-exec, Don-Johnson-*Miami-Vice*-in-reruns kind of guy write about graying and lonely Gloria in New Hampshire? Because, to put it bluntly, she's there, or rather, she's *not* there. Phil is challenging himself. He writes believable male protagonists, but his women are weak. Hence Gloria, about as different from young and never-married Phil as it's possible to be. He's afraid his descriptions are vivid but too extended, so he writes about a place he knows only vaguely from magazines and those reports on the evening news every four years in February when New Hampshire holds its primary. He sets up a strongly interior situation. He's confident he writes striking and realistic dialogue, so he creates an instance where Gloria exchanges the merest pleasantries with Tom and anybody else at the grocer's. In general, however, any dialogue that takes place is inside her own head.

Note, though, that Gloria and Phil share certain things. They both live alone, do their own shopping, are perhaps filled with a little longing to have somebody to divide that task with. Some of Phil's buddies played baseball, and he's a pretty faithful Red Sox fan himself. In other words, though he's creating characters very different from himself, he's also creating ones who, where particular elements are concerned, he can get inside of and identify with.

Phil's story may not be one he should immediately pop in the mail to *The New Yorker*. But it is one that in many ways forces him to work on what he has concluded are weaknesses in his prose: It makes him deal with a female character of a different age and background, does not allow him to coast on dialogue and action, and lets him explore his *imaginative* capacity. The fact that this may not be the finest story he's ever written is beside the point. Phil is educating himself as a writer, and perhaps, twenty years hence, in his second best-seller, Gloria will reappear as a major secondary character, a sixty-five-year-old woman who has won the state lottery and bought controlling interest in the Toledo Mud Hens as a wedding gift for her new, second husband, Tom Frankel. For now, however, Phil's simply stretching some new muscles, seeing what he can do to create a character not himself, a situation not his own.

I have, filed away, a series of pieces I wrote in my late twenties that I refer to as the California stories. They were written in the very early

'80s, when so-called minimalism was all the rage, and are quite unlike anything I've written before or since. I have the suspicion they are not very good, and I never tried very hard to publish them. I've never doubted, though, the value of having taken the time to write them. Like our invented Phil, I was trying to write in a manner I'd not attempted before, inventing an easy and a more dislocated voice than I had in most of my other writing, which, as you might expect, bore some resemblance in its strengths and weaknesses to Phil's.

Having written about Gloria, it may be time for Phil to have another look at his earlier work. Perhaps, from what he has learned in writing about a New Hampshire widow, he can bring to bear certain lessons on all those young-jocks-on-the-beach tales he produced previously. From the perspective of a man who has created something very different from them, he can tighten, rework, alter characters. Once he has seen what he can do, he's then free to make changes in what he has already done.

THE COMMUNITY OF WRITERS

I often tell people about the arrival of the edited manuscript of my first novel, *Mean Time*. I opened the envelope and there discovered the marginalia and emendations of my editor, who happened to be Toni Morrison. In glancing through the pages with their careful notations, I felt like shouting: "My baby! My baby! What have you done to my baby!"

Then, finally, I sat down and actually read the epilogue of the novel as Morrison had edited it. In those concluding pages, all she did was pencil through certain words and phrases. I got to the last two lines, which she had emended thusly: "The spring would bring flowers surely. And it would bring snakes."

I read it again, and again, and had to admit that the removal of three little words made for a more powerful and sinister conclusion. That pair of hard consonants ("deh," "keh") added emphasis to the sibilance of the word "snakes," like a hiss. The effect of a drumbeat— thump, thump—of the two-syllable sentence fragment at the end gave the book closure. There was simply no question it was better. And with that realization, I found that elsewhere in the novel Morrison's changes and queries were almost always exactly right.

This demonstrates the importance to you of a good editor, which is to say, a good audience. While writing is a solitary pastime—just you and your characters and that blank page or glowing screen—it is, finally, social. We write so that others might read. Too, readers see things in the text we may not—not just symbols or your particular authorial tics, but problems in development or characterization or expression that had not occurred to you.

It's probably useful, if you haven't done this already, to associate yourself with other writers. The ways of doing this nowadays are legion. Most all academic institutions—junior colleges, colleges, universities, extension schools, adult education programs—offer some kind of course in creative writing, and though professors may be good or bad and fellow students fine or terrible, somewhere in this mix you should be able to find a common soul. And if not, it is always worth trying again. Having taught such courses for many years, I can say that the chemistry of any single group is unpredictable. There is no way of knowing how a collection of individuals, putting their fiction on the line, will respond to each other. Some classes gel effortlessly, whereas some remain like oil and water, never commingling at all.

In addition, there are a plethora of short-term programs, often in the summer, in which writers of various levels of experience get together for a weekend or a week to read and critique each other's work. I once had something like contempt for these get-togethers, which I saw as little more than a means of separating aspiring writers from their money. But after participating in a few and, more importantly, after talking with aspiring writers who have participated in them, I have come to realize that for many people they offer a chance, as E.M. Forster said, to "connect," to find other writers who can provide that necessary and sympathetic critic and reader.

Finally, if you prefer, you can simply keep an eye out for a classified ad in your local alternative paper or a flyer at your local bookstore or literary cafe about the formation of a writers group, or you could post said flyer yourself. You may hear from one or two individuals; you may hear from a dozen. But regardless, you should be in contact with others with ambitions similar to yours, who can not only critique your work but also share with you both the exhilaration and frustrations of the writer's lot.

For the apprentice writer, such interaction is a terrific defense against the loneliness and occasional despair that is simply part of the territory. Accumulating enough rejection notices to paper your bathroom seems an exercise in masochism. Beyond this, such associations can be of use long after you have begun to make a mark as an author. I know of a novelist, winner of the National Book Award, who remains part of an informal group that has met, month to month, for the last fifteen years. She is not the only member of the circle to have enjoyed success, but all of them remain committed to the mutual support they've lent one another since they first met, all untried and unpublished, more than a decade and a half ago. This is an audience that truly knows her and knows her work. They have watched both her and it mature, and their responses to her writing are deepened by that intimacy they enjoy.

The Selfish Motives of Critique

Remember that you can learn as much or more from critiquing somebody else's efforts as you can from their critiquing yours. Again, it is a bit like looking at somebody else's child instead of the one you brought into the world. You can sort out the virtues of little Barbara and Bobby, but also see their flaws, in a way you can't quite bring yourself to with your darling Baxter. In the story of one of your colleagues, let's call her Alicia, one who has taken the time and trouble to be as honest as she can with you, you may encounter a tendency to overwrite, to employ a vocabulary, a diction, that seems inappropriate to the tale told. In talking with her about the piece, you point this out. Some time later, rereading a story of your own, you note that you yourself, from time to time, commit the same kind of error. It may be that you would have seen this particular problem eventually, but recognizing it in Alicia's work has, perhaps unconsciously, sensitized you to this issue.

A writers group or workshop can descend into a mutual admiration society, which may make everybody feel good but is not especially useful in improving anyone's prose. When dealing with the writing of others, you need to employ both seriousness and sensitivity and expect the same as regards your work. In your reservations, be firm but also be helpful. Lighting into a story, giving no quarter, merely makes the author defensive and angry. If possible, when you perceive a problem, try to suggest a way that, within the realities of the text involved, it might be dealt with. In Alicia's overwritten passages, edit them down; demonstrate how she might strengthen her story by cutting back on the high-flown language she has employed, just as, years back, Toni Morrison demonstrated to me how *Mean Time* might be improved with some judicious pruning of the prose.

IMAGINING A FUTURE

After you have made your inventory, after you have thought about and written some stories that address the particular problems you have found in your fiction so far, after you have looked back again on your earlier work, you might indulge in a bit of daydreaming. Where would you like your writing to be in ten years?

This isn't merely a question of your imagining that mansion on Maui, the Pulitzer Prize (which as a kid, I used to refer to as the Puzzler Prize, which sometimes seems more appropriate) or that Academy Award-winning film based on your stunning best-seller. Instead, what do you want to accomplish, not just in bulk but depth, within the next decade? Phil, for example, might decide that, within the next few years, he wants to write a novel—or at least one of those longer short stories he seems to specialize in—with an older, female protagonist who is the mother of one of his tanned, young protagonists. That is his goal. It may not be realized, and where his imagination takes him may be someplace else entirely. But having it in mind gives him a certain direction, permits him—in those dark nights of the soul that all writers experience, when fingers are frozen and the literary imagination seems to have gone south—to go to a project he has a certain commitment to, to a character he knows, and bring these to life.

There is one further thing every writer should be doing, something that brings us full circle here. That is reading, a topic I'll be taking up in chapter two. You should be reading a great deal, and reading promiscuously. That doesn't mean indiscriminately indulging a taste for dirty books. It means you don't limit yourself merely to a few authors or a single genre. Your ambition may be to write romances like Barbara Cartland's, and if so, it makes sense you should read work by her and by other practitioners of that kind of fiction. However, by looking at other kinds of literature—the quirky, contemporary stories of Mary Robison, for example, or the dark imaginings of the

Czech master Franz Kafka—you may learn certain lessons useful to you in the creation of your own romances or discover that your ambitions are slightly different than you thought they were.

Reading, for the writer, is education. As we learn by doing in writing, we also learn much about writing from reading the work of others. Some of this we accomplish consciously. We act like literary critics and zero in on particular elements in a story. Later, we imitate those elements in our own work. Often, however, the most valuable lessons we accrue are more general and unconscious. Consuming a variety of works by well-established authors will help you better grasp the complexities of character development or the best means of pacing a story, though you may not be aware you're absorbing this information at the time.

Don't feel such lessons are only in the classics. Popular fiction, too, has much to teach, and work by contemporary writers can be just as educational as that of authors long dead. The point is to expose yourself to as broad a spectrum of writing as possible, to writers whose work resembles yours and writers whose work doesn't, so that your own imagination has the widest range of models from which to make your own fictions.

EXERCISES

1. Make a list of the last six books of fiction you read. Are they all novels? All short stories? All of a single genre (literary fiction, mystery, etc.)? Then go out and pick up a book that differs in type from all those you've listed. Read at least the first few chapters.

2. List your six favorite books. Now, explain in a paragraph or two why these are your favorites. What are their similarities and differences? Do all have female narrators? Are they all contemporary novels? Historical novels? Choose the two that seem least related and try to identify certain elements they share. Explain that in a paragraph.

3. Check out the availability of local writing groups. See if you might be allowed to sit in on a workshop or attend a meeting of an independent group.

4. Follow Phil's example. Over the next few weeks, make up your inventory, and then write a story as different as you can from any

you've written before, keeping in mind particularly those elements you've concluded you need to work on.

5. Set aside some time to read, ideally each day, but if that's impossible, each week. Also, budget some funds so you can actually buy books (these can be secondhand paperbacks), or get a library card if you don't already have one and *use* it.

6. Think about that ten-year plan. Jot down your imaginings, where you want to be as a writer, and file them away. In a year, repeat the exercise, and see if your two speculations match.

TWO

CHOOSING
COMPELLING MATERIAL

The person who writes—you, for example—probably came to this pass in the way I and thousands of others before us did. Part of it, surely, is our love of language, that rich and imperfect means we have of communicating with others. Another part is our curiosity about the larger world, about worlds both external and internal, a fascination with experience itself. We writers are interested in life, in *lives*, both our own and those of others, those real and those imagined. We are observers. We are inquirers. We probably have a certain weakness for gossip and a particular curiosity about motivations—*why* someone did or said a particular something.

Writers genuinely like telling stories. Yet we're all aware that we can relate perfectly serviceable tales that divert readers for the time it takes them to consume the stories, but that—in a day, a month, a year or five—they will be as forgotten as a favorite sitcom from 1989 or the name of that girl you met at summer camp when you were fourteen. Where do we find the stories that are not merely entertaining but memorable; those that *compel* someone's attention and remain with her long after she reads them?

For us writers, there are particular issues to confront, particular sources to be tapped, particular lessons to be learned that may help in creating a story a reader finds unforgettable. Let's consider here where these tales might come from, the places we might look for the incidents and plots and characters that appeal to readers and, even more importantly, to our own particular imaginations. Fiction demands an investment of self—not just time and labor, but being—to transcend the limit of time. It must be rooted in our own obsessions in order for us to produce a work that will, in the best sense, obsess our readers.

KNOW THYSELF

The writing of fiction is inevitably a kind of self-discovery, an investigation by the author of who he is—that person he admires and also the one he is not so crazy about. Though it sounds elementary and may even make you feel a little silly, this might be a good time to spend a few days thinking about what truly interests you. Initially, you will probably come up with a pretty conventional list of topics (sex, drugs, rock and roll), after which you may begin to encounter some surprises: Byzantine history, Aunt Martha's divorce, international terrorism.

Taking Note

Carry a notepad with you. When you inexplicably remember something (an incident, a character in a novel, a face), when something strikes you as surprising, unexpected, beautiful (Why are there four wig shops in this one block? Why do I always notice hollyhocks?), jot it down. Be prepared for the fact, by the way, that these moments will frequently strike at the most inopportune times, such as when you are driving, so you end up repeating "hollyhocks" like a mantra until you can pull over and scrawl the word in your notebook. Appearing a little weird is just one of the occupational hazards of a writing career.

Later on, look at what you've recorded and ask yourself, Why do these subjects bear special weight for me? You may come up with a few topics you didn't realize are as important to you as they are (Wig shops? Hmmm. Is my hair thinning? Am I going gray? Did I always hate my hair?) and discover as well that you don't know why others keep haunting you (but I never thought Martha and Frank were a good couple, and I never liked either of them anyway!). You'll find, over time, your evaluations become more complex, more nuanced, more specifically related to issues of substance to you.

As this happens, move beyond the topics per se and try to find the element of each that particularly struck you. Is it the whole eleven hundred years of Constantinopolitan glory and intrigue that grabs you, or is it that last night before the fall of the city to the Turks when virtually the entire population turned out for the final mass, a requiem, at the Hagia Sofia? Is the entire corpus of rock and roll your obsession or the memory of those girl groups circa 1961–64? Did you ever really care why Martha and Frank split up, or were you unnerved by how your cousins Mandy and Oliver reacted so differently to the divorce?

The point here is to push deeper and deeper into your interests, to find out what *really* matters to you. Beyond your pocket notebook, as suggested in chapter one, review what you have written so far, just as Phil did. Are there images, characters, incidents that have recurred throughout your work that you never quite noticed? Phil found himself introducing identical types in his fiction again and again, those party-on beach boys in their early twenties. How was his own experience at that age pivotal to his imaginings later in life, when he had chosen a career path, settled down a little, ostensibly matured? Do you have three stories in which your protagonist is listening to the oldies station on which Lesley Gore insists it's Judy's turn to cry and the Shangri-Las weep for the leader of the pack? Is there a pattern in the children you've created? Are they obsessively well-mannered boys, like Oliver, and obsessively acting-out girls, like Mandy?

To cite a personal example, I have noted that in all four of my long dramatic fictions, as well as in the manuscript of a new one I am presently working on, something explodes. Even in my comic novel, *The Book of Marvels*, a telephone stand gets thrown through a television screen and shatters the image in "a shower of glass and sparks and confused transistors." In all the serious texts, there is a death by fire.

I cannot say precisely why. There is nothing in my own experience or that of those close to me that provides an easy causal link to this particular fascination. Perhaps it was a movie I saw in 1962 starring Roger Maris and Mickey Mantle, *Safe at Home*, which began with a boy being rescued from a burning car—a Studebaker, like my father drove—by his faithful German shepherd. His parents died, but he and his dog eventually got to meet the dueling home run kings. Perhaps it was a fall on a floor furnace when I was two (an event I do not consciously remember); perhaps it was getting spanked in my childhood for playing with matches. It may go back to the photograph I saw when I was seventeen of a lynching in the 1920s. A Freudian would probably say it's just a male thing—the little boy's natural, psychosexual attraction to stuff that blows up and stuff that burns carried over into adulthood. Whatever the reason, though, fire, and death by fire, has licked around the edges of my imagination as long as I can remember.

As you delve into your conscious interests and their sources, consider, too, your dreams and your fantasies. As you doze in the afternoon, are you behind the wheel of a fast car or the counter at the pharmacy? When you think of your life a decade hence, as suggested in the previous chapter, are you in a penthouse in Atlanta or in a trailer on the coast of northern California? Likewise, note the kinds of stories that grip you both in fiction and on the news rack at the grocery store. You may find that some of these aren't very nice. Why do you always read that article about the six-hundred-pound woman? What is it about those descriptions of massacre that keep you mesmerized? Why did you read the entire text of that advertisement for Prozac?

Do not anticipate that you can answer all these questions or insist that you should be able to. As I indicated, I've never figured out the root of my fascination with booms and blazes. This exercise is not psychotherapy; it's intended to let you see what you might never have considered as worthwhile centers for a story. Perhaps, in my case, I should think seriously about a pyromaniac protagonist, or at least about a pyrotechnician. In yours, seek out that six-hundred-pound woman in you; the Serb or Hutu so filled with tribal fury he can commit the unspeakable. Hannah Arendt, the German-Jewish philosopher, wrote a classic study of one of Nazism's most notorious villains, Adolf Eichmann, the man charged with transporting Jews and other undesirables to the death camps. In *Eichmann in Jerusalem: A Report on the Banality of Evil*, she presents us not with an inhuman monster, but with a failed vacuum cleaner salesman who gradually developed into a servile bureaucrat of slaughter. Her portrait of a war criminal caused terrible controversy, in large part because we did not want to see how banal, how horrifyingly normal, Eichmann and his evolution into Nazi deathmaster seemed.

Arendt forced us to confront what the Colombian Nobel prize-winning novelist Gabriel García Márquez years later called "the little Fascist in us all." It is frightening to know he is there, but for a fiction writer, it is also a possible source of great work. William Faulkner, in the implacable and sadistic racist Percy Grimm in *Light in August*, doubtless was in touch with the poison of regional bigotry he had imbibed, as any child of his background would, in the early years of the century. To help set your mind at rest about the entire exercise, note that it is perhaps only by dragging that Eichmann within into the light that we can then truly control him and have power over him.

Keeping a Journal

Beyond your jottings, you may decide you want to keep a journal. This is an old chestnut from the creative writing bag of tricks and a project that is often abandoned after a few weeks or months, chronicling not the banality of evil, but simply banality. I recall the thrill I felt when my father came upon the diary of a maiden aunt of mine who had recently died, and even more my disappointment when I encountered endless notations like this.

> March 14, 1927: It rained.
> March 20, 1927: Jennings brought the car.
> March 23, 1927: Sunny today. No breakfast. Read.

In context, given other details I know of my aunt's life, this is not quite so pedestrian as it appears. Hers was, paradoxically, a life both privileged and stunted by a domineering sister who had married money (Jennings was the chauffeur). And having lifted all her siblings' fortunes, my married aunt never let them forget it. The spinster Lolly had, as far as I know, no pretensions of being what the powers-that-be in the nineteenth century literary world condescendingly called lady-scribblers, though I have to wonder if there were other diaries lost, perhaps from her girlhood, when images of Louisa May Alcott and Mrs. Humphry Ward danced in her head.

Even for the committed and disciplined writer, however, after the first heady experience of keeping a journal, the exercise may be one best employed in those instances when something out of the ordinary is taking place: a long journey, a family illness, a period of economic hardship. When the circumstances are ones to which you are not accustomed, the chronicling of your days may indeed draw attention to things you had not really thought about, details of a new consciousness you had not accessed and elements of your conventional world you had never paid attention to.

Note this last carefully. It recalls what, in the first chapter, I labeled defamiliarizing yourself from your experience. I've usually found that I am best able to employ familiar landscapes and locales when I am drawing on memories of them, not when I am confronting them. In your summer R & R at the rented cottage by the lake, your crowded, urban neighborhood may surface in your mind with unexpected vividness. As you shunt from airport to hotel to meeting to airport again on that endless business trip, the details of your daily routine when comfortably ensconced in what you normally perceive as your dull suburban subdivision can suddenly sparkle with uniqueness in your mind's eye.

Otherness

Beyond this, the experience of otherness—you as foreigner; you as nurse; indeed, you as sufferer—is a direct and obvious entrance into lives not your own. If you feel up to it, writing your responses to being bedridden for three weeks may not only help you pass the time, but can provide the opportunity for a new, empathic response to those who are ill, elderly, disabled or merely lonely. Setting down the difficulties of asking for a bathroom in Riga not only may give rise to a story set in Latvia, but can bring you face to face with the kinds of challenges the political or economic refugee, struggling with a new language and culture as she waits the counter at your local convenience store, faces every time a customer walks through the door.

This exercise in capturing otherness allows you to become more adept at encountering those others in yourself. These might be the beautiful and tubercular Mimi, sadly wasting away in Alexandre Dumas the Younger's *The Lady of the Camellias,* or some heroic soldier of fortune or selfless saver of souls. It might also be the monstrous survivor who is Bertolt Brecht's Mother Courage or Joseph Conrad's murderous Kurtz at the very heart of darkness. Great fiction, as I just noted, helps us understand not only those who are virtuous and admirable, but those who are wicked and miserable. The author who can at once create a character thoroughly evil who is comprehensible, who moves us even as he horrifies us, whom we detest even though (and perhaps because) we understand somehow whence his evil comes, is someone who has tapped into his own otherness, who has found that part of himself capable of the most heinous acts, and in bringing that hidden demon to light moves and, indeed, educates us all.

KNOWING THYSELF EVEN BETTER, AND EVERYBODY ELSE FOR THAT MATTER

In my first creative writing course at college, the professor, the writer Darcy O'Brien, presented as the first rule of fiction: "Write what you know." Armed with that advice, I produced a story for the following class based upon an incident that had occurred over the weekend. I turned it in, and the class responded to it.

They hated it.

O'Brien hated it.

I was crushed.

My next story, entitled "The Great James Knox Polk Centennial Celebration of 1898," was a down-home romance involving a country fiddler and the daughter of a local preacher. It was set in Pineville, North Carolina, a small town near where I lived as a child, where a rather phallic monument on the site of Polk's birthplace graced the summit of a small rise. Despite the fact that I could not fiddle, had last seen Pineville some five years before and had obviously not been around for the centennial of Polk's birth, the piece met with considerable praise all around.

I henceforth abandoned autobiography as a source of my fiction.

I present this anecdote to demonstrate how oftentimes what seems perfectly reasonable counsel can, from writer to writer, be of varying value, though it is also not quite true that I have never used autobiographical material in my work. Inevitably, jobs I've had, landscapes I've seen, cars I've owned, things I've said have all finagled their way into my novels. Though I have yet to write another story overtly recounting a real experience of mine, autobiography in the broadest sense—the sum total of our real lives, our fantasy lives, our dream lives—is probably *always* operative in what I (and you) write.

As O'Brien observed, for many writers the obvious and logical place to begin their fiction is in what they know. There are those who have experienced something so dramatic, so searing that its impact upon readers is virtually certain. Tim O'Brien, the author of *Going After Cacciato* and *The Things They Carried*, has distilled his year in the Army in Vietnam into heart-wrenching art. Vietnam is a wound he revisits again and again, and these revisitations move and remind all his generation how wounded they and their country have been by that singularly ill-augured war. Nadine Gordimer not only watched but was deeply involved in the transformation of South Africa from a racist and repressive police state to a nation taking its first, halting steps into real democracy and has chronicled that transformation in her novels and short stories.

Refining Reality

Most of us, however, lead lives less dramatic than these, so how can experience serve us? For a guide, one might look to Thomas Wolfe, an author more neglected now than in his time. In many ways, his life *was* his work. Product of a large and eccentric family in Asheville, North Carolina, Wolfe employed large swatches of his experience virtually unalloyed in his novels. I knew a woman, who grew up in Asheville, who had a copy of *Look Homeward, Angel* in which real names had been penciled in over those of Wolfe's characters.

The Wolfes of Asheville, who became the Gants of Altamont, were a pretty wild clan. Even so, their experience in the larger scheme of American life from the turn of the century to the 1930s—the loss of two children to disease, marital discord, a ne'er-do-well eldest son and a spoiled and ambitious youngest one, a violent, drunken, yet somewhat romantic father and a practical and grasping mother—was not that far from the realities of many contemporary, less self-dramatizing families, those of the people next door or down the block. Wolfe's later novels, which followed Eugene Gant and later another obvious persona—George Webber—to the university, to the big city, to Europe, were not dissimilar in that sense. If they did not precisely parallel the experiences of most readers, they were familiar enough in dreams if not realities to allow readers to feel a closeness and kinship to Wolfe's characters that made his foreshortened career one of triumph before his death at thirty-nine.

However, as a number of Wolfe's biographers have noted in defense of him as a creative artist, his novels are not merely autobiography with names changed to protect the innocent and not-so-innocent. *Look Homeward, Angel*, despite its allegiance to the broad outline of the author's childhood, is more a chronicle of what *might* have been, *ought to* have been, *almost* was than a faithful rendition of Wolfe's growing up as best he could reconstruct it. In using autobiography, remember that you can change things—recast conversations, shuffle events, add or eliminate actors in the drama—all in the interest of greater clarity, impact and tension. A common lament of apprentice writers is, "That's how it really happened!" The problem is, readers *have* reality. What they are looking for is *fiction*, which is generally neater, more compressed, sharper-edged than quotidian experience.

I recently read a piece by a young author which was centered on the last days of his father's struggle with cancer. The story was short, less than a dozen pages, and there was little question that its point—and the locus of its power—was a son's impotence, grief, fury at the fact of his father's death. In those twelve pages, we met the boy's mother, girlfriend, three sisters, one brother-in-law; two social workers; a doctor; a nurse. In discussing the piece in the workshop, readers found fault with the vastness of the cast. The sisters seemed interchangeable, social worker A existed primarily to give place to social worker B, the brother-in-law appeared only for an instant to shout news of the final crisis.

And predictably, the author protested: "But that's how it was!"

But how it really was is less dramatic and concentrated than it might be. Three sisters could be one. The girlfriend might sit the deathwatch instead of the brother-in-law. The medical and social welfare figures could be eliminated altogether, or dealt with in a narrative paragraph or two. The value of this, beyond eliminating what we might call character clutter, is that it allows the story's real point, its universal resonance—the child's loss of a parent—to speak more forcefully and movingly to the reader. It focuses us upon the young protagonist's actions, feelings and state of mind, *his* particular drama, by reducing the distractions of the comings and goings of figures not germane to the story's emotional heart.

What the author needed to do was *refine* reality. This often is not easy, particularly with events close to us in time. Part of the problem here may have been that this young man did not yet possess sufficient distance from the loss of his father to rework the experience, to distill its many elements to those essential for a powerful story.

This question of distance is complicated, and relevant not only to something as inherently potent as a parent's passing, but to less dramatic and less personal material as well. I tried, when I was in college, to write a story based on my summer job in a convalescent hospital. At twenty years old, being an orderly exposed me to much I had little knowledge of: medical procedures, the frailty of the human body, the various indignities of old age, not to mention disease and death and actually washing and dressing the corpse of someone I had known. Nonetheless, my patients were not family.

The story I started never went anywhere. It was pompous and cluttered and self-conscious. The big problem was sorting out what was truly important *to me* from that summer and what I thought *ought* to be important. Events, remarks, personalities all had the same valence, all seemed equally weighted in my imagination. It was only years later that I was able to write about that experience, having winnowed out what was truly and personally significant about it. The material eventually found a place in *The Book of Marvels*, which is about a thirtyish and recently divorced woman in a small town who has to find a way to support herself. In writing about Lila Mae's daily grind, I was astonished at how much I did remember of that job, but surely there was a great deal more I *didn't* remember, things that had settled into my unconscious because they failed to impress me as much as what I did recall. I worked as an orderly during the summers of 1970 and 1971. I wrote successfully about people and events of that time in the summer of 1988.

Ordinariness

As I said already, writers (who are no different from anybody else in this sense) often don't see their own lives as inherently interesting, dramatic or complex enough to provide the grist for fiction. Just as Dorothy Gale in *The Wizard of Oz* had to learn that when she went looking for her heart's desire, the place to begin was her own backyard, it is worthwhile to consider not merely what is particularly powerful in your own life—as in the foregoing example of a father's death—but what is soundly conventional. While the dailiness of your temporary job at the Exxon station or the time you spent in Paducah on a desultory visit to Aunt Martha (remember her?—she divorced Frank) may not be of sufficient interest to keep a reader reading, it may provide the necessary grounding for a more intense story you want to tell. As with Wolfe's novels, a reader is often attracted to a world that, if not entirely familiar, is one in which she can imagine living. There is a power in extraordinary events that unfold against a background of determined ordinariness. Indeed, we are often fascinated not by the horrible crime or spectacular act of bravery arising in high society or the extreme conditions of war or space exploration, but by happenings involving people more likely to be our neighbors and co-workers.

To cite a grim example from this last decade: Despite the hoopla surrounding the O.J. Simpson trial, it is another crime committed about the same time—that of Susan Smith of Union, South Carolina, who drowned her sons in a county reservoir—that finally haunts our dreams. O.J.'s glitzy world of Bel Air is one of American fantasy, one of Judith Krantz novels and *Dynasty* reruns. His trial pivoted, in the end, on large, public issues of race and of spousal abuse.

Union, on the other hand, is close and cozy, the prototype of that "real" America our politicians evoke in their thirty-second commercials, the small town we try endlessly to reproduce in our cul-de-saced suburbs. Everyone in the Smith case *seemed* so hardworking, unexceptional, normal in almost every way. This was not the world where the nation expected a drama of infidelity and incest and filicide, as if the classical Greek tragedies of *Phaedre* and *Oedipus* and *Medea* had all been rolled into one.

Ordinariness need not be interrupted by such catastrophe, however, to make fine and lasting fiction. Ernest Hemingway's stories often feature acts of sudden violence. In "Indian Camp," for example, a boy accompanies his doctor father to the delivery of a Native American woman's first child. It is a difficult labor, and in the end, the woman's husband, unable to bear the pain he has unintentionally inflicted upon his wife, kills himself. However, Hemingway was just as able to craft a gripping story out of an incident in which nothing happens. He introduces us to two teenage boys in a small-town railroad station, throws in a few lumberjacks, their cook and some prostitutes also waiting for the train, lets us and his protagonists listen to an argument about a dead boxer and fashions it all into one of his most resonant and moving works, "The Light of the World." Therein, the sad grown-up lives of those around the boys convince them that, whatever happens, their course in life will be "the other way from you."

To provide a more contemporary illustration, Charles Baxter resurrects an incident everyone remembers and infuses it with both wit and mystery. "Gryphon" deals with a substitute teacher in an elementary school classroom. But what a substitute! Miss Ferenczi teaches that 6×11 is sometimes 68 instead of 66, that "if you don't like a word, you don't have to use it." She carries a purple purse and a checkerboard lunchbox. She speaks of the "cosmic power of the pyramids" and her visit to Egypt where she was shown "an animal in a cage, a monster, half-bird and half-lion." Eventually, she oversteps, reading the Tarot of two of the students.

> "This card, this nine of swords, tells me of suffering and desolation. And this ten of wands, well, that's a heavy load."
> "What about this one?" Wayne pointed at the Death card.
> "It means, my sweet, that you will die soon."

Wayne tattles to the principal, and needless to say, Miss Ferenczi is shown the door. Obviously, she was quite, quite mad. And yet . . .

The story's narrator, Tommy, picks a fight with Wayne over his betrayal. Though it is never stated, for him, perhaps for the other children as well, this strange woman with her "substitute facts" and gnostic nostrums represents something very powerful they do not quite understand, something more powerful than the rote learning they are accustomed to. She is fantastical, and perhaps fantasy itself. She represents a kind of freedom, a child's imagination in an institution that is, Baxter seems to say, dedicated to stamping out children's imaginations. Miss Ferenczi may be a fairy godmother or she may be a witch, or both, but in this setting with which every reader can identify, she embodies a rare and potent magic, quite possibly that transformatory magic that is the writer's art practiced by Baxter himself.

Every day (well, maybe not every one) presents you with surprises, with little examples of courage, with moments of moral choice. In that job at the gas station, did you see the fourteen-year-old swipe a bag of chips off the counter rack when you turned around to make change? What did you do? Tell him to put it back? Report him to the boss? Tell his father out there gassing up the family station wagon? Or did you let him get away with it? He was hungry; he was daring; he reminded you of precisely what you did at his age. Why did you respond that way? And how did your decision make you feel?

Other People's Lives
Where real experience is concerned, there is a final source to remember. Writers are magpies or birds of prey, depending on your point of view. Not only do you have your own life to plunder for material, you

have the lives of everyone around you. If every picture tells a story, so every person has stories to tell. Listen to others—their anecdotes and true-life adventures, those of friends, relatives and strangers. Many is the time I have cheerfully appropriated details and incidents related to me by others, ones that struck a chord in my imagination. The prologue of my second novel, *Mrs. Randall*, involves a horrific forced miscarriage that was, early in this century, the unfortunate fate of the adolescent aunt of one of my best friends in college.

A wonderful resource, frankly, are the elderly, people of lives near complete who have accumulated a wealth of tales and wisdom. They are often willing to talk about themselves and their memories, perhaps in part because many of the incidents are now thirty or forty years past and many of the people who took part in them are conveniently dead. My grandmother had a very interesting life of her own and was further a storehouse of family lore, not merely from her own turn-of-the-century generation but from her mother's and grandmother's generations. Through her, I accumulated stories from as far back as the 1840s, and bits and pieces of these are woven like strings in a nest through my novels.

This applies as well to all those who are in some way different from you. Engage the guy at the dry cleaners in conversation on a slow day, or talk to the teenager who mows your lawn. These tales may provide ready-made plots, characters, settings and so on for your fiction. And those adulterers and angels of mercy from your own past plus those charming ne'er-do-wells and pouty do-gooders from your friends' family stories may lead you to that hidden part of yourself where sinner or saint resides. From the germ of a notion a casual anecdote has planted, a full-blown fiction may arise.

KNOW THY TRADITION

> ... the old, veritable truths of the heart, the old universal truths lacking which any story is ephemeral and doomed—love, honor and pride and compassion and sacrifice.

Since Faulkner accepted his Nobel prize in 1951, many have accused him of speaking in clichés in the foregoing passage. Yet, he does seem to have gotten it about right. There are certain subjects, particular stories, specific conflicts that transcend the moment and speak directly to the human heart. Romance and love, sex and passion, birth and death, bravery in the face of danger and constancy in the face of suffering: These roots, it seems, anchor great literature in the soil of human experience.

But how do you find the particular material that will make your fiction stand out, make it strike a sympathetic chord with the collusive reader I have talked about and make your book one that keeps her reading in every spare moment she can find? Unsurprisingly, one of the first places to look is within the tradition, in the canon of works that have stood the test of time.

But wait, you say, that's not kosher! I'm merely ripping off somebody else's good idea! Hold on. Take a deep breath. To paraphrase T.S. Eliot: "Good writers borrow. Great writers steal." Our notions of originality derive from the Romantics and the cult of individualism that arose toward the end of the eighteenth century. Before that, imitation was not merely the sincerest form of flattery, but a given in the production of great literature. The Roman poet Virgil looked to Homer's *Iliad* for the form of *The Aeneid*, and it was Virgil whom both Dante and John Milton saw as their guide (Dante in the most literal way!) when they sat down to produce their great Christian epics, *La divina commedia* and *Paradise Lost*. The dramatists of the English Renaissance ransacked every source they could find—Italian novellas, historical chronicles, broadsides that were the contemporary equivalent of the tabloids, not to mention each other's plays. It has long been assumed that even Shakespeare's most famous work, *Hamlet*, is based upon an earlier and now lost treatment of the same story—likely in two parts, perhaps by Thomas Kyd—referred to as the *Ur-Hamlet*.

Myths and Legends

In seeking compelling material, first go back to the oldest expressions of our collective imagination, the various mythologies sacred and secular that have permeated our consciousness for centuries. Begin with the Bible and the Apocrypha, particularly those books centered on narrative: Genesis, Exodus, I and II Samuel, I and II Kings, Daniel; Judith, Susanna and the two books of Maccabees; The Gospels, The Acts of the Apostles, The Revelation of St. John the Divine. In these, you'll find the Joseph who inspired both the German master Thomas Mann (*Joseph and His Brothers*) and Andrew Lloyd Webber and Tim

Rice (in their first musical, *Joseph and the Amazing Technicolor Dreamcoat*). You'll come upon feuding brothers (Isaac and Esau, to name but one of such seemingly endless pairings), tragic overreachers (King Saul), the poor boy made good (King David), scolding outsiders (Samuel and Isaiah), mystic seers (Daniel). You'll encounter dirty old men (in Susanna), the herald of revolution (John the Baptist) and the Good Samaritan. In St. John's phantasmagoric vision of the end of the world, writers as diverse as the sixteenth century's John Bunyan (in *The Pilgrim's Progress*) and the contemporary master of horror Clive Barker have found inspiration.

Some years ago, a student in one of my workshops gave us a story of a girl, a member of a primitive tribe, who was raped by a man from a neighboring tribe. Her brothers demanded vengeance, but those related to the rapist proposed instead that the miscreant marry his victim. As further proof of their sincerity, they offered to do whatever else might be asked of them. The brothers agreed to the marriage, but on the condition that the other tribe embrace the brothers' religious faith and that the other tribe's men undergo a particularly uncomfortable ritual. This, too, was accepted, and those men were circumcised. "On the third day, when they were still sore," the brothers of the violated girl slaughtered them all.

This is the story of Dinah, told in Genesis 34. As you might expect in as patriarchal a text as the Old Testament, Dinah remains a pretty one-dimensional character. What our author did in his retelling of the tale, however, was to make her the narrator of the story. His plot was ready-made, as it were, but he endowed it with a unique point of view, and so made it fresh. His is ineluctably Dinah's story, filled with her reactions, her emotions, her ambivalences. Oddly enough, a couple of years later I saw a performance piece presented by a largely Puerto Rican troupe out of New Jersey who also used the story of Dinah, though in their version, the action was moved from ancient Palestine to contemporary New York. The accents were thick, the speeches peppered with obscenities, and the tale of the avenging brothers, who could not countenance that someone should "deal with our sister as with an harlot," was as modern as it was faithful to the biblical text.

After the Bible, try the Roman poet Ovid's *Metamorphoses* or the books of mythology compiled by Bulfinch or Edith Hamilton, and refamiliarize yourself with the battles, jealousies and peccadilloes of the classical pantheon—Zeus and Athena and all the rest—and the stories of those ancient kings and queens who inspired the first great dramas of the Western stage: Aeschylus' *The Oresteia*, Sophocles' plays about the Theban Oedipus, Euripides' *Medea*. Or turn—preferably with Richard Wagner's four-opera cycle *The Ring of the Nibelung* playing in the background—to that even darker tradition of the Germans and Scandinavians, the tales of the doomed Aesir of Valhalla, who from the very beginning of time awaited "The Twilight of the Gods." Try out some of the legendary texts of northern Europe that have been preserved. Even the most jaded contemporary reader can be stunned by the appalling mayhem of *Njál's Saga*, where the bloodletting makes the latest Freddy Krueger film look tame, and the entire cast seems made up of "natural born killers."

Take a look for the first time in a long time at those folk and fairy tales you delighted in as a child—the exploits of the Knights of the Round Table, Snow White, Sleeping Beauty, Hansel and Gretel. Certainly, there are few places you can go that will give you greater inspiration if you're thinking about a story of a wicked parent or stepparent! And how many variants have we seen in prose and film of the story of Cinderella, that good-hearted and exploited girl who defies the odds and makes a match with Prince Charming? If yearning for a little variety, investigate the legends of China and India, of the native peoples of both North and South America, of Africa east and west. Read the *Gilgamesh*, the great Babylonian flood epic, in which Gilgamesh and his faithful sidekick, Enkidu, sometimes seem more than a bit like Huck and Jim on the Euphrates.

It cannot hurt, as well, to look to other fields—anthropology, literary criticism, psychology—to discover what kind of tales these specialists have found have a peculiar hold on the human imagination. Otto Rank's *The Myth of the Birth of the Hero* traces the intriguing similarities of mythologies throughout the world and across history, focusing on those that relate to such grand, heroic figures as Moses and Osiris. Many of the essays of Freud and Jung consider the hows and whys of our attachment to certain stories and individuals regardless of our century or station. Robert Graves' *The White Goddess* and Joseph Campbell's *The Hero With a Thousand Faces*, as well as the classic tome of armchair anthropology, James Frazer's *The Golden*

Bough, can provide you with ideas of those archetypal tales that have moved men since time immemorial. Despite the squeals of traditionalists and the sometimes intimidating jargon of the texts themselves, pick up an anthology of essays of women's studies, queer theory, Marxist analysis—anything that might let you see the world through new eyes.

The reason to read these sources is not particularly to write allegories or to retell point for point the story of the Hebrew Ruth or Norse Loki or Greek Leda, though from time to time, particularly with an intriguing twist, authors have done precisely this. John Gardner appropriated the epic *Beowulf*, but his *Grendel* is a novel told from the point of view of Beowulf's nemesis, the ruminative and rather put-upon monster, rather than from the Anglo-Saxon hero's perspective. Likewise, Jorge Luis Borges' powerful though tonally very different short story "The House of Asterion" reveals at the end its narrator is The Minotaur, waiting resignedly for the arrival of Theseus, the Athenian prince who will destroy him.

These stories, which you likely last had a look at when you were in high school, serve to remind you of conflicts and desires that seem as relevant today as they did thousands of years ago. Certainly, in Steinbeck's novel of turn-of-the-century California, the two sons who present different sacrifices to their father need not have been named Caleb and Aron, and the book itself need not have been titled *East of Eden*, for us to see that this tale of brothers in conflict is related to the story, within the Judeo-Christian tradition, of the first pair of brothers, Cain and Abel.

Such tales are useful for the plots they can furnish, the characters (or character types) they provide you and the flights of imagination to which they can lead you. There is little question—and again, the title makes the source quite obvious—that Faulkner's Thomas Sutpen represents some kind of degraded, nineteenth-century Mississippi King David, anguished before the death or madness of his sons, in *Absalom, Absalom!* However, though Faulkner's plot broadly follows the biblical one in I and II Samuel, he takes tremendous liberties with it to fit his artistic purposes. He injects the issue of race into the story, replaces the incestuous rape by Absalom with the threat of incestuous and miscegenational marriage, has the monstrous Sutpen murdered and so on.

Such liberties can extend even to the tone of your story. The English writer Tom Holt takes the dark, myth-based plot Wagner fashioned for his operas and uses it to create a delightful and extremely funny fantasy novel, *Expecting Someone Taller*. Therein, a rather dull English accountant, on a late-night drive down the highway, hits a badger. Remorseful at his carelessness, he gets out of the car to see if the poor creature is dead. He is dying, but turns out to be no ordinary roadkill, but the evil dwarf, Albrecht, who has ended up in possession of "The Ring of Power," the magical amulet that is the locus of Wagner's Germanic saga. Albrecht has always known that one day he would be overcome by a hero to whom he would have to relinquish the Ring, but frankly he was "expecting someone taller." The novel then takes off as a satire of both contemporary mores and the risks of absolute power, featuring appearances, of course, by various of the figures in the operas. The entire book would be simply impossible without the pre-extant text that is Wagner's, just as his cycle would never have been composed without the endless retellings over history of those ancient Germanic legends.

The Canon of Great Literature

Beyond myths and legends, we are, we must be, readers of more worldly fictions. Some years ago, I asked in an introductory fiction course how many of those enrolled regularly read novels and short stories. In a disarming display of honesty, only about half the class raised a hand. This brings up not only the question of why someone would want to write fiction if she doesn't bother to read it, but, even more importantly, how she can hope to master any skill without studying the masters. Aspiring divers watch videotapes of Greg Louganis. The neophyte investor scans *The Wall Street Journal* and quizzes those more savvy about the stock market on their experiences. The young concert violinist listens again and again to recordings of Itzhak Perlman and Gregor Piatigorsky; the garage musician, to Nirvana and Led Zeppelin.

And so, the writer reads. There are, on every bookshelf, in every library, endless examples of fine prose that any serious practitioner of the writing craft should seek out not merely for the delight they may offer the soul and the senses, but for the lessons they offer in structure, in pacing, in expression. Any book of the sort here before you is presented with this notion in mind. I have to assume that you read and read a lot, that in addition to this volume and others like it, in addition to the time you spend before computer or typewriter or legal pad, you have a more than passing acquaintance with Anton Chekhov, Ernest Hemingway and Flannery O'Connor, as well as with more ephemeral texts—be they thrillers, mysteries or your weekly magazines and daily newspapers.

These assumptions of a person constantly and consistently honing his skill in a variety of ways should apply to all writers: journalists, columnists, humorists; scholars writing on medieval architecture, German politics, feminist theory; purveyors of celebrity biography and those manuals whose themes range from discovering your inner child to mastering the Internet. For writers of fiction, however, in addition to these essential studies, there are further demands, an extra dollop of effort that is required to lift work into the realm of art.

Fiction writers, as a subset of that larger community of writers, often seem a self-dramatizing and self-important lot, looking down their noses at those other wordsmiths who, in all likelihood, are making a better living than your average novelist. And it is indeed true that nonfiction works can, from time to time, have an impact not dissimilar from what we anticipate in fiction. Some years ago, I remarked to someone that I had been "moved" by Walter Russell Mead's *Mortal Splendor: The American Empire in Transition*. Moved? By a book about public policy? But that was an honest response. In his study, the author had woven a spell that made the dilemma the United States faces in its definition in a changing world seem human, almost tragic, as the title itself indicates, taken from a poem by Robinson Jeffers, "Shine, Perishing Republic."

Still, the success of Mead's book depended finally upon his capacity to engage his reader intellectually, not emotionally. Emotion is, however, the lifeblood and the defining essence of compelling fiction. In novels and stories, we must go beyond the skills of all fine writing to discover our own particular strengths and weaknesses, desires and fears, fantasies both light and dark. Fiction demands a peculiar level of self-knowledge. The fiction writer must have a special element of self-appraisal and a generosity that offers up what is most personal, even when it is embarrassing or disturbing, masked though it may be in imaginary guises.

The poems and novels and plays we continue to read across decades and centuries, we must assume, are read not only because they are promoted or sanctified by those powers dominant within the culture, but because they really do speak some truth, exemplify some profound reality that continues to be relevant over time. Sit down again with Shakespeare, as Jane Smiley did before she wrote her novella *A Thousand Acres* with its three daughters and vain and aging father, her rendition of *King Lear* on the Iowa plains. Reacquaint yourself with the hesitant Hamlet, the ambitious Macbeth, that Othello who loved not wisely but too well. Read Milton, Melville, Dickens, the Hawthorne whose *The Scarlet Letter* gave rise, one hundred and more years later, to John Updike's *S*. One of these might inspire you to undertake a Christmas carol or a major fish story. Twain's *Huckleberry Finn* is undoubtedly the granddaddy of so many buddy tales in American literature it is impossible to even estimate their number. The works of other writers can provide the seed for your own work or the spark that ignites the idea you already have for a story. They may show you the larger resonance your idea possesses and suggest a structure for how it might develop.

Revisiting *Jane Eyre*

To give you a detailed illustration of how this process works, consider the use of Charlotte Brontë's *Jane Eyre* in Jean Rhys' 1966 novel, *Wide Sargasso Sea*. Rhys was born on the island Dominica in the West Indies, daughter of a Dutch doctor and a native white mother. At sixteen she went to England and, a few years later, married a relatively feckless Dutch painter with whom she shared a decade's rootless life on the Continent during the 1920s. Four novels, published between 1928 and 1939, established her as a merciless chronicler of both the bohemian life and of the dangerous liaisons inevitable between the sexes. After World War II she plunged into oblivion, and it was only after some of her stories were reprinted that she was ultimately tracked down to Cornwall, where she was at work on her final and most famous novel.

In *Jane Eyre*, one of the most interesting characters, and surely the most mysterious, is the "madwoman in the attic." Mr. Rochester's first wife, Bertha, has gone insane and is secretly kept imprisoned upstairs. Brontë no more than alludes to the couple's history.

Rochester, as a second son, had gone to the Caribbean as a young man to make (or marry) his fortune. There, he wed Bertha. Ironically, not long after, he ends up lord of the family manor, Thornhill Hall, due to the deaths of his father and older brother. Jane learns of Bertha's existence immediately before she herself is to marry Rochester. Faced with his deceit and the specter of barely avoided bigamy, Jane flees. Subsequently, Bertha escapes confinement again, sets fire to Thornhill and leaps to her death from its parapets.

In Brontë, Bertha exists as a ghostly threat. What Rhys does in her novel is give the madwoman flesh. From those vague hints in her source of Rochester and Bertha's past, she fashions the story of their disastrous relationship. The Creole heiress is as incapable of understanding the morose English adventurer as he is of comprehending her and her decadent colonial heritage. Rhys does not "gloss" *Jane Eyre*, that is, merely retell or elaborate upon the earlier story from Bertha's perspective. She creates an entirely separate piece of art, a prequel to Brontë's story, one that occurs almost entirely in the Caribbean. It fits with the nineteenth-century text only in the masterfully condensed part three, which finds the madwoman in her attic prison, having long since lost her reason.

> I got up, took the keys and unlocked the door. I was outside holding my candle. Now at last I know why I was brought here and what I have to do. There must have been a draught for the flame flickered and I thought it was out. But I shielded it with my hand and it burned up again to light me along the dark passage.

We can see here how Rhys used *Jane Eyre* as a jumping-off place for her own novel and why the figure of the first Mrs. Rochester might have particular resonance in her imagination. The child of a European and a Creole, one who grew up steeped in the complex and often dark history of imperialism in the Caribbean, one who, as an adolescent, went to England, Rhys was surely inclined to look sympathetically upon Bertha. Her twenty-some years in obscurity, as well, seem a less odious but perhaps not much less lonely kind of imprisonment. Here, the seeds of individual experience, nurtured by the light of a minor but unforgettable character in a classic novel, blossom finally in the harrowing book that is *Wide Sargasso Sea*.

MAKE IT NEW

An issue to bear in mind is that certain stories, images, archetypes may have a particular resonance in the contemporary world they did not always possess, that changes in history, in social conditions or the means of production or class structure and so on may suddenly make a forgotten tale ring new. We must wonder if Rhys' book would have had the impact it did if it had been published in the 1930s rather than in the 1960s, when the perception of the realities of colonialism were far harsher than earlier in the century. Consider that Marlowe's *Dr. Faustus*, after the Renaissance, slumbered for nearly two centuries before Goethe resuscitated the story in his very different telling, *Faust*. The tale of the bargain of a man with the Devil for infinite wisdom and power struck the Romantic consciousness, there on the threshold of the industrial revolution, with particular force. Certainly, in the two centuries since, the Faustian bargain has figured large in our imagination.

In popular culture, the spate of films and fictions of the 1950s about alien invaders who enslave, either physically or mentally, God-fearing Americans seem now obviously inspired by a paranoia arising from the birth of space exploration and the perceived threat of Soviet and Chinese hordes and internal Communist subversion. More recently, the transformation of the vampire from the campy image of Bela Lugosi into a truly dangerous and romantic figure, as shown to us in Francis Ford Coppola's film *Bram Stoker's Dracula* or the fabulously popular novels of Anne Rice, have much to do with the AIDS epidemic, the confluence of love and death, blood and wasting. The vampire once again has become not a figure of fun, but the emblem of the dangers of passion.

Do remember, though, that it is not often possible to determine which old tale will suddenly seem new. Rice began her "Vampire Chronicles" in the mid-1970s. More to the point, Rice's choice of subject, as her pseudonymous work such as *The Claiming of Sleeping Beauty* indicates, has always tended toward erotic exoticism (or is that exotic eroticism?). Rice cannot be accused of simply cutting her works to fit the historical cloth. Rather, history itself accidentally provided them a new and terrible resonance.

In reviewing the canon, trust your own creative judgment and imagination, what titillates you or fills you with dread, not your hopeful clairvoyance regarding tomorrow's trends or catastrophes. There are many great stories whose greatness you recognize, but you are seeking those with which you have particular affinity. At best, while reading the paragraphs preceding, you suddenly recalled the Bible story, the myth, the Shakespeare play or Russian novel that truly ravished you at twelve or twenty or thirty-five. Go back to it. Reread it. Is this that same old story we talked about in chapter one? The same old story, the archetypal tale, that most moves you as a reader may, in your hands as writer, move others just as effectively.

KNOW THY HISTORY

Great literature, of course, is not the only source of great stories. Reading history can provide material for a historical novel and also a more profound understanding of character, of politics, of human interaction. Suetonius' brief biographies in his *The Lives of the Twelve Caesars*, chronicling the Imperial Roman court in the first century, can still serve any fiction writer as a gossipy primer in the depths of human depravity, beside which the goings-on in a Danielle Steel novel look almost sedate. Don't believe me? Do remember he is writing about the likes of Nero, who had his own mother murdered (along with several thousand other people), and of Caligula, who had his horse declared a god and was none too respectful of human life himself.

The contemporary, popular histories of Barbara Tuchman or Walter Lord bristle with the intrigue, bravery and stupidity of real men and women of the past. In *The Guns of August*, the former shows us how kings, empresses, generals, government ministers and populations in general blundered their way into the First World War. Lord's *A Night to Remember* follows a great and unsinkable ship from the moment of her conception to her premature end in the freezing waters of the North Atlantic. There is no doubt this book was the first resource consulted by Beryl Bainbridge for her recent novel about the *Titanic* sinking, *Every Man for Himself*. We should hardly be surprised. What novelist would not yearn for a character like the engineer Thomas Andrews, the man who designed the ship, who was aboard when the liner struck the iceberg and who, after investigating the damage, had to tell the captain that this marvel of human achievement would sink in two hours? He knew as well, of course, that its lifeboats could accommodate only half the passengers and crew.

To his credit, Andrews went down with the ship.

History and the available historical record—memoirs, collections of letters, oral histories, scholarly investigations—can be integral to a fiction's very existence. Leo Tolstoy's *War and Peace* and Stephen Crane's *The Red Badge of Courage*—still arguably the two greatest novels of war ever written—were both the products of men who had no experience with the events they re-created. They had, however, steeped themselves in the lore of the Napoleonic era and the Civil War respectively and then let their imaginations guide them from there. You might, in investigating a period of history that particularly appeals to you, encounter a story that captures your imagination, as Gore Vidal did numerous times, from the life of the apostate Roman emperor, Julian, to those of such American figures as Aaron Burr and Abraham Lincoln. Indeed, by focusing on such great men in the nation's history, Vidal fashioned an entire cycle of novels tracing the development of the United States from the Revolutionary period to the mid-twentieth century.

In my own novels, both those set earlier in the century and in contemporary decades, I've found myself making use of a variety of nonfiction sources. Anthologies of Vietnam recollections allowed me to create with confidence the war sequences in *Letting Loose*. For *Mrs. Randall*, I read Kevin Brownlow's history, *The Parade's Gone By . . .* , to get some notion of the world of silent pictures to which my protagonist, Gambetta Stevenson, fled in 1918. For *The Professor of Aesthetics*, numerous memoirs and popular histories of gangland Chicago provided the details I needed for the amoral Jay Skikey's career as a mob enforcer.

You may find that a particular plot or character already extant in your mind might better function in a time other than our own, that the lines of a story may be bolder and more powerful if it occurs in a place of sharper class differences, greater physical danger, more rigid moral codes or more pervasive and obvious corruption. Hawthorne encountered his profoundest fictional home, after all, not in his real world of Emersonian optimism, but in the brooding dusk of New England two centuries before. Southern writers, as we've noted, returned again and again to the world of their grandfathers to deal with the demons of race and class and decorum that still held the region in a stranglehold.

Bear in mind that the converse of this may be true as well. As that contemporary retelling of *Romeo and Juliet* worked wonderfully on stage for Leonard Bernstein, Arthur Laurents and Stephen Sondheim, so too might the relocation of a particular historical person or event in a modern setting. Might there not be a novel with particular force in a late-twentieth-century rendition of, say, a life like that of Emily Dickinson? The illicit passion of Paolo Malatesta and Francesca di Rimini led to the murders of both in 1289, and their story has since been related many times by writers from Dante on down. Could you put a new spin on this famous tale by shifting the action from a medieval court on the Adriatic Sea to the realm of the Michigan militia on the shores of Lake Huron?

Many writers, particularly in the last twenty years, have employed historical incidents or characters in works that do not fit the mold of the traditional historical novel, that long line born in Sir Walter Scott's Scottish fantasies that has subsequently flowered in guises as various as A.J. Cronin's evocations of the court of the Plantagenets and Margaret Mitchell's Civil War epic, *Gone With the Wind.* The late modernist fictions of the 1960s and 1970s—Thomas Pynchon's *Gravity's Rainbow*, John Barth's *The Sot-Weed Factor*—employed particular historical moments (the final days of World War II and colonial America respectively) to tell tales that, in their hearts, comment more upon existential, political and philosophical concerns of the authors' own times than upon the particularities of the 1940s or the eighteenth century. Robert Coover's *The Public Burning*, a wild fantasy set during the McCarthy era and centering on the execution of the Rosenbergs, is in many ways less about that period than about the 1970s, full of worries about image, government duplicity, paranoia. This might well be expected. Its protagonist, after all, is Richard Nixon.

KNOW THE WORLD AROUND YOU

Beyond history, or subsumed within it perhaps, there are always the current events printed in your daily newspaper or broadcast on the evening news. Over the years, I have been struck with how many times apprentice writers have produced their most original pieces when they undertake the imaginative leap into a circumstance half a world away. These have included stories about starvation in Ethiopia, the ongoing troubles in the Middle East and Amerasian children in

Vietnam. Lawrence Thornton's prize-winning novel *Imagining Argentina* was begun the night he watched a documentary on PBS about The Mothers of the Plaza de Mayo, who at great risk demonstrated week to week against the military regime that had "disappeared" their children. Thornton, in this particular book, did very little research into Latin American realities. As the title indicates, he wished to *imagine* the horror for himself, in an *imaginary* place, a sinister Argentina of his own invention that could capture the fear and revulsion he himself felt as he contemplated people vanished as into air.

The newspaper and other media can also serve you, though perhaps not as effectively as they once did, in other ways. Before computerized typesetting, most dailies regularly offered a bounty of peculiar stories, often of only a couple paragraphs or so, that recounted amusing or bizarre occurrences from around the world. Such items still appear occasionally as news or can be encountered in columns like Cecil Adams' "The Straight Dope" or such independent subscription publications as *News of the Weird*.

I still have posted in my office a squib from the *Los Angeles Times* of 1977 that recounts the burial of an anonymous corpse. The undertaker in a small town in Arkansas had kept the body for seventy-odd years in the hope that someone would eventually come along and identify him. From that strange tale, a few years later, I fashioned the epilogue of my second novel, *Mrs. Randall*. I took great liberties with it, of course, but that is what a fiction writer does. I made the undertaker a mysterious and cultivated figure who had chosen his profession for reasons only implied after a trip to Europe before the First World War. To a teenage visitor, he relates how, many years before, a woman had come and asked to see the unidentified body, who she claimed might be a friend of her brother's. But when she saw the corpse, the undertaker understood not only that she knew the man, but that she had loved him. None of this was in my source, of course, but that made no difference. I wanted a grand and romantic conclusion to what was an unabashedly romantic novel.

It must be said as well that, from the first, I found that peculiar story compelling. It is true that I had a certain connection with southern Arkansas, where I had spent a few days as a small child on visits to what were locally referred to as kissin' kin, people related to me collaterally rather than by blood. But more than that, I was filled with curiosity as to *why* the mortician would preserve the body; I was moved by the notion that an anonymous burial would not suffice, something that perhaps has to do with my own fears regarding the loneliness of death, of loneliness in general, and by a naive attraction to the notion of the kindness of strangers, even if that kindness is bestowed upon a dead man.

Once again, just as with myth or with that great novel of the past, it is not the strangeness, but the personal, compelling strangeness of that filler story that will determine whether it is of use to you or not. Your creative self must be intrigued by it. It has to touch you in a special way. And that touching, I would suggest, is involved with particular issues at the very core of you and your own experience.

KNOW THY DREAMS

You have determinedly reviewed the canon of great literature. You have read Homer's *Iliad*, the heroic tragedies of John Dryden, the socially conscious novels of Émile Zola, and still, the earth has not moved, the bells have not rung, no fireworks have shimmered through your imagination. None of the classic stories from the ancient, medieval or modern world has particularly struck you, certainly has not compelled you toward a creation of your own. Contemporary fiction casts no spell on you, history doesn't shake you, the newspaper strikes no chords. Your own life is a wash. Your family history is stultifying in its dullness, and those of your friends are a numbing cavalcade of clichés and conventions.

Now, where to turn?

Let's go back to the beginning of this chapter, where we talked of knowing thyself and touched on the idea of your dreams and fantasies. Sit down for a moment. Close your eyes. Drift. What you are looking for is an image. It may be something you've seen, something you've imagined, something you've dreamed. What is significant is that this is the image you remember. Among all the possible images you might recall, this is the one that comes to you.

Get it firmly in your mind. Now, describe it. Note the details. Is it a place? A face? A scene? Begin to pull back from it, just as you would with a camera. What do you see? Do you hear voices? What are people saying?

This is not a New Age exercise. It is part of the Romantic heritage of artistic creation which, despite endless literary movements since, still dominates our vision of the writer's lot. Samuel Taylor Coleridge asserted that his fragmentary poem "Kubla Khan" came to him in a dream, helped along, it is true, by a stout dose of tincture of opium taken to relieve what must be one of the most artistically fortunate attacks of diarrhea in history.

The concept of the inspired image—the product of sleep or daydreams or foreign substances—is a serious one. Faulkner repeatedly claimed that the most complex of his novels, *The Sound and the Fury*, began with nothing more than a single vision: a little girl with muddy drawers high in a tree, her brothers on the ground beneath her as she peeks through a window to observe her grandmother's funeral. James Dickey's novel of the Georgia backwoods, *Deliverance*, grew out of a daydream of a man standing alone on a high cliff, a dream that came to Dickey while reclining in a hammock in Italy in 1962. In my own experience, you may have realized that my novel *Mrs. Randall* sprang from three images I've mentioned. The first was that corpse maintained all those years in Prescott, Arkansas. The second, that family story of my college friend, whose aunt's illegitimate child was aborted by her own sisters. And the third? That photograph of a lynching I talked about, seen in a book entitled *Mississippi Black Paper* when I was in high school: a picture of the charred corpse of a man burned alive in the 1920s, surrounded by the stiff, smiling members of the mob who had murdered him.

These images, clear as snapshots, were indelibly imprinted on my memory, and each is the center around which the book's three sections—the epilogue, prologue and body of the text respectively—revolve.

There is no question you have to be a mite careful about depending on dreams for the genesis of your fiction. There is no carte blanche to kick back and while away the years imagining the great book you'll publish someday. A onetime roommate of mine with literary ambitions, on nights when both of us were a bit in our cups, would describe to me the novel he was going to write. There were moments of his narrative so achingly right I can recall them now, twenty years after the fact. Perhaps some statute of limitations has expired, and I can guiltlessly appropriate them. My friend, now a successful attorney, never set down a word of that tale.

Yet, Edison's remark-become-cliché that genius is 10 percent inspiration (the rest is perspiration) is not to be dismissed lightly. Those images you inexplicably keep, those that come to you from nowhere, speak of some wonder, some horror, some joy that intersects with some profound element that makes you who you are. Trolling through your unconscious—that happy act of daydreaming—should not become a means to avoid the terrifying moment of sitting yourself down before the blank page. But the wandering mind, like the body that sets out with no particular destination, can lead us to unanticipated riches. Don't presume all your naps in the hammock on a balmy afternoon will be as inspiring as James Dickey's. Don't anticipate that if one glass of wine loosed your imagination, three will send it soaring. But do remember that there are times, riotously self-justifying as it may sound to your friends, when in those moments of apparent relaxation, you are really hard at work.

EXERCISES

1. Keep a journal for a month. Don't feel you must dutifully record every day's events as in a diary. Include those you feel are significant, but include as well your thoughts on what you are reading, dreams you found interesting, stories others told you and so on. At month's end, choose four entries you think might bear consideration as the basis for stories, and try to figure out why these four particularly struck you.

2. Read a book of the Bible, any one, to see if there is an incident you can imagine recasting in a contemporary setting. Write a scene or two. Do the same with a book of mythology or anthropology.

3. Choose a favorite literary work and reimagine it. Alter something basic: the point of view, the setting, the time. Then, jot down half a dozen differences that would exist between the original and your own imagined text.

4. Spend a day (or at least a couple hours) with someone of a generation, class or locale different from yours. Try to get the person

to talk about his experiences, be they in work, in love, at leisure. Write two pages expanding upon one anecdote you've been told.

5. Choose two events, one contemporary and one historical. Write a scene based on each, respecting the time in which they occurred. For example, evoke the religious violence of today's Northern Ireland and the "Gunfight at the O.K. Corral." Next, take the scenes you've written and turn them on their heads, for example, shift the sectarian battles of today back in time, and set the gunfight in a contemporary context.

6. Over the space of a week, close your eyes and relax and let images drift through your head. Jot them down, and then choose two or three of them and see if you can elaborate on those visions.

THREE

WORDS, WORDS, WORDS

You've got that contemporary, urban retelling of "Hansel and Gretel" in your head, a hard-hitting exposé of deadbeat parents, kids adrift in the jungle of the big city and the dog-eat-dog (witch-eat-child?) world we live in. You're ready to write the prequel of *Great Expectations*, explaining, from her boyfriend's point of view, just how Miss Havisham got jilted all those years ago. You've planned a great novel based on one overlooked blunder at Gettysburg that changed the course of the Civil War. There's a single image of inexplicably carnivorous hollyhocks searing your brain that will blossom into an unforgettable epic of ecological vengeance. So let's get about the business of constructing a compelling fiction. Grab the hammers, saws and wrenches. Raise the roof beam, set the studs, tighten all those nuts and bolts. Let's get with it!

Let's not . . .

Yet.

Before I discuss precisely how to put together a story that will stick with your reader, it's worth taking a little time to consider what that story is put together with. And that, of course, is words.

According to the novelist Cynthia Ozick, "A novel is, first of all, made out of language, it is language that determines whether a novel's storytelling trajectory will land it in the kingdom of art or the rundown neighborhood of the hackneyed." We can quibble with Ozick's assertion. A great many immensely popular books are written in a language that is charitably described as "workmanlike," a term that brings to mind nothing so much as the ditty from the mid-twentieth century about "ticky-tacky houses"—red, blue, pink, yellow—that "all look just the same." Still, from time to time, there is a truly great talent who possesses an utterly tin ear when it comes to words. The most often-cited example is the American naturalist Theodore Dreiser, who, despite a prose style so barren it hardly constitutes a style at all, gave us *An American Tragedy* and *Sister Carrie*, novels which by sheer force of plot and character capture the glittering energy and dark hypocrisies of America at the twentieth century's dawn.

Generally, though, Ozick's point is sound. How many times have all of us had the experience of reading a review of a book or hearing its plot related, then buying it and finding ourselves oddly uncompelled by it? Thirty years after the fact, I can still recall my disappointment when I read the novel (which shall remain nameless) upon which one of the two or three signature movies of the late 1960s was based. The plot and characters were the same but, frankly, the director had done a far better job bringing them to life than had the writer.

Great fiction is not solely a great story. It is a great story well told.

And for that telling, inevitably, we are thrown back on language.

Objectively, you could assert that having only words places writers under some severe limitations. Think of the resources a film director can draw on: music, the varying registers of the human voice, the concrete presence of actors, sound, special visual effects, the *image* itself projected on screen. A Jean-Luc Godard or Martin Scorsese can marshall all these forces, in *addition* to words, to stimulate his audience's imagination.

And what do we writers have? A highly imperfect system of signs that can by their very nature only intimate what is being evoked. When Federico Fellini wants to show us that ocean liner as it sails past the small village in his movie *Amarcord*, he can capture the dreamy magic of the huge ship as it appears to his child protagonist and project it before us for all the world to see. We, conversely, can only suggest it on the page, use words that are approximate or ambiguous. Consider *set*. It has sixty-four different definitions in *The Oxford English Dictionary*. *Belie* is its own antonym. How many of us have precisely the same color in mind when somebody tells us something is taupe?

This may not be as bad as it sounds. Those signs allow our collusive reader, who comes to a work with her own imagination, her own stock of experience and dreams, to construct her own nuanced vision of what we have set on the page. Let's say you and your friends sit down to watch the videotape of the 1956 production of *Moby Dick*—a sincere if somewhat flat film directed by John Huston. All of you will see Richard Basehart as Ishmael, Gregory Peck as Ahab and a less than convincing portrayal of the title character by something akin to an Army Surplus dirigible. Huston controls what all of you have in your minds.

Conversely, if you and these same friends sat down and read *Moby Dick* aloud to one another and could, by some magic, each project on the wall what your minds' eyes created in collusion with Herman Melville's prose, those images would all be different, probably not in their broad outlines, but in the details: the shape of Queequeg's head, the gait of the lamed Ahab, the expression of terror on Ishmael's face when his Polynesian roommate prays at his makeshift altar. Words are a kind of sophisticated Morse code by which we telegraph information from one imagination to another. They are decoded by the receiver, producing in his head an image similar to, but distinct from, the one the author had in her head when she translated it from vision to words. That image is distinct from reader A to reader B, B to C and so on ad infinitum. Each act of reading transforms a work; every reader creates the work anew.

LEARNING TO LOVE THE MOTHER TONGUE

The words we employ are English words, and as writers, we could do worse, despite the fact that English is a particularly messy language. Those who possess it as their native tongue are lucky if for no other reason than it is so difficult to learn. English grammar results from a vain and pedantic attempt to impose imperial Roman order on a language that is, at base, barbarically Germanic. Indeed, some of the earliest English grammar books (Alexander Gil's *Logonomia Anglica*, for example) were themselves *written* in Latin, which was probably not a very good augury. Think back to those lessons in the eighth grade when you learned a particular rule, only to turn the page to discover a list of exceptions to it. Even something so apparently straightforward as pluralization can get pretty dicey.

> You form a plural by adding an "s" to the singular, except when the word ends in an "s" already, or an "x" or "z", or an "sh" or "ch", when you add "es". Of course, when the word ends in a

"y", if that "y" is preceded by a vowel, you add an "s" ("Guernseys"), but if it's preceded by a consonant, you drop the "y" and add "ies" ("fillies"), except if it's a proper name, when you again just add an "s" (the "Bachardys"). Then there are words that end in "f' (it's "safes," but "leaves"). Don't forget "mice," "geese" or "children," or certain words derived from Latin (datum, data; alumnus, alumni), and . . .

Makes *i* before *e* except after *c* (yes, yes, "when sounded like *a* as in . . .") look simple, doesn't it? Imagine trying to play baseball if every eighth batter or one whose name began with *K* got five strikes instead of three.

You get the idea.

If we really are strictly bound by the laws of pluralization, all sorts of supposedly immutable rules of the language are, whether intentionally or not, broken constantly by everyone from the man on the street to the prissiest grammarians to the great geniuses of literature. "Never begin a sentence with a conjunction," we are solemnly warned. Now, look at the final sentence of the lionized poet John Milton's famous essay (on education!), *Aeropagitica*, which begins "But to redress willingly and speedily what hath been erred . . ." Perhaps he was playing hooky the day they talked about conjunctions, though more likely he wanted to throw particular emphasis on the thought with which he ends his argument. The same holds true for the old chesnut that asserts we should never end a sentence with a preposition. What would you make of someone who, rather than saying, "What are you waiting for?" says, "For what are you waiting?" Affected? A strange visitor from another planet who hasn't quite got the language down yet?

A Brief History of a Bastard Tongue

Our garbled grammar and much else eccentric about the language are the results of history. We speak a tongue derived from two distinct linguistic families, Germanic and Romantic, with a tiny number of Celtic ghosts flitting around the edges. Native Britons were conquered by Romans, and their Latinized descendants by Teutonic tribes at the beginning of the Dark Ages. Those Angles and Saxons and Jutes had to put up with assaults from their relatives, the Danes, and finally their kingdom fell to the Normans, themselves gallicized Vikings. So

Anglo-Saxon and a French dialect came together to give us what we call English, which has undergone endless evolution ever since.

The mongrel quality of English, maddening as it often is, is nonetheless the source of its greatest strengths and, hence, some of your greatest opportunities as a writer. From very early in its development, English possessed a bigger vocabulary than any other Western language, one that even today is guesstimated as half again as large as, for example, French. The initial reason for this is those conquests I mentioned earlier. When the Normans came with their Norman French, many words in their vocabulary were simply integrated into the predominant Anglo-Saxon tongue, often in revealing ways. The reason we eat "mutton" instead of "sheepmeat" is, at least speculatively, that the victorious continental lords sat at their tables and carved up "*mouton*," the French word for the animal the peasants were tending out on the local heath. We have "bricklayers," but wouldn't it be more elegant to be a "mason"? Are you a down-to-earth "stonecutter," or are your ambitions rather loftier, so that on your business card you're a "sculptor"?

As these examples indicate, English combines an extensive Latin-based vocabulary with a more limited (but more frequently employed) Anglo-Saxon one, which means we often have two words for something where other languages have but one. We may be "scared" (from the Old Norse *skirra*) or "terrified" (from the Latin *terrere*), both these roots meaning "frightened." A flower may have a "good smell" (*god*—Old English; *smellen*—Middle English) or a "pleasant odor" (both brought to us from Latin via French). Does the villain in your story use a "dagger" (French *dague*) or a "knife" (Old English *cnif*)? Is your princess a "lady fair" (from the Old English *hlaefdige faeger*, a light-complected breadkneader!) or a "beautiful damsel" (from the Latin *bellus* via the Old French *beaute*, and, again from Latin through Old French, *domina/dameisele*)?

It is these kinds of choices that allow Macbeth's exclamation regarding his bloody hand after he has murdered King Duncan.

> . . . No, this my hand will rather
> The multitudinous seas incarnadine,
> Making the green one red.

Of course, Shakespeare's character is saying the same thing twice. The second line is anchored by two mellifluous Latinisms, "multitudinous" and "incarnadine." And what does *incarnadine* mean? "Bloody, crimson, like flesh," derived from the same root as *carnivorous*, the Latin *carnis*. The third line, conversely, is composed solely of short, sharp Germanic words, with "make red" replacing "will incarnadine."

The history of our language has also inclined us toward a greater latitude in enlarging and enriching our vocabulary, a willingness to simply appropriate words from other tongues if they prove useful. British and American imperialism, along with the vast waves of immigration to the New World from all parts of the Old, have given us a linguistic palette that few other languages can rival. Consider this.

> She's a diva and he's a macho poseur—all that kvetching over
> a pair of khaki mukluks on the futon!

All right, so that's pushing the envelope a bit, but this is a completely comprehensible English sentence. And take note of its Ellis Island of provenances: "diva" (Italian), "macho" (Spanish), "poseur" (French), "kvetch" (Yiddish), "khaki" (Hindi), "mukluks" (Inuit), "futon" (Japanese). Stringing it all together are short, hearty Anglo-Saxonisms: "a," "and," "all," "that," "over," "of," "on."

Learning to Love Another Tongue

You would think, with our jerry-built grammar and polyglot vocabulary, we would be master linguists, but the sad fact is that Americans in general make Shakespeare's possession of "little Latin and less Greek," as his contemporary Ben Jonson put it, look like the accomplishment of a U.N. interpreter. It may seem wildly reactionary to suggest that every writer, and especially one who is at a key moment in his development, ought to know or study a foreign language, but the notion has much to recommend it. It is not a question of your mastering French or Arabic, or even attaining a degree of fluency in it. Rather, it is the idea of simply hearing how Russian sounds, seeing how Portuguese is put together, noting the likenesses and differences with this English you know. If nothing else, the experience will enlarge the palette of your vocabulary. It was while studying Spanish that I came upon the word *fausto*, which means "lucky." This added to my appreciation of the irony in the name of the hero of all the various versions of the story of Faust, the man who sells his soul to the devil for the possession of infinite knowledge (some luck!). I also got to put it in the mouth of my self-consciously elegant protagonist in the novel *Mrs. Randall*. He seemed just the kind of guy who would drop a highly ambiguous Latinism like that into a remark about his detested father: "Perhaps, if there is a destiny to things, Mrs. Randall came to live in Franksville because of my father, in whose faust astrology there was no place for extended suffering."

Thinking about another language helps you think seriously about your own, encourages you to seek new and distinctive modes of expression within it. If a foreign language is simply *too* intimidating, at the least consider taking a course in sociolinguistics, reading a history of the English language or rediscovering the racy medieval world of Geoffrey Chaucer's *Canterbury Tales*. Any of these can help focus your mind on the richness of the tool at your disposal. If you're absolutely convinced you would make an utter fool of yourself trying to pronounce anything as esoteric as Italian, then take Latin—mother or stepmother of so many tongues, and handily dead. Despite its occasional usage by the Roman Catholic Church, we really don't know exactly how the classical poet Horace pronounced *"Dulce et decorum est, pro patria more"* ("It is sweet and glorious to die for one's country") or how Caesar said *"Veni, vidi, vici"* ("I came, I saw, I conquered"). A little bit of Latin will allow you to see where a great many words and structures of English come from, not to mention the opportunities it will provide for you to show off and make your friends feel provincial and deprived.

With English, you possess a perversely complicated but marvelously supple instrument, one that gives you an array of selections, especially in vocabulary, unknown to the Dutch or the Greeks. Is that swirl of color at sunset "maroon" or "chestnut"; that remark "sharp" or "barbed"? In the chapters upcoming, I'll return again and again to the variety and subtlety of English, the ways it can shade and nuance the meaning of your story, the ways it can make your prose more compelling.

VOICE AND STYLE

In texts on writing, in most workshops offered in fiction, in most classes that center on literary texts, early on we inevitably encounter some reference to an author's voice. As you'll see, this is an elusive concept, but as such one we might as well tackle here, since often (though not always) it is associated with the writer's language—that is, with her words, syntax, sentence cadences and so on. Voice can be a key factor in holding a reader's attention, in keeping her turning those pages. It is sometimes the most seductive element of all in a piece of prose, a sensual bond between writer and reader, the element that transforms someone who "likes" the books of a particular author into a die-hard fan.

The problem is that simply defining what voice is, much less providing any useful guidance in developing one, is akin to capturing Saint Elmo's fire in a jar.

Voice

Virtually everything you read is in strictest terms written in something nobody really speaks, something we often grandly and vaguely call Standard American English. The boundaries of this language are pretty fluid. Think of the prose you encounter in *The Weekly World Star* vs. that of *People* vs. that of *Newsweek* vs. that of *The New Yorker*. The level of vocabulary and complexity of syntax differ significantly from one publication to the next, and yet all are more or less written with the same attention to particular linguistic norms.

What we think of as literary language is a bit different from the standard. This is surely what Ozick has in mind when she talks about a language that will place a work within "the kingdom of art." It is one that tends to be more vivid, more given to metaphor, in many ways more personal. It often speaks to us in that identifiable voice we come to think typifies a writer. There's little question, for example, that a Hemingway paragraph is immediately distinguishable from a Faulkner sentence, and often not nearly as long. You can judge for yourself.

> Down the street came dancers. The street was solid with dancers, all men. They were all dancing in time behind their own fifers and drummers. They were a club of some sort, and all wore workmen's blue smocks, and red handkerchiefs around their necks. . . .
> —Ernest Hemingway,
> *The Sun Also Rises*

> Her voice would not cease, it would just vanish. There would be the dim coffin-smelling gloom sweet and over sweet with

> the twice-bloomed wisteria against the outer wall by the savage
> quiet September sun impacted distilled and hyperdistilled, into
> which came now and then the loud cloudy flutter of the
> sparrows like a flat limber stick whipped by an idle boy, and
> the rank smell of femaleold flesh long embattled in virginity . . .
> —William Faulkner, *Absalom, Absalom!*

The Faulkner sentence continues for another seven lines of print.

Too much can be made of this notion of a distinctive voice, in that a writer can at least appear to have many voices, drawing on a variety of resources and crafting fiction from them all. The Faulkner who wrote the widely anthologized "A Rose for Emily" and other stories for *The Saturday Evening Post* during the same years he was composing *Absalom, Absalom!* could, on those occasions, sound almost Hemingwayesque. Here's the opening to the story "An Odor of Verbena."

> It was just after supper. I had just opened my *Coke* on the table
> beneath the lamp; I heard Professor Wilkins' feet in the hall
> and then the instant of silence as he put his hand to the door
> knob, and I should have known. People talk glibly of presenti-
> ment, but I had none. I heard his feet on the stairs and then in
> the hall approaching and there was nothing in the feet because
> although I had lived in his house for three college years now
> and although both he and Mrs. Wilkins called me Bayard in
> the house, he would not more have entered my room without
> knocking than I would have entered his—or hers . . .

Now, I did say "almost." You can see how the sentences here are much shorter and the language less convoluted than in the previous example of Faulkner's prose. "It was just after supper" is about as good a simple, declarative statement as you can find. Admittedly, though, when he hits "I heard his feet on the stairs . . . ," Faulkner's flowing Mississippi rhetoric bursts through. Ideas bloom out of other ideas, the conjunctions and dependent clauses start to blossom, and that single sentence ends up longer than the preceding three combined.

Let's look at a more contemporary illustration, one that demon-strates more vividly how knotty a problem we're dealing with. Com-pare these two passages.

I should say at this juncture that Beersley, though undeniably brilliant, tended also to be somewhat mercurial, and I could see something had set him off. Perhaps it was the beastly weather or the long and poorly accommodated trip, or perhaps he was feeling the strain of overwork, called out on this case as he was soon after the rigorous mental exercise he'd put into the baffling case of the Cornucopia Killer of Cooch Behar.

The girl seemed to consider this, reaching out a slim veiny arm to brace herself against the car. "No matter," she said, slurring the *t*'s, "he'll turn up." And then, as if she'd just taken stock of the whole scene—the ravaged car and our battered faces, the desolation of the place—she said: "Hey, you guys look like some pretty bad characters—been fightin', huh?" We stared straight ahead, rigid as catatonics.

The one sequence is arch, self-consciously British ("beastly weather," "rigorous mental exercise"), teetering on if not falling into parody. The other is gritty, down on its luck ("a slim veiny arm"; "slurring the *t*'s"; "our battered faces"). However, both are by the same author, taken from different stories in T. Coraghessan Boyle's *Greasy Lake*. Which voice is his real voice?

The answer, of course, is that both of them are, or perhaps more accurately, neither is precisely Boyle's voice. Both Faulkner's and Hemingway's voices are most overtly expressed in their style. Faulkner can't resist those semicolons and conjunctions, stringing concepts and actions and history together in long, sinuous sentences ripe with an elaborate language filled with words he has invented ("coffin-smelling," "hyperdistilled," "femaleold"). The voice of a writer such as Boyle, on the other hand, arguably exists on a deeper, less obvious level. He is an ironist, often a prankster in his stories, and those qualities more than his style per se constitute his voice, whether he is writing humorously or seriously. His language and syntax are less significant than his tone in identifying his work as specifically his.

So is your voice as a writer stylistic or tonal or something else entirely? My advice, though it may seem like a cop-out, is "don't fret about it." In the end, your voice is something you discover. Like Columbus happening upon America in his search for India, you're most likely to find it when you're not consciously looking for it. A voice evolves, it *becomes* the way you compose, the way you naturally set things to paper in the very broadest sense. It may be quite evident, it may be more subtle, but it is less something you work at than something that establishes itself largely without your knowledge.

Style

Just to make everything more difficult, however, remember that style itself can be self-conscious. In the two selections from Boyle, we can see how he needs and employs a distinct style. His purpose—not to mention his setting, the kind of characters he's creating and so on— varies from one piece to another. Most obviously, he alters his style by using a different diction, a different kind of language, in the story "Rupert Beersley and the Beggar Master of Sivani-Hoota" (the title speaks for itself, don't you think?) than he does in "Greasy Lake" (with an epigraph from a song by Bruce Springsteen).

Still, the line between style and voice is often obscure. The writers Anne Bernays and Justin Kaplan, who have individually or collectively written in virtually all prose genres, have this to say about style.

> Style, or *"voice"* [my emphasis], is an elusive but pervasive characteristic of written prose and hangs on vocabulary, sentence structure and variation, idiom, pace, purpose, mood—and more. Some years ago John Updike complained in an interview that no matter what he wrote it always ended up sounding like John Updike. Why was he complaining? Most of us spend years trying to develop a distinctive and recognizable voice.

Updike's work does manifest a particular, mid-twentieth-century focus on certain issues, put over in a way that always at least suggests the fiction might be his. Boyle, on the other hand, is a wildly versatile writer, one noted for an almost ventriloquistic range. He is a veritable choir of styles. Each, however, is drawing on the linguistic resources he has accumulated over the course of his life. In this context, think a bit about all the different dialects and dictions you are familiar with and employ, that you mix and match. This is what a linguist calls an idiolect—your own, unique way of speaking. The most overt examples of the breadth of individual idiolects are probably found among members of different racial or ethnic communities or particular subcultures, some of which you may be a part of. The eloquent African-

American attorney who this afternoon urged the judge to "take serious note of the implications of the plaintiff's amicus brief" could tonight, around the poker table, warn his bluffing buddy: "You do be smokin' tonight, but I don't believe you got grapes in that hand." The gay autoworker on the assembly line wants to know, "So, what's the beef with the new shop steward?" while at the barbecue on Saturday he asks, "So what's the dish on David's new boyfriend?" Years ago in New York City, walking down the street with a Nuyorican friend, I was surprised when he pointed to a distinguished old post office and said, in a bilingual idiolect: "*Mira ese* building, *que* nice."

"But I'm just boring and white bread," some of you protest. "I don't have those kind of resources to draw on." Tut, tut. Listen to the various levels of language you use every day, what a linguist calls registers. You greet your boss's business associate ("So nice to see you again, Ms. Pilfer") in a different manner than you greet your spouse ("Hi, sweetheart") or your old friend at last month's high school reunion ("Yo! Milbeck, you turkey!"). You tell Ms. Pilfer your day's been difficult, your spouse that it was crummy, Milbeck that it sucked. Phil's evocation of Gloria's thoughts and experiences, back in chapter one, is sure to differ in expression from his tales of beer-drinking slackers down on the beach. He'll be seeking those elements of his own idiolect that would reasonably be employed by a woman, one some thirty years older than he, who lives in a region distinct from the one he inhabits.

Diction and Dialect

Diction represents a serious authorial choice you make in narrating a story and in the voices of its characters. You may opt for some variation on Standard American English—a straightforward, relatively stripped down, almost journalistic prose, like Hemingway's, or a dense, highly metaphoric, self-consciously literary one like Faulkner's. For the sake of argument, let's assume you are writing a first-person narrative about a working-class New Yorker in the 1930s. This is how Thomas Wolfe framed that voice in "Only the Dead Know Brooklyn."

> So like I say, I'm waitin' for my train t' come when I sees dis big guy standin' deh—dis is duh foist I eveh see of him. Well,

> he's lookin' wild, y'know, an' I can see dat he's had plenty, but
> still he's holdin' it; he talks good an' is walkin' straight enough.
> So den, dis big guy steps up to a little guy dat's standin' deh,
> an' says, "How d'yuh get t' Eighteent' Aveneoo an' Sixty-sevent'
> Street?" he says.

We can argue that Wolfe is overdoing it here, trying too hard to capture the sound and rhythm of a brand of English that must have seemed strange to him, a Southerner with a Master's degree from Harvard whose prose ran more toward the rhetorical, the Latinate, the poetic. But he opted for the first person in this story. He had to abandon his standard diction. He cannot *tell* us in the narrative that his character turns the diphthong *th* into a *d*, that he drops his final *g*'s and *d*'s. He has to show us.

This kind of linguistic transcription should be used sparingly. You want to capture the peculiarities of speech, its flavor and color, without turning your text into a scholarly article or what appears to be a screed against the way some people speak. If you look at humorous texts of the last century, you will encounter endless forgotten stories written in various dialects. Many of these now strike us as virtually unintelligible, and, for the most part, their intent was condescension. Many were merely mean-spirited, playing off the voguish bigotries of the day.

Oftentimes, you can choose one or two tics of speech—the dropped *g*, the double negative, the repeated use of particular kinds of metaphor—to *imply* a particular voice. These cue the reader, collusive as she is, as to how the speaker sounds, and the reader will then "hear" that voice with the proper shadings even though you don't transcribe them absolutely on the page. Likewise, in narrative, a simple statement can often suffice.

> "Well, is that all?" he drawled.
> "Just park it out in front." The long, flat "a" let me know
> Billy's last name might as well be Boston.

Pull down your copy of *The Adventures of Huckleberry Finn*. Many readers overlook (and indeed, many editions fail to include) Mark Twain's two notes to the reader that precede chapter one. Here's the more famous of the two.

Persons attempting to find a motive in this narrative will be prosecuted; persons attempting to find a moral in it will be banished; persons attempting to find a plot in it will be shot.

It is the second, however, that if less amusing is more important.

EXPLANATORY

In this book a number of dialects are used, to wit: the Missouri negro dialect; the extremest form of the backwoods Southwestern dialect; the ordinary "Pike County" dialect; and four modified varieties of this last. The shadings have not been done in a haphazard fashion, or by guesswork; but painstakingly, and with the trustworthy guidance and support of personal familiarity with these several forms of speech.

Twain is not a writer we often think of as a "painstaking" craftsman, and yet the note makes it apparent he was proud indeed of the fact that Jim, Huck, Aunt Sally, The Grangerfords, the Duke and the Dauphin speak not one language, not some literary language, but the languages they would, in reality, speak. He is not making fun of anybody, at least of the way anybody talks. The explanatory makes clear he respects the differences he has heard. Twain, in his boyhood and youth, in his journeys as a riverboat pilot up and down the Mississippi, had been exposed to dialect after dialect, and he wants us to hear them as we read. Listen to Jim and Huck in conversation.

> " . . . I ben a-buyin' pots en pans en vittles, as I got a chanst,
> en a patchin' up de raf', nights, when—"
> "*What* raft, Jim?"
> "Our ole raft."
> "You mean to say our old raf warn't smashed all to flinders?"

For Huck, it's an "old" raft, for Jim, an "ole" one. Huck uses the verb "warn't" rather than "wasn't," and the noun "flinders," derived from Norwegian (!), rather than the conventional "pieces."

You sigh. The American language has changed after all. The inflections and metaphors of region or place have grown gradually more homogenized due to easy travel and television. There is some truth to this, though perhaps less than we think. Carbonated drinks are still "pop" in the Midwest, after all, and "soda" in the East. Southerners say "hey" for "hi," and continue to use "yonder" ("over yonder in the garage"), which is archaic elsewhere. New Yorkers wait "on line" rather than "in line," while Canadians "queue up."

Jargons

Regional variations of vocabulary are but one of the resources upon which you can draw. You need not wander far afield to encounter the special dictions you use. Your job, sports, music and dance, your hobbies, your particular generation—all these employ particular idioms (a linguist's jargons) that may be useful in characterizing the figures who populate your story, in finding *their* voices. The weekend touch-footballer, in urging a friend to carry through on a project, tells him, "Don't punt." The couple in their seventies can still "cut a rug," while their grandchildren "go clubbing." Remember when *bad* went through a period of meaning "truly good"?

Back in my graduate student days, I was enchanted by the film *Altered States*, directed by Ken Russell with a screenplay by that old master Paddy Chayefsky. What struck me was less the weird special effects that allowed the star to become a primordial ape-man and ultimately a Day-Glo blob of protoplasm than the *language* the characters spoke. The argot of the young scientists—a colloquial and often vulgar diction peppered with complex terms and turns of phrase drawn from biology, physics and chemistry—struck me as absolutely right, exactly how these researchers would sound. Indeed, it was the way my friends and I spoke in those days—though our conversations blossomed with arcane terminology from the humanities, not from the hard sciences: "You can't say it's just some goofy reification!" "Are you pulling that ditzy present absence argument again?" "Marcusean one-dimensionality won't cut it unless you rejigger the axiomatic norms."

I'm not entirely sure *I* understood what I was saying, but it sure made me feel hip.

As with variant spelling or grammar, don't overdo it. In many ways, what these idioms do is create a particular atmosphere or aura. Too much specialized terminology can leave a reader foundering, which means your story is sinking. If you know a great deal about cars, and you have a character, DeWayne, who is an aspiring mechanic, spice your story with a dash of transmission fluid here and a sprinkle of ball bearings there, but stay away from catalytic converters or alternator brushes unless these are truly significant in the tale you have to tell.

Remember that a reader can often figure out certain terms by the context, and also that your narrator or characters can define something, so long as the definition fits logically into the text. Perhaps DeWayne's sister, Patrice, has come by, and he (briefly) explains some piece of automotive arcana to her. Perhaps the physical description of a thrown rod or a carburetor—not merely how it looks, but how it sounds or feels in his hand—can be the means to provide the reader with whatever information he needs to know.

DESCRIPTIVE STRATEGIES

DeWayne's experience of life at the garage—what it looks like, what it smells like, the noise and bodily sensations of the physical labor such work entails—leads us toward another facet of language and its uses in raising your work out of Ozick's "rundown neighborhood of the hackneyed." Sensual description is one of the most powerful weapons in your writerly arsenal, and, let's be honest, one of the things that attracts us to our particular interests is the stimulation of the senses they offer. The carpenter has a distinct and visceral appreciation of the heft and odor of different woods, the exact function and feel of every tool. The committed cook enjoys the resistance of dough between his fingers, the smell of garlic and olive oil asimmer. Listen to how John Steinbeck, in *The Grapes of Wrath*, captures the controlled chaos of a country stove in a mere two lines.

> She picked up the fork and combed the boiling grease and brought out a curl of crisp pork. And she set a pot of tumbling coffee on the back of the stove.

"Combed" and "curl," "boiling" and "crisp," coffee that's "tumbling" in the pot: The sensory vividness of Steinbeck's description ends up implying far more than is stated. Though there is no mention of them specifically, you can feel the heat from the cooking, smell the hot grease and hear the coffee roiling over the flame. The sensuality of the combed-out curl, of the coffee tumbling subtly links the pleasure of food to physical, almost erotic, pleasure. Steinbeck's tools here are simple ones: verbs, nouns and adjectives. But he has chosen them judiciously, creating the kitchen and that breakfast in two brief sentences.

Consider another example. One of the oddest things I have noticed about jock stories in workshops is how, so often, they fail to include the immediate and intense physicality that gymnastics or football or baseball must involve and which their participants obviously enjoy. A baseball bat has weight; the well-used pigskin has a special smell and texture; the balance beam demands a constant monitoring on the subtlest level of strains and stretches so that an entire routine appears effortlessly explosive.

This is the contemporary writer Michael Martone in the mind of an Olympic swimmer in his story "Highlights."

> . . . I would think about that while swimming. Growing gills, webs, flukes. Evolving backwards . . .
>
> While I swam, parts came loose and floated free. My nipples slid down my chest. My chin sheered away. My toenails shed like scales. There were fingers in my wake.

Notice how Martone captures for us the feel of swimming, of water sluicing over the body as the swimmer torpedos through the water. Unlike Steinbeck's, Martone's description is not merely verbal, not only dependent on the words themselves. It is overtly *metaphorical*. The sliding, sheering, shedding the character feels all relate to the larger, overarching image of a man being transformed into a fish— arms to "flukes," feet to "webs." The sensuality of the experience is further emphasized by the magic of the character's envisioning his own metamorphosis.

Using All the Senses

In description, it's useful to remember that we humans have become overly dependent on our eyes. Some scientists argue that our other senses have become mere adjuncts to our sight so that, for example, rather than reacting to a sound itself, we immediately *look* to see where a sound is coming from. Our creature cousins use hearing, touch and so on far more extensively than we do. It is not that visual description is a bad thing, but often a metaphor drawn from a different sense is more powerful. How many of us have had the experience of finding ourselves in sudden tears when a particular song comes on the radio, one that instantly transports us back to a moment spent with a long-lost friend? How many have had a forgotten memory triggered by the smell of baking cookies or that peculiar mix of chalk and wax and a summer's disuse that is the odor of the first day of school? The aural, the tactile, the olfactory can have a kind of impact that the purely visual does not.

Look up for a moment from your reading. What's the first thing you see? A magazine beside the bed? A glass of iced tea? A bush in the backyard? Consider how you might describe that object employing a sense other than sight. The slick, glossy paper of *Time* or *Esquire* has a distinctive smell. The sweat on a cold glass on a hot day makes whatever is inside seem all the colder. The wind through a bush can sound like a steady rain. The unanticipated rightness of a description can make your prose, and hence your story, one that burrows past your reader's conscious appreciation and settles itself in her own store of images.

When working in that convalescent hospital, I was feeding a stroke patient with a mouth syringe one morning. She was in bad shape, needless to say. To pass the time, I often spoke with her roommate, a feisty, Southern woman in her late eighties named Rona. I do not remember why now, but one morning, I was more or less ignoring Rona, who rolled her wheelchair over to the door of the room, which happened to be across from the kitchen. Normally, at that hour, there was much banging and slamming of trays and glassware and cutlery. The staff, however, must have been on break. As Rona sat there, she sighed, leaned back in her chair and said, "Quiet as cotton outside."

That was more than twenty-five years ago, and that image has stuck with me ever since. It is a remarkably complex one if you think about it. Cotton is a fiber. It is soft. It can be used to swathe or muffle something. Softness is a tactile sensation, but also an aural one, synonymous with quietness. We talk about soft music or a soft voice. In her metaphor, what Rona did was conflate the two sensory experiences into one, so that the quiet of the hallway seemed to her as soft as the feel of cotton.

Sources of Metaphor

Rona's growing up at the beginning of the twentieth century in the rural South was, doubtless, the source of this metaphor. As I've noted, such specific regionalisms find their way into our speech less and less as America grows endlessly more suburbanized. Still, the suburbs themselves, the contemporary workplace, your hobbies and other pursuits can provide a host of distinctive images. Sitting here at the keyboard, it occurs to me that in the right context an evening sky could glow "blue as a PC screen." Remember DeWayne, our aspiring mechanic? Let's say his sister Patrice is mad at him, and he's describing her sudden rage to his boss. Rather than, "She got real angry," why not, "She was hot as a Mustang with a busted radiator"? Look at how Susan Dodd's protagonist, in the story "Hell-Bent Men and Their Cities," mines an extended and unexpected image from our over-carbonated culture: "His eyes, the color of cola with tiny pinpoints of light like fizz, washed over her face and made it tingle."

What images are lurking out there on the grocery shelves and in the offices and rec centers of the vast sprawl surrounding our major cities?

His mind was as neat as a just-mown lawn in Larchmont.

The triplets were as identical as three split-levels from 1974.

The ricochet made the sound of a broken racket string.

Nancy had the heart of a corporate raider in the middle of an unfriendly takeover.

As I've noted before, writers too often dismiss their own experience as gray and dull and thus inappropriate as a source of plots, characters or metaphors. In the case of the last, they fall back on trite and conventionalized descriptions that have been so often used they mean nothing: "clear as a bell," "pretty as a picture," "sweet as pie." Or dull as dishwater. On the other hand, you've got to be careful of being *too* creative. Language and metaphor should illuminate your text, help the reader envision what you envisioned. They should not draw undue attention to themselves by violating the overall tone of your story. We'd be more than a little surprised if, when Patrice enters the garage, we were told "DeWayne looked up from the greasy engine and saw her. She looked serious, angry, *la belle dame sans merci*." Unless you've established that DeWayne has been brushing up on his Keats (or his French), that particular phrase is likely to stop the reader dead.

Still, strive to be distinctive. Be conscious of the world around you, and integrate what you see, smell, hear, taste and feel into your imagination. One of the reader's greatest delights is that mot juste, the very *right* word or phrase, that captures exactly, uniquely, what is being portrayed.

THE PECULIAR POWERS OF THE PRINTED WORD

As the image drawn from smell or taste may be more powerful than the purely visual, words on the page are in a certain way stronger than those spoken (yet another example of the primacy of sight). We *see* each word in a way we don't actually *hear* them when spoken. Let's say you have a surly fifteen-year-old as a character, kept after class by his teacher.

> "But, Tommy, why set the trash can on fire?"
> "Umm, well, I thought like, ya know, it might like, ah, get Sarah to like talk to me, ya know?"

That may be the way this teenager talks, but, as suggested earlier, you can probably get away with only a couple of his tics: one "ya know," one "like." You are capturing that aura of real speech that cues the reader to how Tommy speaks and, we can hope, ultimately to how Tommy thinks and who Tommy is.

Talking Dirty

The greater power of the printed over the spoken word arises particularly when it comes to swearing. Four-letter words (as we rather quaintly call them, though they seem to become ever more polysyllabic) are now so common that, in certain contexts, they seem to function more as classic "time-buyers"—"umm," "ahh" or a drag on a cigarette—than as real and significant words. A rule of thumb I once heard: As you hear a character pepper her speech with obscenities, write them all down and then take out half of them. The word in black and white is stronger than the word uttered. This perhaps explains both the popularity of graffiti and the fury it causes: The written word assaults us in a way the spoken one doesn't; we hear it in our heads when we read it.

Vulgarities in narrative or dialogue are always tricky. In introductory workshops, the question inevitably arises: "Can we use swearwords?" The answer seems apparent: If the narrator or character would use this kind of language, it is dishonest to wash his mouth out with soap and have him shout, "Gol darn it!" when he hits his thumb with a hammer. A drill sergeant normally has a dirtier mouth than the director of activities at the local Methodist church; a society matron will likely avoid words a young fashion model would use without a second thought. DeWayne and his buddies at the garage are unlikely to be too delicate in their speech, though they may well rein in their tongues a bit when Patrice is there.

As said, most obscenities have become so much a part of daily speech that their very power has been undermined. Not long ago, I noted that "asskisser" appeared in *Time* magazine (ironically followed within half-a-dozen words by the notion that the person so described was an "ass----"), but remember that, up until the 1950s, most writing— from the most elegant poem to a story in *The Police Gazette*—got along quite nicely without such expressions. It was not that these words did not exist, nor that they were not in common use. A look at any diction- ary, particularly one of slang, will show you that most of our common swearwords go back hundreds of years. I remember being fascinated in high school that in Norman Mailer's novel of the Second World War, *The Naked and the Dead*, all the soldiers were regularly muttering, yelling, hissing, snapping, "Fugg you." What an example, I thought, of the evolution of the language in a mere twenty years!

The banal truth, of course, was that Mailer's publisher did not want to break the long-standing taboo against what used to be considered the most resonant American dirty word, and so he was forced to alter it. Times have obviously changed, though if you're uncomfortable with profanity, remember that Shakespeare, Austen, Dickens, James and Forster did fine without it. Also bear in mind that certain publica- tions—not merely religious journals, but many magazines both large and small—still frown on such language. Particularly foul-mouthed characters may limit the market for your story. Is that foul-mouthed mode of expression integral to your character? If so, you cannot hon- estly censor her, though even then, there are evasive maneuvers you might take.

"What are you telling me, DeWayne?" Patrice's hands went to her face, and she swore. "I never, never thought you could try to pull such a . . ." She swore again. ". . . stunt! After all *I've* been through! All this . . ." She swore a third time. "I can't believe you'd, you'd . . ." She gasped for breath, then let go with a string of obscenities that would have made a sailor blush.

This may seem a little clumsy, though you might argue that making the reader *imagine* the words coming out of Patrice's mouth gives them a distinct power that your actually spelling them out lacks. Think of Alfred Hitchcock's notions of horror, as in the famous "shower scene" of his film *Psycho*. Unlike in the "splatter" movies of the 1980s, we do not actually see Janet Leigh reduced to a knife-tattered pulp by Tony Perkins. Rather, in a series of quick cuts, we see the blade descending again and again, Leigh struggling, the shower curtain pulled off its rings—pop! pop! pop!—as she falls and, finally, the blood-streaked water swirling down the drain as the shower continues to patter, all of this in black and white. Hitchcock's idea was that it was far more frightening to let each viewer come up with the gory details of the scene in his own head than it was to impose the director's own particular horrific version of it. You may not be surprised, remembering the opening of this chapter, that Hitchcock is often referred to as a particularly literary director.

MIXED CODES

We should note that, in fiction, there is a great deal of mixing codes. That is what those aforementioned graduate students and young researchers were doing in *Altered States*—combining an everyday argot with the most highly specialized scientific vocabulary. In third-person narrative, self-evidently, it is very common for the narration to be written in one diction and the dialogue in quite another. Both literary texts and endless thrillers, crime novels and horror stories mix and match their dictions. Characters speak one way and the description of their thoughts and actions and surroundings emerges in terms that differ radically from the kind the characters themselves would employ.

In his novel *Midnight Cowboy*, James Leo Herlihy writes of a naive young Texan, Joe Buck, who goes to New York to seek his fortune as a gigolo.

> "May I sit down?"
> Joe was flustered and pleased. "Oh hell yes." He got to his feet and began to shuffle chairs unnecessarily, unhinged by his

sudden role as host. The visitor put out his hand and said, "Perry."

"W-what's that?"

"My name, Perry, P-e-r-r-y."

"Oh, yeah, oh, yeah." He took the young man's hand and shook it. "Joe Buck," he said. "Want a cigarette?"

Obviously, nineteen-year-old Joe is unlikely to think of himself as "flustered" or "unhinged" or as playing the role of "host." But of course, it is Herlihy who is narrating the story, not Joe, and hence his diction can be far more sophisticated than that of his character.

On the second page of my first novel, *Mean Time*, the ex-con, Dewey, is described this way.

> . . . on that Friday, when he heard the gate slam behind him and emerged into the world a self-proclaimed promise of chaos, he felt the thrill of the dawning fulfillment of some minor destiny, one that had transformed him from a boy who thought killing had less to do with malice than with honor to a man convinced of the regnancy of evil.

Not exactly the kind of imagery you would expect from a small-town killer, but one of the things a narrator can do is find the words to describe the inchoate anger or longing or desire of his characters and voice them in a way the character never could. Dewey would not have said it that way, but, for me, that was what Dewey was feeling: After ten years in jail, he had become a man determined to avenge himself on the world, a devil or exterminating angel.

The mixing of dictions can be employed in even more surprising ways. I was once in an airplane flying west, reading Toni Morrison's *Tar Baby*. Some movie was playing, and I was studiously ignoring it, pulled into the story of Jadine and Sonnie Boy and London and the Isle de Chevaliers. Then I came to a paragraph that made me want to stand up and say, "Shut off that stupid film. Listen to this! Just listen."

I will not quote the entire passage, which runs several hundred words, but I will give you a good selection. As Jadine takes off on a plane from the Caribbean to London, the narrator employs an extended metaphor about the ants of the island, about their queen who mates but once in the air and from that mating founds an entire new hive of ants, "Bearing, hunting, eating, fighting, burying."

... somewhere between the thirtieth and fortieth generation she might get wind of a summer storm one day. The scent of it will invade her palace and she will recall the rush of wind on her belly. . . . She may lift her head then, and point her wands toward the place where the summer storm is entering her palace and in the weariness that ruling queens alone know, she may wonder whether his death was sudden. Or did he languish? And if so, if there was a bit of time left, did he think how mean the world was, or did he fill that space of time thinking of her? But soldier ants do not have time for dreaming. They are women and have much to do. Still it would be hard. So very hard to forget that man who fucked like a star.

This is, obviously, a brilliant example of mixed codes, of one slamming Anglo-Saxonism invading and so throwing into relief the sweetly sensual, almost folkloric, evocation of the ant-queen. Out of this, we comprehend the pride and passion of Jadine, her depth and earthiness, and too, what she has lost.

It is not by luck that Toni Morrison won the Nobel prize for literature. I would wager, more than anything else (plot, character, theme), it is her absolute and perfect ear for language that distinguished her among a hundred international talents.

THIS MAY SEEM TRIVIAL, BUT . . .

The final test of language in any piece of fiction is, Is it appropriate? Appropriateness does not have to do with some standard of what is elegant or edifying or polite. Remember that Twain's *Huckleberry Finn* was initially rejected for inclusion in the Concord, Massachusetts, library's collection. Despite all the author's care to capture the way people actually spoke, the book was judged to be coarse and common. The fact that Huck and Jim and the Duke and the Dauphin and so on were themselves coarse and common—mostly outsiders, mostly poor, mostly just trying to survive in the rough-and-tumble world of mid-nineteenth-century America—mattered not a whit to the refined sensibilities of the library board, but it of course matters to us and mattered to the author. This is one of the reasons *Huckleberry Finn* still lives today, while other better-mannered texts of the era gather dust on the shelves in Concord, if they have not already crumbled into dust or been sold by the pound at the fund-raiser of 1901.

Appropriateness means that the words fit the broader, deeper, distinctive reality of your story. They are in synch with the characters you've created, the situations they find themselves in. Mailer's soldiers swagger and swear (even if hobbled by a skittish Random House) because they are seventeen or twenty-three and frightened and lonely and ten thousand miles from home, anxious to prove their manhood not just to others, but to themselves. They will inevitably speak in a way very different from Jane Austen's Emma or Margaret Atwood's neo-Puritans of *The Handmaid's Tale*. When it is the characters who are speaking or narrating, you are concerned with capturing *their* voices, the quirks and kinks and eccentricities that will distinguish the way a preacher or a rebellious teenager or a corrupt ward heeler sounds.

Appropriateness has to do not only with the utterances of specific characters, not merely with that voice of a character who is narrating in the first person, like Huck. It also applies to other kinds of narrative. Metaphors should be drawn from the world a story grows in. DeWayne is as unlikely to employ that image of Nancy's heart being that of a corporate raider (what knowledge or interest would he have in unfriendly takeovers?) as he is one drawn from Keats. Phil's imagined Gloria is probably not going to think in terms of rap and putting the pedal to the metal. Morrison's Jadine, straddling various worlds, can logically mix her codes, in a way Herlihy's callow Joe Buck would never do. The language of your story will be determined by who it is about, where it's taking place, when the action occurs, who is narrating the tale.

To conclude this consideration of language, let's append two last admonitions. One may strike you as trivial and the other as self-evident, but they are both worth pondering when you think about your prose.

Punctuation

First, be aware of your punctuation. This sounds like your sixth-grade teacher Miss Applegate, but, believe me, she may not have been just an old-fashioned stickler for rules. The way your prose reads is determined, in no small part, by how it is "pointed." If language is music, words are its notes, and punctuation its rests. Try to imagine a song or symphony in which the rests are not marked. There really is a difference, for example, in the way we hear (or don't hear, I suppose) a period as opposed to a comma.

Patrice looked nervous, addled, vulnerable.

Patrice looked nervous, addled. Vulnerable.

Patrice looked nervous. Addled. Vulnerable.

You can see here how altering the punctuation alters our perception of Patrice's condition. In the first instance, using commas, the three adjectives are essentially equivalent, the three elements interchangeable ("vulnerable, addled, nervous" would work just as well). In the second, the emphasis is thrown onto the word that stands alone. Patrice's vulnerability has a special weight. It is the final, important consequence of her nervousness and addledness. In the third configuration, equivalency is once again established, but each element has a kind of autonomy. Our attention is specifically drawn to each one.

The pointing influences how we scan a passage. The poet Paul Dresman once suggested to me that the difference between a dash and a parenthesis is the difference between horizontal and vertical. The horizontal dash propels us forward through a sentence: "He staggered forward—faster, faster—in search of his lover." The vertical parenthesis, conversely, creates a wall, sets the intensifying adverbs apart: "He staggered forward (faster, faster) in search of his lover."

Most marks of punctuation don't fit quite so neatly into a geometric scheme, but they cannot be ignored. Listen to the phrases in your head, determine where emphasis should fall and punctuate accordingly. Think of the difference between a sentence that ends in an ellipsis and one that ends in a dash.

"Are you suggesting that . . ."

"Are you suggesting that—"

The first indicates that the speaker simply stops speaking, the words timidly evaporating into the air. The second suggests that her speech is cut off, that she's been violently interrupted.

Overwriting

Finally, after all this praise of words: Beware of overwriting, that awful showing off of your thesaurus. Remember your companion in chapter one, Alicia in your imagined workshop? Apprentice writers sometimes get a little tipsy on language itself—adjectives and adverbs proliferate uncontrollably, images clash and clang, syntax gets stretched on the rack and Latinisms sprout at every turn. Our first serious, creative relationship with words is often characterized by precisely the kind of cow-eyed, moony intoxication we associate with any first love. Look at what can happen to "Anna's white cat delicately licked his paw."

> Anna's feline, brilliantly colorless as the sparkling snows of towering Alpine peaks, raised his clawed appendage with infinitely feminine grace and, extending a pink, file-like tongue from his bewhiskered snout, laved his multipadded paw.

Overwriting can occur in a specific passage or even a sentence in a story. A workshop member, in a tale about the death of his grandmother, used a wonderful word, "glossolalically," in the piece's final sequence. His colleagues balked at the choice, not because the word was inaccurate but because it was, in the context of the conclusion, too arcane, self-conscious and arresting. Those who knew what it meant ("related to speech in an unknown or imaginary language, as in the religious practice of 'speaking in tongues'") stopped to admire it: "What a great word!" Those who didn't recognize it, of course, stopped as well ("What the . . . ?"). The problem was that in the course of a story's final gesture, the last thing an author wants is for the reader to be booted out of the shared imaginative experience by the use of an unusual word.

Related to this is the fact that writers tend to *modulate* their language in accord with what is occurring in the story. The language tends to grow more intense, more elaborated at moments of high tension in a piece or at its conclusion. The final passage of Thomas Wolfe's last novel, *You Can't Go Home Again*, literally scans as iambic pentameter (ta-TUM ta-TUM ta-TUM ta-TUM ta-TUM): "To lose the earth you know, for greater knowing; to lose the life you have, for greater life." Once again, a musical parallel is apt. This is like that swelling we anticipate as a symphony draws to a close. Be careful of "increasing the volume," complicating the orchestration of your words at moments when it is not called for. You don't want your reader to assume your story is ending when, in fact, there's another three pages to go.

In your work, never dismiss the power words themselves possess. You can tell the finest story, but if the language is dull or overwrought or inappropriate, your tale will not have the impact you desire and it deserves. Be conscious of all the opportunities English provides. Think of Morrison, think of Boyle, and of Marlowe and Shakespeare and Milton and Melville as well. Listen to your own speech, that of your friends, that of strangers at the market or the bus stop. In all of these places, you can find language that is alive, language that compels your attention and can be brought to bear on your own work. Never forget that the words are one of the most important elements in compelling your reader to enter into and stay with your story, or, as Ozick would have it, that words are the necessary vehicle in transporting your story into that "kingdom of art."

EXERCISES

1. Jot a list of twelve to twenty words at random. Try to determine, on your own, whether they are Latinate or Germanic in origin. Then list what you consider to be some synonyms, at least one of which should be drawn from a linguistic family different from that of the original word. If you start with *futon*, you might list *couch* (French, as in *coucher*, to go to bed), *sofa* (the Arabic *soffah*, a raised place on the floor) and *davenport* (from—we think—the name of a manufacturer or the place where these were made—Davenport, Iowa, perhaps?). Then, come up with a sentence or two where *one* of the words would be most appropriate (e.g., "Adele couldn't stand the Ohio humidity one more minute. She stacked four records on the Victrola, turned on the fan her aunt had just received from Montgomery Ward and settled back luxuriously on the davenport").

2. Review your fiction again. How many different styles can you identify? How are they distinguishable? Do you see what might be a specific voice emerging? What characterizes it?

3. Isolate four elements of your quotidian self—job, hobbies, age, gender, geography, etc. Write a paragraph in which the language and metaphors are particularly drawn from each of these.

4. Try reproducing exactly the speech of someone you know who has a distinctive manner of expressing himself. Then edit the passage

you've written so that it reads smoothly—without, however, losing the specific flavor of the utterance of your acquaintance. Next, rewrite the passage, maintaining the content of what is said but casting it in a diction that is as different as you can manage.

5. Look at works by three of your favorite writers. How do they employ language to achieve particular effects? Do all three use more or less the same verbiage and the same linguistic techniques, or do they differ? How? Now, as closely as you can, try to imitate these writers.

6. Choose three or four paragraphs from your work. Try "repointing" them, shifting emphases by punctuating them differently.

FOUR

MAKING A STORY

So far I have touched on readers and writers, on sources of material, on language itself. I hope the import of each of these in our undertaking is self-evident. Now, let's turn to the basic element of storytelling—plot—to see how a text can be put together.

In this chapter and those following, various schema will be laid out that, I hope, will help you produce more memorable fiction. Before I begin, however, there is one point you should always keep before you: Writing should be pleasurable. It should be fun, not in that laugh-riot sense of whoopee cushions and roller coasters, but in that way a professional athlete feels about her sport. The tennis or basketball star works hard to achieve something approaching perfection in her endeavor. A writer should do no less. At the same time, however, that player of games should never lose the visceral joy that a stunning backhand or balletic layup provides. Fine fiction demands constant and intense labor, but one of the grand rewards of writing is that, in the end, we should feel an enjoyment that other kinds of work too often do not provide their practitioners. Remember, as we wend our way through what follows, that what you are doing as you put your stories together, take them apart and reconstruct them once again—grueling as the task may sometimes be—ought to be the source of a fulfillment that approaches the spiritual. Writing is play, a connection to the innocent self full of wonder that all of us once were.

IN THE BEGINNING

There is an oft-reproduced facsimile of the first page of T.S. Eliot's typescript of his classic poem *The Waste Land*. Eliot had sent the draft to his friend and fellow poet, Ezra Pound, for his remarks. On that opening page, Pound drew a huge slash that extended through three-quarters of the lines and in the margin scrawled "START IT HERE!"

The line beside that notation, of course, is "April is the cruelest month . . ."

Among other things, this anecdote illustrates the usefulness of a good editor: just how important it is not only to aim for objectivity in reading our own efforts, but to seek the counsel of others whose judgment we respect. A workshop or writers group, as we've noted in the first chapter, can be your best friend. The story about *The Waste Land* emphasizes how even so astute a critic as Eliot did not recognize the place his most famous work really began.

It is fair to say that we, as readers, tend to make up our minds about a book by an author we do not know within the first half-a-dozen pages if not the first few paragraphs. This is also notoriously true of editors with limited time and a stack of manuscripts reaching for the sky. Your story's opening gesture may be the single most important part of it. If you do not grip the reader in those first minutes, she may abandon your story, and then, no matter how fine the rest of the work, you have lost her forever.

Pound knew a powerful line when he saw one. Often, when we write, we *don't* necessarily know that. We become accustomed to a passage, used to a text beginning with a particular scene, and so do not entertain other options. Getting started on any piece of writing is difficult, and we are loath to alter those initial words that got us going in the first place. But it is essential, after a work is done or even well under way, to look hard at how rudely those opening few lines demand attention.

I still have the original manuscript of that first novel of mine, *Mean Time*, written on foolscap, typed single-spaced on an ancient Royal portable. I often show the first page of it in classes I teach, complete with strikeouts and inserts. What is most interesting is an initial descriptive paragraph, completely lined through. It is not so bad—a little pompous and abstract, but not poorly written. But then, the second paragraph begins: "Dewey got out of the penitentiary on a Thursday, but it took him till the following Monday to get home."

Even I, very early in my career, recognized that the stark evocation of a man just out of prison was a far stronger way to lead my first chapter than a showy bit of description. In those twenty or so words are rooted a thicket of questions: Who's Dewey? What was he doing in the penitentiary? How long's he been there? Why does it take him five days to get home? Where's home?

The discarded paragraph, however, may have been absolutely necessary, not for the book that is *Mean Time*, but for its real, physical writing. Eliot apparently had to go on for three-quarters of a page before he wrote the line with which, we now think, *The Waste Land* must begin. Likewise, I—rather less immortally inspired, perhaps—had to type something about a landscape before Dewey Monroe, on foot and embittered, could begin his trek home from prison and my novel could open with a line that grabs the reader's attention.

I have seen this countless times in countless manuscripts. When you sit down to write, whether facing an entirely new project or a new chapter, you sometimes need to warm up. I know of writers who, each day before they began their serious work, dash off a letter to get their minds accustomed anew to the written word. A frequently used analogy is that of a cold car. Those first few lines you put down, that paragraph, that page, is a "rev." You are heating up your creative engine—getting the oil circulating, blowing the accumulated gunk out of the fuel lines, allowing the pistons to pump, puffing a little exhaust into the air before you pop your story into gear and lean your foot on the accelerator. This is often absolutely necessary. Then, however, look critically and carefully at those opening moments. This is your big chance. You want a reader who is swept up by the fluid motion of your story, one who doesn't even realize what has happened before he's helplessly barreling down the road of your imagination beside you.

This does not mean, as students occasionally complain, that a shot must ring out in the first line, or a truck must carom into a bridge abutment, or your protagonist must take a pratfall down a flight of stairs, though something like that is certainly not illegitimate. As august a form as the epic, from Homer's *Iliad* on down, traditionally begins *in medias res*—in the middle of things—after the action we will be privy to has already begun. When we open Dante's *Inferno*, we don't hear all about his birth, education, girlfriend, early career, political affiliations and so on. Many of those come up in later cantos. In that first moment, however, the middle-aged Dante is lost in a dark wood, and the very gate of hell is gaping before him.

Establishing the Focus

A good beginning usually gives us some clue as to what the story will be focused on: a person, a place, a set of social interactions, an overarching event. Dickens gets us into the thick of things immediately in *A Christmas Carol*, introducing in a single paragraph both his main character and the one who will be the harbinger of his transformation.

> Marley was dead, to begin with, there is no doubt whatever about that. The register of his burial was signed by the clergyman, the clerk, the undertaker, and the chief mourner. Scrooge signed it. And Scrooge's name was good upon 'Change for anything he chose to put his hands to.

Faulkner, meanwhile, starts *The Hamlet*, unsurprisingly, with specific geographic fact: "Frenchman's Bend was a section of rich river-bottom country lying twenty miles southeast of Jefferson." Louisa May Alcott opens *Little Women* with a conversation.

> "Christmas won't be Christmas without any presents," grumbled Jo, lying on the rug.
>
> "It's so dreadful to be poor!" sighed Meg, looking down at her old dress.
>
> "I don't think it's fair for some girls to have plenty of pretty things, and other girls nothing at all," added little Amy, with an injured sniff.
>
> "We've got Father and Mother and each other," said Beth contentedly from her corner.

This may seem a shade heavy-handed, but recall Alcott's audience of adolescent readers. And note all that she accomplishes in this short exchange. We know what time of year it is; the size and makeup of the March family; their economic status. Perhaps most importantly, we've been given an idea of what Alcott's four "little women" are like: Meg's concern with status, the youngest, Amy's, sense of injustice, Beth's serenity and Jo's feisty boyishness—she, after all, is sprawled on the floor, hardly an appropriate place for a ladylike teenage girl of the mid-nineteenth century.

A first sentence can tell us we are in a different time or place, as George Orwell's does in his *1984*: "The clock was striking thirteen . . ." This effect may also be achieved far more subtly. The modern Argentine master Jorge Luis Borges writes at the outset of "The Circular Ruins": "No one saw him disembark in the unanimous night . . ." Translators have quibbled endlessly over that adjective "unanimous," with perhaps the most widely distributed version of the story in English rendering the phrase as "No one saw him disembark in the impenetrable night."

That translation, however, is simply wrong. *"Noche unánime"* in Spanish makes no more sense than "unanimous night" in English. But in the story, it makes *perfect* sense. This is the tale of a man who "dreams" another, creates him out of his own unconscious, only to discover at the story's climax that he himself is but a dream of someone else. The night, then, is indeed unanimous, the product of "one mind," the word's Latin significance. That first, unexpected and unexplained adjective is not merely the sign that this is likely to be a strange tale indeed, but it is also a clue that points to the solution of the story's central mystery.

Consider the opening sentences of three novels of the past twenty-five years.

> A screaming comes across the sky. It has happened before, but there is nothing to compare it to now.

> Many years later, as he faced the firing squad, Colonel Aureliano Buendía remembered that long ago afternoon when his father took him to know ice.

> At an age when most young Scotsmen were lifting skirts, plowing furrows and spreading seed, Mungo Park was displaying his bare buttocks to al-haj' Ali Ibn Tatoudi, Emir of Ludamar.

What screaming, and when did it happen before? What firing squad, and hadn't this man ever seen ice? What is this Scotsman doing with his pants around his ankles before an Arab potentate?

Each of these authors, Thomas Pynchon (in *Gravity's Rainbow*), Gabriel García Márquez (in *One Hundred Years of Solitude*) and T. Coraghessan Boyle (in *Water Music*), has snagged us in much the same way that I attempted to in *Mean Time*. We reach that initial period, and we are immediately asking the question, What is going on here? This, perhaps, is the most frequently employed and simplest opening gesture there is, the immediate and overt appeal to the reader's curiosity.

Do note, however, how the three authors proceed. Pynchon breaks into a new paragraph, and the apocalyptic terror of those first words resonates through the prose of the next two pages before we are ever introduced by name to any of his characters.

> It is too late. The Evacuation still proceeds, but it's all theater. There are no lights inside the cars. No light anywhere. Above him lift girders old as an iron queen, and glass somewhere far above that would let the light of day through. But it's night. He's afraid of the way the glass will fall—soon—it will be a spectacle: the fall of a crystal palace. But coming down again in total blackout, without one glint of light, only great invisible crashing.

Pynchon creates a terrible tension by refusing to tell us exactly what is happening, or to whom, while images of darkness and destruction multiply. Our reading is driven forward both by our curiosity and a kind of gory voyeurism. The story's ultimate explanation will take some eight hundred pages.

García Márquez apparently proceeds in quite a different manner. Rather than a world in collapse, an aborning world comes before our eyes, that of the "long ago afternoon" when a boy came to "know ice."

> Macondo in those days was a village of twenty houses of mud and cane built on the edge of a river of diaphanous waters dashing over a bed of smooth stones, white and enormous as prehistoric eyes. The world was so new, many things still lacked names, and to mention them you had to point with your finger. . . .

We are taken back into an Edenic place to watch the story unfold. It will be long into the novel before we discover how Aureliano Buendía ended up before the firing squad, and indeed, precisely which Aureliano Buendía this is, in a novel in which generation after generation bear virtually identical names.

And Boyle?

> The year was 1795. George III was dabbing the walls of Windsor Castle with his own spittle, the *Notables* were botching things

in France. Goya was deaf, De Quincy a depraved preadolescent. George Bryan "Beau" Brummel was smoothing down his first starched collar, young Ludwig van Beethoven, beetle-browed and twenty-four, was wowing them in Vienna with his Piano Concerto no. 2, and Ned Rise was drinking Strip-Me-Naked with Nan Punt and Sally Sebum at the Pig & Pox Tavern in Maiden Lane.

And what does this have to do with Mungo Park in the court of Ali Ibn Thoudi? "All in good time," Boyle might chorus with Pynchon and García Márquez, "all in good time." As with the other two writers, Boyle gives us a surprising image, captures our attention and then *withholds* information. If the most successful opening gestures grab us by the lapels, they also must not tell us too much.

Managing Information

One of the most common errors of apprentice writers is what I refer to as frontloading. In the combined enthusiasm and terror of beginning a piece of fiction, we are tempted to get out as much as we can, as much as we know, as much as we can make up as we go along about our characters and their situations.

> Beverley picked up the phone to call her boyfriend, Dave. She was very excited because she was sure Dave was going to ask her to the prom. He was six-feet, two inches tall with brown hair and green eyes, and played linebacker on the Waller High Stallions. They made a perfect couple. Beverley, at five-foot three, with a voluptuous figure and great taste in clothes, looked so good beside him. At least, that is what her best friend Anne said. Anne was a little plain, but she had a good heart and she and Beverley had known each other since second grade.
>
> "Hello, is Dave there?" Beverley said.

Actually, this is not quite as bad as it sounds if we are talking about a first draft. After all, in the act of composition, we are hearing the story ourselves for the first time, and we have endless questions about what places look like, how people move, what car our protagonist drives, what our villain eats for lunch.

However, in rereading our work (whether the next day or when the entire draft sits before us), we then have to ask how much of this information is significant at all and, even if it is, whether it belongs in the first few paragraphs. It usually doesn't. A compelling story is like a striptease or getting to know someone who will become a lifelong friend. Like Gypsy Rose Lee or the man in the tuxedo on the stage of Chippendales, a good story, after an initial bump and grind, gradually reveals itself. Like that friend, it is the ongoing discovery of a story's eccentricities and surprises that keeps us awonder about it and anxious to know more.

Don't go overboard! You do not want to deceive your reader. Too often, in our initial efforts, we're tempted to structure things toward a punch line, keeping the reader in the dark regarding the most salient piece of information about a character or situation. This becomes what I've known writers to call the *Twilight Zone* syndrome: amusing, ironic, occasionally even memorable, but too often merely clever. Even Rod Serling—creator of the eponymous television series and a serious and complex man—had his reservations about this method.

Writers frequently miss even the facility of a fine *Twilight Zone* episode. The effect of their stories is vaguely satisfying, but it is dependent on pulling one over on the audience, and as happens with a joke, the audience is able to recall next day only the howler that came at the end. As you learn about that body under the clothes, as you learn about that person beyond a mere name, so the reader wants to learn about your character and her story, see her quirks and facets.

When I was in my early twenties, my roommate and I, in need of some extra summer cash, decided we would become pornographers. There was a local house that published explicit material, and, professionals that they were, they responded to our query letter with guidelines for their aspiring authors. The list was long, and some of the suggestions have little place in this, a family publication. But it did include a very intelligent piece of advice.

The publishers pointed out that their novels were displayed on racks, and their readers would usually come to the store with no particular title in mind. Rather, they stood at the rack and thumbed through one or two or a dozen books and then made their selections. Hence, the "open me anywhere" rule, which translates, less colorfully than the publishers expressed it, as "something must be happening on every page."

In good fiction, as opposed to pornography (or action films for that matter), this can be carried too far. But you want a reader to sense an ongoing broadening and deepening of character, event and significance. As said, don't fool the reader. The novelist John Rechy has made the legitimate point that, over the long haul, you are not withholding information as in the opening gesture, but rather managing information, controlling its ebb and flow throughout the text. Your goal is to allow the reader to discover your story with fascination and innocence, just as you did; to make her feel as compelled to know it as you were when it unfolded before you.

CONFRONTING PLOT

So, you have an opening. You've avoided frontloading and craftily planted just enough information in that opening passage that your reader can't help but plunge on.

Now what?

Obviously, if you've chosen to write a piece based on an extant source—"Cinderella," Shakespeare's *Othello*, the wartime adventures of poor divorced Uncle Frank or what happened to you at the supermarket last week—then you know more or less where your story is headed. Let's assume, though, that this isn't the case, that you've constructed an opening scene arising out of an image, a single incident. This happened to me with my third novel, *The Book of Marvels*. I sat down at the keyboard one day and, in my mind, heard a woman talking on the phone. I had no idea who she was, what she did, to whom she was talking. Within a brief period, however, I had the answers to all those questions, and soon after that, I was deeply into the story of Lila Mae Bower Pietrowsky.

These days, there is no single way to plot a story. Writers are always looking for new ways to tell their tales, and changes in the world we live in alter the way they are told. The rise of the middle class in the nineteenth century made for far more novels that focused on problems inherent to those of that economic status. The formulation of psychoanalytic theory and those of other schools of psychology had a tremendous impact on the way characters were presented in the fiction of our parents and grandparents. Even new technology can provide new narrative strategies. I recently read a student novel that consisted entirely of e-mail messages. Nicholson Baker's *Vox* is composed of one phone conversation.

Nonetheless, we can still generally describe what a traditional plot is and how you go about coming up with one. Plotting remains a frightening leap into a void, so stay loose. In all aspects of writing, but especially in plot, looseness—a willingness to improvise, reimagine and so on—is everything. As Hamlet says: "The readiness is all."

To Sketch or Not to Sketch

I often ask introductory writing students, about two weeks prior to the date an assignment is due, to write me a précis, or summary, of what they intend to show to the workshop. The first reason for this is obvious. It's a way of discouraging those texts you know were put together frantically less than twenty-four hours before they were handed in. Having to synopsize the piece means the apprentice writer will have given at least some thought to the story he is going to tell before grinding it out at the keyboard.

A second reason, however, is that I want the author to have some notion of the *sequence* of the action, how events in the story are going to connect with one another, how characters are going to interact and grow, and toward what the story is finally headed. I don't want to know that the upcoming story is about loneliness. I want to know it's about "a girl named Margaret who lives with her maiden aunt in a small town called Willoughby in 1989. One Tuesday, she wakes up and decides to go for a walk. She has no friends, and her aunt . . ."

You may like to have everything sorted out before you put a single word on the page, or you may trust the muse to snuggle up next to you after you've put down that opening scene or swatch of dialogue. Oftentimes, we work both ways, employing one method with one story and the other with a different one. With *The Book of Marvels,* I simply let the action flow for some time, but I do not always write that way. Someplace, I still have squirreled away the outline of my second novel, *Mrs. Randall*, full of scratch-outs and carets, the bulk of which I planned meticulously before I set about composing it.

The advantage of sketching an outline or synopsis is simply that it keeps you on course, especially when the work in question is long. Some notion of the story's development, its key scenes, its most significant characters provides, if nothing else, a certain confidence for the writer that she is in control of things. On the other hand, some writers believe that *any* kind of structuring that does not arise naturally in the text's composition is stifling, that an outline is little more than a straightjacket. You may want to experiment with various techniques to see which works best for you.

Truth and Consequences

But even to get this far—that is, to the point of conceiving a plot—you need to have some notion of what a plot is. E.M. Forster's remarks on the matter in *Aspects of the Novel* are so well known they have almost become a cliché, but they are worth repeating. He says that while "The king died, and then the queen died" is a story, "The king died and then the queen died of grief" is a plot.

He is using the the word *story* here to mean a simple sequence of events (as he puts it, what the most primitive reader is looking for, saying, "And then? And then?"). To avoid confusing terms, let's call Forster's first formulation data, a simple statement of fact. The second one, however, is indeed a plot. What makes it a plot is that it is about *consequences*. Events in it are *causal*. The meaning of the phrase "the queen died of grief" is that she died be*cause* of her grief. Something has happened (the king's death) and, as a consequence of that, something *else* happened (the bereaved queen died).

Think of the sequence Forster sets up in more quotidian and contemporary circumstances, in ones that might be familiar to you.

> After Luther broke up with Patrice, she went out with his best friend, Ali, out of spite.

> Though Luther liked diving better, his father had always wanted to play pro baseball, so Luther went out for shortstop.

> Given Patrice's brother DeWayne had always been favored in the family, she deferred to Ali as she had to Luther.

These are the bare bones of plots—"stories," according to me if not Forster—because they imply motive, action taken on the part of characters for particular reasons. You might argue that fiction is a bit like religion. Indeed, the atheist argues they are one and the same. Fiction, at least traditionally, assumes that there are explanations for things, that we can *understand* life. Fiction is, in its way, a defense against chaos. Whether we truly believe it or not, most of us *want* to believe there is a logic to living, and fiction reinforces that.

But still, you say, *How* do I put a plot together?

It may help to turn to a dramatic model. Think of your story or novel as a traditional play, one divided into three acts. Act one involves that introductory gesture with its presentation of the piece's significant characters and their world, and then, normally, the revelation of a problem—something that interrupts the flow of everyday life for the characters involved.

This is followed by act two: the rising action. As a consequence of the problem, characters take certain steps, interact in new or different ways. The problem introduced in act one grows more complex, more threatening, and often the characters are called upon to do things they would not ordinarily do. There is an increasing sense of foreboding, a feeling that the problem cannot be contained and that this failure will lead to dramatic change.

In act three, these complications lead to a moment where the order that characterized the world at the story's outset is altered. This is followed by the denouement, the falling action, in which the consequences of this change are somehow dealt with by the imposition of a new order, or not dealt with, leaving the reader with a sense of a character, life and a world out of control. The classic formulation of the former, of course, is "they lived happily ever after." An example of the latter may be found in Herlihy's *Midnight Cowboy*, which we talked about earlier: Nineteen-year-old Joe Buck, who began as a self-confident gigolo-in-training, in the end finds "he was scared. He was scared to death."

Primitive though it is, this kind of tripartite structure does describe, *very* broadly, how most stories, both dramatic and comic, work. Indeed, it describes how most scenes within stories work: The action rises, there is a pivotal event/statement/gesture and then the action falls.

IMAGINING A PLOT

Let's say your opening is an image, an incident that stuck in your mind. You were out walking the dog, and you noticed a car parked at the curb in front of a house. Inside was a man, just sitting there. As you approached, he got out and started to walk toward the porch. As you passed in front of the house, you noticed a woman standing in the doorway behind the screen. Your last glimpse was of him at the door with her still on the other side.

For starters, ask yourself the standard questions of Journalism 101: Who? What? When? Where? How? Why? The answers are the foundation your story stands on. If you know who peoples your story; what events occur; when, where and how your story takes place; and, perhaps most significantly, why the events come about, you're on your way to constructing your edifice of fiction.

Who

You saw that man and woman. Who are they? One of the first things you should do, if not *the* first thing, is learn their names. There's a tendency to think that characters' names are an authorial after-thought, but that is a serious misconception. Indeed, there is an entire area of study known as onomastics that concerns itself with nothing but this issue. Melville's Ishmael can probably *only* be Ishmael, named for the son of Abraham and his concubine, Hagar, in Genesis. The biblical Ishmael is the father of the nomadic Bedouins, wanderers across the vast wastes of the desert as Melville's character is a wanderer over the vast wastes of the sea. Critics have suggested that Faulkner's quintessential flapper, Temple Drake in *Sanctuary*, is quite self-consciously on the author's part both a ruined temple and, in her independence and insatiable sexuality, more man than woman, more drake than duck. Even Hemingway's apparently conventionally chris-tened Nick Adams combines a slang expression for the devil (Old Nick) with the name of the first, innocent man.

Not all names, of course, have overt literary or linguistic roots. Still, as discussed in the last chapter as regards language in general, they usually possess a particular appropriateness. Mickey Spillane's hard-boiled detective, Mike Hammer, might have been Rick Mallet, but Aloysius Kronwinkle probably would not do. There's nothing wrong with the name Aloysius, but it simply doesn't fit an audience's notions of a gun-toting, hard-drinking private eye with a moll on each arm. In the same vein, we can thank Margaret Mitchell's better angel for the inspiration, after her first draft of *Gone With the Wind*, to change the name of her fiery Georgia heroine. One wonders if the novel would have been the runaway best-seller it was if Rhett Butler had directed his "My dear, I don't give a damn" not at Scarlett O'Hara, but at Pansy O'Hara.

We sometimes assume that dubbing our characters "he" and "she," for example, or "A___" and "B___," endows them with a particular universality. Nine times out of ten, this is a mistaken notion. In real life, the first piece of information you learn about a person you meet is his name. This gesture of introduction is not merely polite. Its roots are ancient, arising from the primitive notion that the name of something is magic. Remember that, in Genesis, God gives Adam the privilege of naming the animals "so he might have dominion over them," and in the oldest parts of the Bible, God himself is referred to as Yahweh, a Hebrew word meaning "the unspeakable name." Man can't know the name of God, for to know the name of something is to have power over it.

But, of course, God knows man's name, and, in the cosmos of your imagination, you get to be The Big Guy (or The Big Gal, as the case or your theology may be). Very seriously, when you baptize your characters, you've taken the first step into a heady experience indeed. There are few times in anyone's life when she can play God, but this is one of them. Just as a parent or godparent is enjoined to "name this child" in the christening ceremony, so you, as writer, are enjoined to provide that character with a name he will bear as long as the paper upon which your story is printed takes to crumble to dust.

So, who is the couple?

Before you read any further, name them now.

To avoid skewing your choices, in the plot we're about to weave, I'll call them by the generic names from endless parodies of soap operas, John and Marsha, but don't take away the impression you should be flip about this process. Sometimes you will have to work and work to encounter the name that suits your character, though happily, many times, the "right" name will merely come to you. One of the hardest tasks a writer can face is renaming a character after a piece is finished. Though in one of my novels, along about the third draft, I changed an English character from Malcolm to Basil, I still found myself, long after, referring to him as Malcolm. In *Mrs. Randall*, I still think of the characters with the names I first gave them—those of classmates from junior high school—rather than those they received after the legal department of my publisher suggested the names should be changed.

In any case, it was John and Marsha you saw on the porch. They looked to be somewhere in their twenties, both prosperous enough. John was driving a black Toyota, and the house, apparently Marsha's, was pleasant with well-maintained shrubs and a freshly mown lawn. Still, as you passed by, you couldn't help but feel a palpable tension, though you couldn't put your finger on what caused it.

What

At this point, ask yourself *what*. What's happened, happening, going to happen? John was sitting in the car when you first noted him, as if he didn't really want to get out. Marsha was standing at the door as he came up the walk, but did not move. She didn't draw back, as she might have if he were a stranger, but neither did she come outside to greet him. When he reached the door, they remained fixed, unmoving. What's going on?

The possible answers to this question are legion. But you've already made some decisions. You named the characters. Now you have to determine what brought them to the moment you observed them. They could be brother and sister, casual acquaintances, old friends who had a falling-out and haven't seen each other in years. Let's say, though, that they are a couple. They have been romantically involved for a year. The last month or so, the relationship has been rocky. John called Marsha to say he was coming over, and now he's arrived.

This is where you walked in. All you truly know is what you observed, John's journey from car to Marsha, but you have invented a plausible scenario to explain the scene you witnessed. Having done that much, it is simply a question now of inventing what happened after you walked away. Did Marsha slam the door in John's face? Did he say, "It's over, Marsha," turn on his heel and go back to the car? Did she fling the door open so they could passionately embrace and swear undying devotion to one another? As before, it's up to you.

Suppose John has decided to break off the relationship, but now can't quite bring himself to do it. He and Marsha speak haltingly through the screen for a while, then she steps out onto the porch. They talk some more. Perhaps she lights a cigarette and he joshingly admonishes her about it. They smile, talk more intimately and then kiss. They arrange to see each other the next evening. It's grown dark. Marsha goes back inside as John returns to his car. He gets in but does not turn on the ignition. He sits, just as he was doing when you first saw him.

When and Where

So, you have a sequence of action—a shade rough, but still, the skeleton upon which to build a story. Now, presumably, *when* and *where* should be easy questions to answer.

It ain't necessarily so.

Thus far, John and Marsha have existed in the contemporary world in which you encountered them, one of automobiles and lawn mowers, a vaguely suburban environment (John's driving to her house, not taking the subway). The issues we've touched on in this imaginary piece—ending a relationship, John's apparent ambivalence about committing himself to that particular course of action, the suggestion that Marsha shouldn't be smoking—ring with the topicality of articles in *Vogue* or *Details* or the "Modern Living" section of your daily newspaper.

But what if John were driving not a Toyota but a Model A? What if his jokiness about Marsha's smoking had to do not with the dangers of tar and nicotine, but with the potential scandal of a "nice girl" smoking in public? These are not idle questions. Those issues just mentioned in the previous paragraph are not, after all, ones that have suddenly emerged full-blown in the last twenty years. Relationships and men's nervousness before commitment, at least, have been around since time immemorial. And smoking, since Europeans first imported tobacco from the New World, has evoked controversy throughout the centuries on the basis of good health and good manners.

The when and where of your story may indeed be bound by particular historical and geographical realities. It would be difficult to set a story in a gay disco in 1914, though you might find enough of an analogue in some of the clubs of Harlem of the 1920s. If your story involves a boy and an escaped slave floating down a river, setting it in Arizona in 1986 is probably not going to work. But with our example of John and Marsha, consider whether the issues raised might stand in starker relief if the piece occurred in an urban setting or in the world of young investment bankers or that of ghetto teenagers. Might it be more powerful if it were set during the 1910s, or immediately after the Second World War, with John returning from the service overseas? Remember, in chapter two, we noted the case of Nathaniel Hawthorne, who, though he could write winningly of his contemporary reality in a book like *The Blithedale Romance*, established his immortality with novels and stories that unfolded in colonial New England. The wilder continent and the stricter social regime of the Puritans provided Hawthorne with a world more congenial to his particular philosophical obsessions and his gothic imagination.

None of the options mentioned for our tale of John and Marsha represents a "right" choice. It may well be that the contemporary suburbs are exactly where the story should take place. Still, it is worthwhile considering if its initial temporal setting and locale are those best suited for it.

How and Why

We still have two of those journalistic questions to ask: *how* and *why*. How did this turn of events come to pass, and why did it pass as it did?

To this point, what we have invented here is a pretty conventional scenario, not necessarily uninteresting, but not surprising either. Relationships end every day, after all, or come close to it and mend or stagger along for a while longer before they fail. What makes each such event unique, however, is the details of its happening and the reasons it happens. Indeed, it's often these two elements that transform a piece of writing into a piece of art. The *how*s and *why*s are what most frequently make a piece of fiction compelling.

The details constitute the question *how*: How is John walking as he approaches the porch? How is Marsha standing in the doorway? How do those conversations between the two develop—from the halting exchange on the threshold through the serious one when Marsha comes outside, through the cigarette, the joshing, the more intimate words that follow, the kiss and the promise to meet. How do those voices sound? Do they change as the dialogue changes? What words are spoken? How does the body language of our two characters express what they're really feeling?

As you can see, what you're doing now is fleshing out the various skeletons. First you're molding and shaping the story of John and

Marsha so that, despite its conventionality, the reader begins to see it as *their* experience, *their* specific and particularized relationship in trouble. Further, you're literally fleshing out John and Marsha so that for the reader they feel like real people, with bodies, gestures, quirks. They have specific ways of dressing, moving, talking, *being*. They are no longer just a man and a woman, no longer just any John and Marsha, but a distinctive John and Marsha who are different from any other such couple.

Much of what I am talking about here, of course, relates to what was discussed in the previous chapter: language. You are constantly making choices in terms of nouns and verbs and adjectives, of image and metaphor, in how you describe your characters, and it is those words that will transmit more than simple action. We will know John and Marsha by the way you limn them with language. A cocky gesture or ironic utterance from John will tilt our impression of him in ways quiet or sad ones will not. The way Marsha holds herself may profoundly affect whether we find her a generally sympathetic character or not.

Now, finally, there are the *why*s.

If *how* gives your characters flesh, *why* gives them life: a past, a future, a personality, a soul. John arrives to break up with Marsha, and he doesn't do it. Why not? Perhaps it is that he doesn't really want to, that he really does love her and is simply uncomfortable at the prospect of committing himself. Perhaps it's that he's uncertain as to what he wants to do, or knows he wants to end the relationship but is too weak to act on his own desires.

Let's assume, however, that he really has planned to break up with Marsha but as a consequence of some other experience, something Marsha herself doesn't know about, he can't bring himself to do it. Was it watching the ugly divorce of his parents? Was it having his own heart broken when some other woman gave him his walking papers?

Perhaps we should find something more dramatic. What if John (who began, you will remember, as that figure you saw sitting in his car when you walked the dog) had been in precisely this same situation before? Say it was fall rather than spring, that it was four years ago and that the woman standing in the doorway was his college sweetheart. Her name was Sally. John drove over to break up with her too. Today, what he can't see until he is to the porch is that Marsha is simply waiting for him, whereas Sally was waiting for him with a boxcutter held to her wrist.

Whew! Now there's something that certainly might put John in a bit of a stew about calling it quits with his girlfriend. Such an event in John's past might not only make him wary of the moment of truth with relation to Marsha, but her own calm and self-control might be such a relief that he would abandon his initial intention altogether. In the end, though, he would be back in his car, realizing he hasn't done what he set out to do, haunted by a woman he hasn't seen in four years and continuing a relationship that is unfair both to Marsha and to himself.

As with all the other questions along the way, this particular answer is no more the "correct" one than a whole slew of other possibilities. It does provide, however, a context for what happens, a past, a psychological angle on John's actions. In so doing, it endows his character with a depth that simple weakness or dithering wouldn't. It makes this encounter specific, distinguishes it further from all the other botched breakups inside or outside of literature.

Fact and Fiction

Having answered these journalistic questions, remember that, unlike journalism, fiction must convince us of its logic. It is oddly bound—precisely for being made up—by certain laws of plausibility that reality (which the reporter at least ostensibly writes about) can escape. Reality needn't seem real, because it simply is. Verisimilitude, one of those key elements of realist fiction, means "to have the appearance of truth." But such an appearance, ironically, must hew to a higher standard of credibility than the sometimes bizarre twists and turns of everyday life.

When I lived in Boston in the 1980s, there was a banner headline in the *Boston Herald* in "Doomsday type" (that is, the three-inch letters that demand our attention and that we associate with tabloids) announcing the death of a former professional hockey player. It was summer, and he and his wife were asleep in their brass bed. The bedroom window was open. A thunderstorm rolled through. A bolt of lightning leapt from the sky and through the window and blew off the man's head, leaving his wife unharmed.

This was simply true, and yet, I think you can see, if you tried to write a story in which this occurred, it would seem wildly improbable. It would work, perhaps, in a comedy, and a very broad one at that. In a dramatic piece, the author would have to set up all kinds of fore-shadowings—frequent lightning strikes in the area, the conductivity of the bed and so on—to justify this spectacular conclusion. Even then, there is something so outlandish about the unfortunate man's demise that forcing us to take it seriously would be a challenge for the most skillful writer.

Our notions of plausibility have grown even more stringent in the last century or so. Many readers now find the coincidences and reversals of fortune of many novels of a hundred years ago simply laughable. What a stroke of luck that the criminal who so intimidated Pip in his boyhood in *Great Expectations* ends up a kindly man of means, and the father of Pip's beloved Estella to boot! How remarkable that Jane Eyre hears mysterious voices calling her at the very minute the gravely injured Mr. Rochester is speaking those words hundreds of miles away! Even in genres in which fantasy is a given—in science fiction, for example—a more skeptical and sophisticated audience demands a rigor of thought and development in contemporary authors that those who published in *Amazing Stories* in 1935 were never held to.

Perhaps that's why it seemed better to have that boxcutter in Sally's hand rather than Marsha's. In the story we've invented, Sally, offstage, represents a kind of intensity or pathology, a kind of tragic or pathetic grandeur, that these days we read about in the newspaper but have a little trouble accepting in fiction, or at least in serious fiction. This is probably our loss, another sign of the cynicism of our times, but we as writers, though we can choose what century to write *of*, can't choose what century to write *in*. Keep your eyes on the humanity of your characters, their tones and gestures, their foibles and dreams. As with John and Marsha, it is from those little dramas of loyalty, of frailty, of ambivalence that great fiction—compelling fiction—arises.

WHOSE STORY IS THIS ANYWAY?

At this point, let's throw you a curve.

So far in our imagined story, I've opted for John as the narrative center of the piece. He seems a logical choice, if for no other reason than, from our chance observation on the street, he was literally the active character, the person who moved from car to porch. Still, we should entertain the notion that perhaps the tale ought to come to us from Marsha's perspective.

Remember that even in the composition of a story, much less later when you are revising it, you are not married to your outline or your initial concept. As it emerges on page or screen, a story may well differ—perhaps subtly, perhaps drastically—from what you thought it was. Oftentimes, stories pull in particular directions. When this happens, you should almost always follow. If an unexpected character (say, ahhh, Marsha) begins to command more attention than you originally imagined she would, let her. If the action seems to be veering away from what you assumed was a key incident (the kiss, maybe) toward some as yet unimagined one, let it. Sometimes these momentary meanderings lead to dead ends, which means you simply retrace your steps back to what you knew was the main line of action in the first place. On other occasions, however, the apparently capricious inspiration is drawing you toward what and who are truly important in your work in progress, toward what you *ought* to be writing. Mystical as it sounds, your story knows itself better than you do.

Maybe the focus of your piece, which you originally saw to be John, is in fact Marsha. You may not realize this until your first draft is done, or you may recognize it somewhere along the way. It's quite possible, for example, that since the inspiration for the story was John sitting motionless in his car, the right perspective in the piece is that of the character who, like you, observed him there, that is, Marsha. Maybe she in fact does know about the boxcutter incident with Sally. Does she manipulate the situation given that knowledge? Is she filled with sadness for John, torn within herself between her own desire to maintain things as they are and her realization that John is unable to break away as he wants because of what happened years before?

There are other possibilities as well. Perhaps things might be more interesting if presented from the point of view of an observer—you, the passerby, or another character as yet not invented. Is there a snoopy neighbor next door? Does Marsha have a friend or new lover visiting, or is she divorced and the mother of an eight- or twelve-year-old child? Even Sally, the former girlfriend with the boxcutter, might function as a narrator. Is the scene something she fantasizes? Is she stalking John and hence the observer? Does she have friends in common with John or Marsha? Has she had the encounter related to her and is now relating it to us? Any one of these might work. But which is the one that most engages you as author?

That's the most basic question, but not the only one, for as we have noted, there is another party to be considered here, your collusive cohort in the enterprise of fiction, the reader. There is nothing wrong with asking yourself what character would make the most *compelling* center for the story. Who, in the circumstances you've created, is most likely to evoke sympathy? That, of course, can be heavily influenced by you in the way you lay the story out, but when constructing the tale, you may well want to consider what audience you are trying to speak to and whom its members would most easily connect with.

Omniscience

One option, of course, is to adopt the stance of an omniscient narrator, that is, one who is all-knowing (see, you're getting the chance to be a divinity again). Up until the twentieth century, this was a frequently employed narrative technique, and remains so in a great deal of popular fiction. Omniscience allows the storyteller to enter into the heads of any and all of her characters. Hence, in an omniscient narrative, readers can know what John is thinking *and* what Marsha is thinking, all at the same time, and indeed, what the passerby and the snoopy neighbor are thinking as well.

This godlike power of the omniscient narrator has apparent attractions for a writer, supplying the means to create a text in which most all ambiguities are resolved because we are aware of what each character's perspective on the given situation is. Conversely, this technique has particular disadvantages and limitations. In the first place, omniscience tends to create a certain distance between reader and text, an awareness that the story is mediated by the author. In so doing, it emphasizes the artifice of the narrative. It makes us conscious of the fact that we're being told a story, that we are getting information that the characters involved do not necessarily share, indeed, that it may be impossible for them to share. Further, in terms of that management of information we spoke of earlier, omniscience may make it difficult to maintain the mystery of a piece, with information seeming not so much managed as manipulated. If the author can move freely into the mind of any character, can the fact that Winnifred actually knows

Constance is her long-lost daughter fairly be withheld from the reader until page 178? Finally, though omniscience can provide a story with a feeling—or at least the illusion—of objectivity, it can also prevent us from forming the kind of bond with a particular character we might feel if the narrative were framed in a different, more limited, more personal way. This bonding is neither an idle nor some kind of late-twentieth-century touchy-feely concern. It can be crucial in both attracting and holding your reader's interest.

In what we've come to call postmodernism, we sometimes encounter a variant on omniscience, the self-referential text, in which we are reminded, usually by overt authorial intrusion, that what we are reading *is* a text, an invention. The contemporary Latin American writer Luisa Valenzuela can stand as an example in her novel *The Lizard's Tail*, a terrifying historical fantasy/satire based on modern Argentine history. It centers on the bizarre figure of José López Rega, known in the book as The Sorcerer or Witch Doctor, who played the role of Rasputin in the political family of Juan Perón both before and after the president's death. Here's Valenzuela's beginning to the second part of the book, entitled "TOo."

> I, Luisa Valenzuela, swear by these writings that I will try to do something about all this, become involved as much as possible, plunge in head-first, aware of how little can be done but with a desire to handle at least a small threat and assume responsibility for the story of the so-called Sorcerer that is slipping from my hands, taken over by him, who had been the Papoose from Trym Lagoon, a very precise and well-mapped place, now transformed into the diffuse and undiscoverable Kingdom of the Black Lagoon with him, a mere witchdoc, as Lord and Master. He's already expanding its borders and hopes to invade all of us after having invaded me in *my* kingdom, the imaginary one. I know now that he, too, is writing a novel that superimposes itself on this one and is capable of nullifying it.

The present popularity of this kind of narrative is perhaps a reaction to the long reign of realism in the novel. Valenzuela, herself long-expatriated from her native country at the time the book was written, is both communicating her own disquiet before the fact that a thoroughly evil, repellent and very real-life character is, in a sense, possessing her, and also drawing our attention to the fact that this is, in the end, a book, a product of her own imagination.

This technique is not entirely innovative. Many novels of the eighteenth and nineteenth centuries were full of references to the "dear reader." Forster, in his Cambridge lectures in 1927, was quite impressed by the French writer André Gide's *The Counterfeiters*, which includes a character who is writing a novel called *The Counterfeiters*. Still, Valenzuela and others in the last twenty-five years are uniquely concerned with emphasizing text as text. They are not merely "including" us by talking to us directly, but bringing us into the process of their creation of the fiction itself.

Third-Person Narrative

A traditional omniscient narrative has to be written in the third person: "John felt," "Marsha thought," "He recalled," "She retreated into the house after he left." There are, of course, other forms of narrative in the third person. One might be called third-person hyperobjective, a kind of mirror image of omniscience in which knowledge is limited entirely to observation. Instead of entering into the consciousness of all of the characters, we enter the consciousness of *none* of the characters. All their emotions, their reactions and so on must be externally expressed in some manner or another—words spoken, tone of voice, body language. The hows we talked about previously become all-important here.

This may seem like a tall order, but you're actually quite familiar with this kind of narrative thanks to theater and film, though playwrights and screenwriters sometimes find this technique too restrictive. Shakespeare employs soliloquy to allow characters to think aloud and tell the audience what they are feeling or considering. In movies, we sometimes hear a voice-over in which vital information or personal emotion is expressed. The most extreme example is probably in the American dramatist Eugene O'Neill's *Strange Interlude*, in which those on stage simply interrupt the action to directly address the theatergoers and confide in them their inner thoughts.

Such narration can be quite striking, though it is often difficult to maintain over the long haul. The French *nouvelle roman* ("new novel") of the 1950s employed this technique, with books filled with minute descriptions of "surfaces"—of objects, landscapes, modes of dress. In contemporary fiction, a similar technique enjoyed something of a vogue during the early 1980s as an element of so-called minimalism. This encouraged a terse, stripped-down prose that often left the reader to come to his own conclusions based on inferences he was able to draw from the situation presented. Unsurprisingly, minimalism worked best in the short story, as those of such figures as Raymond Carver or Ann Beattie demonstrate.

There is another kind of third-person narrative, however, referred to as third-person limited, or central intelligence, narrative. In this kind of telling, our knowledge of what is going on is restricted to what is perceived, felt, told to a single consciousness within the story. This method offers rich possibilities in that, of course, the partial view of things on the part of the "intelligence" that is moving through the story may, in fact, be misleading. The character through whose eyes we are seeing is, after all, a character with particular foibles, prejudices, shortcomings, and we as readers may recognize that she is misinterpreting or overreading the events surrounding her.

Henry James pioneered this kind of narrative, though perhaps the most famous single example is the final story in James Joyce's collection *Dubliners*. In "The Dead," the self-satisfied Gabriel ultimately realizes the emptiness of the bourgeois world that he has made his own. The worst blow is the revelation by his wife, Greta, of her first and greatest love, one shared chastely and fleetingly with an adolescent boy named Michael Fury who died of pneumonia. Long before Gabriel achieves his bleak awareness of the emptiness of his life, we as readers have recognized its hollowness. Joyce's genius in the story is that, despite our discomfort with Gabriel's smugness, we finally sympathize with him and his new and (for him) terrible knowledge of himself.

The central intelligence narrative lends itself to irony and ambiguity, which may account for the fact that it is probably the most popular stance in contemporary fiction. We cannot be entirely sure that the relating and interpreting of events we are witnessing are not, in fact, overdetermined by the narrative consciousness through which we are receiving it. Should we entirely trust what we are hearing? In this, of course, the central intelligence in the third person bears considerable similarity to the kind of story that is most familiar to us, and which is most commonly employed by apprentice writers: the first-person narrative, told to us by an "I."

First-Person Narrative

Everywhere, every day, everyone employs first-person narratives. We tell our friends at work about the baseball game we attended the previous evening, we review the day's events with our partner, we relate the drama and frustration of the traffic jam on the freeway to our next-door neighbor and bore some hapless teenager with the tale of our five-mile walk barefoot through the snow to attend school. The very familiarity of this kind of storytelling is both its greatest virtue and its problem.

An "I" narrator tends to put an audience at ease immediately. This is someone confiding in us, someone, apparently, we are to trust, who is going to take us through her story in a way we are accustomed to. The earliest practitioners of the novel in English—Daniel Defoe and Jonathan Swift—used it. Dickens begins *David Copperfield* with "I was born. . . ." Melville's narrator in *Moby Dick* instructs us, "Call me Ishmael," while we meet Huck Finn with the line "You don't know about me without you have read a book by the name of *The Adventures of Tom Sawyer*. . . ." *The Great Gatsby, The Catcher in the Rye, The Stranger* by Albert Camus are all masterpieces that feature a first-person narrator.

Nonetheless, the first-person narrative is not always the same. Sometimes, as in Dickens and Camus, Twain and Salinger, the "I" speaking to us is the central figure of the story. This is the most common strategy in this kind of storytelling: He who relates the tale is also its protagonist, which, of course, mimics most of our own narratives about ourselves in everyday life. In such instances, the character's own voice often increases the intimacy of our response to the story. Camus' Meursault, put off by society's deceptions and evasions, involves us in his own alienation both by what he tells us and the flat and unemotional language he employs that exemplifies his spirit's condition. In the same way, though with a wildly different voice, Holden Caulfield winnows his way into our affections at least as much by how he tells his story as by his story itself.

> I ran all the way to the main gate, and then I waited a second
> till I got my breath. I have no wind, if you want to know the

truth. I'm quite a heavy smoker, for one thing, that is, I used to be. They made me cut it out. Another thing, I grew six and a half inches last year. That's also how I practically got t.b. and came out here for all these goddam checkups and stuff. I'm pretty healthy though.

Fitzgerald's Nick Carraway, the "I" of *The Great Gatsby*, functions differently. He is a secondary character as regards the central thrust of the novel—the doomed love of Gatsby for Daisy Buchanan. He is an observer/investigator, unfolding the larger story before us as it unfolds for him, partaking of its action at the same time he is, in a way, among but not of the novel's central characters. This allows him a kind of distance from the passionate goings-on at the novel's core and lets him function as interpreter and judge of what is occurring in a way that a more deeply involved first-person protagonist might be unable to do, at least so effectively.

The upside of first-person narrative, as the quotation from *The Catcher in the Rye* demonstrates, is its immediacy, its familiarity. Holden's "if you want to know," his "that is, I used to be" make us feel he has confidence in us, wants to ingratiate himself to us. First person does have its downsides, however. For the apprentice writer, and especially one who chooses to work with autobiographical material, it is often an invitation to self-indulgence. We must face the fact that we all like to talk about ourselves, and writers are perhaps more inclined toward this than anyone else. I have known instructors who forbade this kind of narration in workshops, precisely because they had read one too many a self-aggrandizing, self-justifying, self-pitying piece of how a put-upon "I" triumphed over witless parents, wicked bosses, snarky friends and unfaithful lovers. This strikes me as extreme, but certainly a writer should always be aware of the potential for running on at the mouth, as well as for surrounding an all-virtuous narrator by others who are no more than straw men.

As I noted in chapter two when discussing the possible problems of autobiographical material, a first-person narrative drawn from our own experience may invite all those "but that's how it really happened" problems—lack of focus, character clutter and so on. It can also result in precisely the opposite problem: a story that is too sketchy. Because the autobiographical "I" is familiar with the setting and characters, he does not recognize the need to provide the details so we the audience see them clearly. A workshop member once presented a very fine boyhood story in class but was shocked at the group's response to the father in the piece, who most felt was a real ogre. The problem was that the character was, in fact, based on the author's own father, whom he loved and respected. However, none of the man's virtues, so naturally perceived by his son, had made their way into the story.

Bear in mind that a first-person narrator locks you as writer into her particular worldview and her particular diction. Remember Phil's project in chapter one, his story about Gloria, the sixty-year-old working-class widow in New Hampshire? If she is to be the first-person narrator of the tale, Phil needs to be conscious not only of the kind of thoughts she would reasonably have, the sort of conclusions she would logically draw, but also the language and metaphor she would employ to give shape to her emotions and ideas, both when she talks and when she thinks.

Let's say Gloria, since her husband's death, has developed a peculiar habit of arranging and then rearranging her pots and pans in the cabinet. As a third-person narrator, Phil might reasonably (if a little puffily) write, "Like Penelope at her loom, unweaving at night what she wove in the day, Gloria shifted saucepans and stewpots from upper left to lower right, from front to back, from side to side." The metaphor does have certain things to recommend it: Penelope, Odysseus' wife, believes herself a widow and does and undoes her work in order to avoid having to choose a new husband from among the many suitors for her hand. Gloria, widowed, is right at the point where she might consider a new romance with her and her late husband's old friend, Tom.

Note, however, that just as we had a hard time imagining DeWayne comparing his sister to *la belle dame sans merci*, this image would likely not work if Phil opted to tell Gloria's story in her own voice. If she's to allude to Homer, there would have to be some explanation for her doing so, in that this is not exactly what we expect from a working-class New England woman of a certain age. Giving her a taste for the classics, which perhaps she's maintained ever since she was in high school, might well add dimension and distinction to her character. But it is something that would have to be established by the author relatively early in the story. Otherwise, the metaphor would simply seem peculiarly false and out of place.

Other Narrative Options

The foregoing—variations on third-person singular and first-person singular—are the stances typical of, I would estimate, 98 percent of all fiction. Still, there are three (actually four) other "persons" in English: first-person plural ("we"), second-person singular and plural ("you" and "you [all]") and third-person plural ("they"). I am unaware of any story employing the third and fourth of these ("you [all]" and "they"), though both are theoretically possible, even if sustaining them for more than a few pages might prove difficult. We could conceive of a fantasy story, for example, about a primitive tribe or a race from another planet that functioned as if they had a single consciousness—"They moved on across the plain," "That night they made love all together," "They shifted in a body to a defensive posture," etc. That notion of single consciousness would also be at work in a "you [all]" narrative, let's say in the evocation of a mob sacking a church or a neighborhood—a group of people functioning as if it were possessed of a single mind.

"We" is certainly a rare pronoun in powering a narrative, at least in consistent use, though one can see how it might be employed by either a royal personage (accustomed to thinking of herself in plural) or someone suffering from mental illness, an individual subsuming two or three different personalities. Indeed, given the fact that even we sane folk sometimes imagine ourselves as not entirely integrated, this narrative stance is perhaps not so far-fetched as it sounds, even if it has not been much employed. There is a novel from the 1980s, *During the Reign of the Queen of Persia*, by Joan Chase, that is told in first-person plural. Chase's conceit is four teenage girls, two pairs of sisters, so intimately linked with one another that they think of themselves as a unit: "we." It's a risky and, arguably, showy strategy, but Chase manages to make it work for her.

Of these unorthodox techniques, the one most commonly seen is the use of the second-person singular, of "you." The Mexican novelist Carlos Fuentes employed it in his first great success, *The Death of Artemio Cruz*, interspersing sections narrated in first, second and third person, all centered upon the title character. A few decades later, Jay McInerney, in his debut novel, *Bright Lights, Big City*, tells the entire story in the second person.

Second person can be quite effective and is not quite so odd or rare a stance as we might think. Colloquially, we often use "you" in telling stories, particularly those we assume to represent some kind of universal experience: "You know how you go to the store, and you're in a real hurry and just need to pick up a couple things. There's always this guy stacking cans, and every time, he's right at the spot where that chili you want is. . . ."

It might be argued that this constitutes merely a kind of universalizing or collusive first-person narrative. That is, when we say, "you're in a real hurry," what we mean is, "I was in a real hurry." The use of "you," however, makes the particular experience into one that all individuals are involved in or familiar with.

Where these less common perspectives are employed, any author should ask herself why this particular choice would be more effective than a more traditional one. In my own experience, in my novel *The Professor of Aesthetics*, those sections that focus on the story's villain, Jay Skikey, are narrated in second person. Now, I'm the first to admit, having written sections in third and first person that concerned two other central figures in the book, I was running out of stances. However, it did seem to me that using the second person in connection with Skikey as opposed to any of the other characters was particularly effective.

> You did not forgive. You took what was offered, demanded more, and killed.

> You pursed your lips, and tasted blood.

> . . . So you stood. Raised the ice pick high into the air. Then, with all the force your young and so recently strengthened body possessed, you brought it down. . . .

The second person makes the reader complicit in Jay's evil. It is *you* thinking these terrible thoughts, *you* doing these terrible deeds.

With longer pieces of fiction, you are not necessarily married to one particular point of view. It is perhaps indicative of the century in which we live, one characterized by considerable skepticism regarding any received truth, that while omniscient narration appears less and less frequently in serious fiction, narratives in which the point of view shifts from one perspective to another have become more common. The touchstone of this kind of variant stance is, interestingly, a Japanese film, though that film is, in fact, based on a short story, also Japanese. The story is "In a Grove" by Ryunosuke Akutagawa, and the film is *Rashomon*, directed by the great auteur Akira Kurosawa. This dark tale of robbery, rape and murder is told to us from four different perspectives: the robber's, a witness's and those of the victims—the violated woman and (via a medium) her murdered husband. Which is the "true" version is for us, as audience, to determine according to our own lights.

With our own projected story, the one about John and Marsha, perhaps it would be most effective to employ John as the "central intelligence" in the first half of the tale, say to the point Marsha lights that cigarette, and then shift the point of view to that of Marsha, getting both sides of the story while maintaining chronological action. As you can see, the number of mixes and matches you could employ, even in our simple fiction, are numerous indeed: snoopy neighbor to John to Marsha to snoopy neighbor again (a kind of frame structure, which we'll discuss later on); John to Marsha to John; Marsha to snoopy neighbor to John; and so on. John and Marsha might narrate their sections in the first person, whereas the snoopy neighbor would be narrating in third. We could employ parallel columns, with John's and Marsha's narratives running simultaneously (don't laugh, I've used this technique). Or perhaps, in the end, it's simply easier to opt for omniscience.

"*Enough!*" you howl.

What's a writer to do?

Happily enough, just as with names, I'd say that the majority of stories come out initially in their "natural" point of view—natural, that is, to your particular and private creative consciousness (or is that unconsciousness?). In most instances, we don't even think about the point of view we are writing from; we simply adopt it. It becomes an issue only when something isn't working in a piece. Perhaps it's that maundering on that a first-person narrator can be prone to, which may be more easily controlled if the story is recast in third person. If that's the case, don't be ashamed of yourself. This is what the legendary editor at Scribner's, Maxwell Perkins, asked of Thomas Wolfe after reading the manuscript of *Look Homeward, Angel*. Perhaps there's a vital piece of information that the narrative center of the story cannot possibly be privy to without some bizarre or contrived turn of events, and hence the writer would be better off opting for omniscience or telling the tale from a different viewpoint or shifting viewpoints from one narrative center to another.

One thing to remember is that if you are going to function as an omniscient narrator, you need to signal your intent relatively early. If we think we're reading a story from the perspective of one character and there's a sudden and momentary entrance into the consciousness of another, we're likely to feel disoriented in the bad sense of the term. Be careful of shifting perspectives too quickly. Shunting back and forth from one point of view to the other can simply confuse the reader.

Finally, don't forget the advice earlier on regarding a story that pulls in a particular direction. If the piece seems to tend toward the actions, emotions, responses of one of the secondary characters rather than your central ones, go with the flow and see where it leads you. You may indeed be "writing the wrong story" or, at the least, favoring the wrong character. Once again: The story knows itself better than you do.

EXERCISES

1. Review the openings to your stories thus far. Do they immediately involve the reader as in the examples I've presented? Write a brief list of their strengths and weaknesses. In at least one story, find a way to start farther into the text than you presently do.

2. Sit down and simply start writing and see where it takes you, at least for two or three pages. By page three, do you have a story? Next, outline an entirely different piece. Make the outline relatively detailed. Now, try writing the first two or three pages of that story.

3. Jot down a list of six names you invent. Let this list sit for three or four days. Then return to it and write a character sketch of the people each name represents. Find a way to alter the name (e.g., Richard Langostino to Dickie the Shrimp). Let those sit, and then write sketches for each of those.

4. One last time, take out those stories of yours and ask in relation to two or three the journalistic questions we discussed before. Do all have answers?

5. Cast around for an implausible event that has occurred—one you've read of or been told about. Try to figure out how you might make use of this (a) in a comic story; and (b) in a dramatic one. How would you have to alter the original event to make it work in these two different pieces?

6. Invent and narrate an incident involving at least three characters. Then, write the same scene again from the point of view of one of the other characters involved.

FIVE

POLISHING PLOT

So you have a plot in mind. You've named the characters, adopted a narrative stance and sat down to pound out that story. You've played the journalist and asked those significant questions, but you're not a journalist after all, you're a fiction writer, and what is at stake for you is different than what's at stake for the reporter from *The Daily Picayune*. Like Detective Joe Friday, all the reporter needs is "the facts, ma'am." But Forster has pointed us in a different direction, and you're after not only facts, but causes and consequences.

Perhaps you've finished a draft, perhaps you are stuck halfway through, perhaps you still haven't made it past that opening gesture and are sitting there, staring at the keyboard and thinking about a one-way ticket to Brazil. At any of these points, you might approach your story, its presentation and how it's put together in somewhat varying manners. It may well be, if you've completed the piece, you can deal with what we discuss in the coming pages in five minutes. In those instances where the text is not proceeding as planned, employing the scheme described in this chapter may help you mold the material in such a way that you escape the impasse or transform a perfectly serviceable fiction into one that is truly compelling.

In the last chapter, I talked of fiction in terms of a tripartite structure that involved rising action, climax and falling action. Having now actually formulated our tale of John and Marsha, let's elaborate upon that notion, thinking about five specific elements that go into the making of a story. As you'll see, these parallel in many ways the journalistic questions, but provide a sequence that allows you to see how your story is developing. To make it easy, we'll refer to these as the 5 Cs.

1. **Coordinates:** establishing the location, temporal setting and characters.
2. **Conflict:** the emergence of the story's problem.
3. **Complication:** the increasing difficulties of the characters in dealing with the problem that has arisen.
4. **Climax:** the moment the problem finally leads to a confrontation, an act, a conversation that alters the lives or circumstances of the characters.
5. **Conclusion:** the consequences of that alteration on the lives of the characters and the world they live in.

COORDINATES

The *coordinates* of a story are, essentially, the answers to those questions *who*, *where* and *when*. They usually need to be established in a general way early in any piece of fiction. As I noted while we were plotting our little drama of John and Marsha, our initial impulses where these questions are concerned are usually but not always the right ones, the ones that make for the most compelling stories we can write. Nonetheless, if the piece lacks the power you feel it should have, perhaps the problem lies in a focus on the wrong character or the setting of the story in a less than desirable place or time. If that is what's going on in your story, substantial recasting may be in order.

Though this may feel like the imaginative equivalent of the crash of your hard drive, don't panic.

Sit back. It is not an easy task to make this kind of radical change—perhaps the most basic there is—but it is not a hopeless one either. In cases like this, there are two steps you can take. First of all, ask yourself what initially attracted you to the material you're working with *and* what it was that kept you working on it. The answers may well differ. We've successfully demonstrated how the image of John and Marsha can be turned into a compelling story, but, for you as a writer, what is compelling *you* to continue with it, compelling *you* to create, may mutate, even if you're not entirely aware this is happening. This is why so much ado was made in the preceding chapter about those unexpected pulls a tale may exert. For you as author, is the story somehow too small—too tightly focused on the problems of this single couple without some greater context to give it more than transitory impact? As Rick says to Ilsa Lund on the airstrip in

Casablanca, considering the war that's in progress: ". . . the problems of two little people don't amount to a hill of beans in this old world." As suggested in chapter four, perhaps shifting the action to a different locale or historical moment might set forth its central issues more starkly. There are other options. Instead of in their twenties, should John and Marsha be in their fifties, facing what may be a final chance for romance? Should some major event beyond their control—war or illness, for example—be looming over them as they confront each other on that porch? Is John facing the draft in 1967? Is Marsha in remission from breast cancer? Maybe your own interest, your own sympathetic attachment to their situation is really centered not upon the two of them, but on others they love and upon whom their relationship will have an impact—that twelve-year-old son we postulated for Marsha, for instance.

If this process leads nowhere, you have a second option, one time-tested by writers for centuries. Let your story rest. Walk away from it. Work on a different piece. You sometimes have to trust your own creative intelligence, conscious and unconscious, to rework the material you've set down; or await some external circumstance you cannot predict to swing your story in the direction it needs to go.

A decade ago, I started a short story called "Remembering Bobbo," set vaguely in the South-Central states of my childhood sometime in the late 1970s. It centered on a man's recollections of his brother, who had been killed in Vietnam ten years before. In the writing, another voice began to emerge, that of the dead man's high school girlfriend. However, after a half-dozen pages or so, the story simply dried up. I had no notion of what I wanted to accomplish with it and, after a few frustrating evenings at the keyboard, set it aside.

In 1991, during the Gulf War, like many Americans I found myself suffering a terrible déjà vu. Hadn't we all seen this kind of buildup of troops and matériel twenty-some years before? As fighting loomed, I found myself at the computer screen, there joined by a secondary character from an earlier novel of mine, *The Book of Marvels*. Fred Bower was a good-hearted but troubled man, an alcoholic Vietnam veteran who had never quite managed to adjust to life after his stint at war. Suddenly, there he was in 1991, sitting before the casket of a lost soldier, an MIA in that war two decades earlier whose remains had finally been repatriated to his hometown. That soldier, of course, was Bobbo, and as time went on, the voices of that brother and girl-friend began to figure into the text. In the end, this became the novel *Letting Loose*.

Before, I had lacked a real catalyst for the story, some external event that would set my imagination in motion. The impending conflict in the Middle East and the memory it evoked of the Vietnam era brought me back to Fred and gave me a place, time and character to get the abandoned "Remembering Bobbo" rolling again. The final canvas, of course, was much larger than the story I had originally conceived. The book became an attempt to deal with a whole series of issues from the last thirty years. Ironically, by the time the manuscript was finished, all direct reference to Desert Storm had been eliminated, though it was that war that had fertilized the seed of those few pages knocked off and then abandoned in the late 1980s.

Before I move on, I have an ancillary but important note. The foregoing demonstrates a very old adage for writers: Never throw anything away. This makes for messy filing cabinets and bundles of computer disks and moans of despair from spouses or housemates, but it will save you much grief. In the first place, in those periods when you go to the well and find it dry as a bone, there is always old material to reread and rework. In that spell between "Remembering Bobbo" and *Letting Loose*, I encountered the second-person narrative voice that allowed me to complete *The Professor of Aesthetics*. You cannot know—cannot be expected to know—precisely how your own life and imagination change month to month or year to year. The piece that lies unfinished is one that may, indeed, simply not yet have been ready to be finished. Fiction gestates surely as a child does, but the period of its gestation can vary greatly. It recognizes when it is ready to be born.

CONFLICT AND COMPLICATION

Problems are perhaps most likely to arise in a story in connection with the second and third of those 5 Cs, that is, with *conflict* and *complication*, the latter, in some ways, being the elaboration of the former. It would seem self-evident that all stories, one way or another, center on conflict, though that in itself doesn't say much. What do we mean by conflict? Where does it reside, for example, in Phil's projected story about Gloria? Are there different kinds of conflict, and if so, what are they? How do we manage conflict to greatest effect?

Conflict

Let's take a step back. A story, traditionally anyway, involves a central figure, who constitutes its *subject*. This used to be called the *hero*, though in our antiheroic age, the more neutral term *protagonist* is probably a safer one. The protagonist has a *desire*, which is his *object*. There is some *obstacle* to the achievement of that desire. That obstacle may be a human *antagonist* or an antagonistic force or circumstance, such as war, political repression or poverty. The story is the sequence of events that leads to the protagonist's overcoming—or not—that which prevents the realization of his desire. Success in this quest implies (though not inevitably) a *comedy*; failure (again, not inevitably), a *tragedy*.

Simple though it sounds, this describes almost all plotted literature we know, from the potboiler to the classics. The lone spy must deliver the essential information to his superiors despite the unrelenting efforts of the enemy to track him down. The "woman with a past" must overcome her own shame and societal disapproval to give her daughter the kinds of opportunities the child deserves. Jane Eyre wishes to marry Mr. Rochester, but there is the obstacle of Bertha; Jay Gatsby wants to marry Daisy, but there is the obstacle of Tom. In Mario Puzo's *The Godfather*, Michael Corleone wants to "go straight," but there is the obstacle of his loyalty to his family.

Admittedly, the formulations above are dreadfully reductionist. The larger and more complex the story, the more protagonists, desires and obstacles we confront. *The Iliad* is the "comedy" of the Greeks, who achieve their desire of the destruction of Troy and the recuperation of Helen. Simultaneously, however, it is the tragedy of the Trojans. Within that overarching story we witness many other tragedies, including that of the Greek hero Achilles, who overcomes the warrior Hector to achieve the object of Greek victory, but through the obstacle of his pride loses his *personal* object of desire, his companion Patroclus, and ultimately loses his own life.

In considering the central conflict in your story, you obviously want to pay close attention to the protagonist—who she is, where she comes from, what elements of her character will incline your audience to sympathize with her position within the action. Generally, this is relatively easy, in that this is whom you presumably have come to identify with most intimately in the piece. However, you need to think carefully about her desire and antagonist as well. You must understand their complexities, that both may mean more than they seem to. In *The Great Gatsby*, Daisy Buchanan is the physical object of Jay's yearning, and yet, it is perhaps less this superficial woman "with a laugh like gold" that he wants than what her younger self once represented to him in terms of charm and grace and beauty. The real, human obstacles to the happiness of Romeo and Juliet are her cousin, Tybalt, her suitor, the County Paris, and both their fathers. Yet these are only the markers of the far greater obstacle that is the longtime enmity between Montagues and Capulets. In the end the Prince of Verona thunders, "All are punished" for this feud, which is the underlying engine of the plot.

But how, you might ask, does this apply to our story about John and Marsha? Where is the obstacle to Gloria's desire, for example, and what *is* her desire, anyway? The conflict in these pieces—and this is not at all unusual in modern fiction—resides for the most part within the characters themselves. One could argue that John's antagonist is Marsha, or even more plausibly, Sally. But most of all, John the protagonist is his *own* antagonist. The obstacle he has to overcome to achieve his present desire, which is to break up with Marsha, is his trauma about what happened when he broke up with Sally. The most significant conflict in the story takes place within John himself.

The same is true, in a more comedic vein, with Gloria. Her antagonist certainly isn't Mikey or Tom Frankel. Her antagonist, in a sense, is absence, that lack of anyone to share her life with. The obstacle to her happiness is her own grief at the loss of her husband, and also, perhaps, her inability to understand consciously that she even has a desire, that of filling the hole left by Mikey's death.

Gloria's conflict, once again, is internal: Gloria as woman and lover vs. her sadness and loneliness. At story's end, with her having thought of both Mikey and Tom, her notion of repainting the kitchen points quietly to a recognition of her desire and a resolution to that conflict. She may or may not strike up a romance with Tom Frankel, but encountering him has allowed her to confront and lay to rest the past and to take the first, tentative step into a future that is different from her present.

Let's now sketch that story of our mechanic, DeWayne, in greater detail, imagining a tale where the conflict is represented more concretely in the action. DeWayne, there at work in the garage, is looking forward to his upcoming date with his new girlfriend, Darlene, and his co-workers are well aware that he is hoping this particular evening to take her to bed. One of them, Louis, loudly encourages that desire, joshing and joking about the pleasures in store. That afternoon, however, DeWayne's sister, Patrice, drops by. She has been dumped by her boyfriend, Luther, whom she quite sincerely loved. He, on the other hand, had never invested much in the relationship and has subsequently both bad-mouthed her to various friends and possibly left her pregnant.

Louis and Patrice, then, give physical form to a conflict brewing within DeWayne himself. He is torn between his body's yearning for Darlene, which Louis keeps pressing him to slake, and his tender emotions toward her, which are associated with the sympathy and love he feels for the wounded Patrice. Louis urges DeWayne to get everything he can off his girlfriend, while Patrice—and even more concretely, Patrice's experience with men—counters Louis' advice with an object lesson in the possible consequences of sex without real commitment.

As fiction, along with the present century, has grown more psychological in its concerns, the story in which the locus of conflict resides within the protagonist herself has grown more and more common. This is not to say, however, that there is no place for a straightforward plot in which protagonist and antagonist are two clearly delineated characters, and in which the obstacles to the former's success are real and solid. This kind of narrative remains what most best-sellers are made of, and some genres—romances and thrillers, for example—are virtually inconceivable without it. Such pieces can fall into mere *allegory*, where characters so overtly represent opposites—good and bad, lust and love—that the narrative seems simplistic. In a tale like DeWayne's, however, that can be avoided with relative ease if both Patrice and Louis are given sufficient shading as characters so as to avoid being mere markers for particular abstractions. This is especially important in the latter instance. Patrice as wronged woman is someone an audience is likely to embrace. Louis, however, will have to be somebody who is more than just Mr. Wink-Wink Nudge-Nudge if we are to feel real conflict in DeWayne's position. I will discuss this at greater length in subsequent chapters, but for the moment, keep in mind that Patrice and Louis, if given sufficient flesh, can make the playing out of DeWayne's internal conflict both memorable and compelling to the reader.

Complicating Conflict, Torquing Tension

If we know what conflict is and how to create it, that doesn't necessarily tell us how to sustain it, how to use it to propel our story forward and keep our reader reading. Obviously, if you're dealing with a plot ready-made—deriving action specifically or generally from the story of Dinah or *King Lear*—your conflicts and their development is largely taken care of. In other instances, however, what to do? At some point in writing a story, be it in the first moments of its conception, in the midst of its composition or when you've completed your first draft, you need to ask yourself what the piece's central conflict is and how to use that conflict to your advantage.

Remember William Faulkner's claim that his novel *The Sound and the Fury* arose from a vision he had of a little girl high in a tree, peeking through the window at her grandmother's laying out, with her brothers below, themselves peeking up at her muddy drawers? From the outset, I suspect, he at least intuited the conflicts inherent therein.

Implicit in that single "snapshot" are some of the most powerful engines of Faulkner's story. First of all, there is a role reversal. There are three boys and one girl present, and it is the latter who has shinnied up the tree. Even now, in our less gender-bound age, we still expect boys to be the more adventurous and physical of the sexes, and yet here, it is the girl who is the explorer, the curious one, indeed, the defiant one—insisting on observing a scene from which the children have been excluded.

This girl, Caddy, is a voyeur, but of course the brothers are voyeurs as well, though the forbidden sight they are observing is not the spectacle of death, but that of their sister, specifically the forbidden part of her body barely covered (and indeed emphasized) by her muddy drawers. As Faulkner's novel unfolds, it is indeed Caddy and later her eponymous daughter who prove the most powerful and defiant of the book's characters, their actions catalyzing the events throughout the story. Beyond that, the three brothers are hopelessly in her spell. The retarded Benjy adores her, Quentin loves her with an incestuous passion that will lead to his suicide, and Jason detests her and her offspring with a loathing quite as intense as Quentin's desire. The author could not know there was so much conflict tied up in that initial image, but—consciously or unconsciously—he was able to encounter and exploit it as his story developed. Throughout the novel, as the perspective moves among the three brothers and finally to the family retainer, Dilsey, Faulkner increases and decreases Caddy's presence, gradually revealing her significance to the other characters in the story.

In our piece centered on DeWayne, we'd perhaps begin with the men at the garage teasing DeWayne about his upcoming sexual conquest, seeking to involve the reader in their leering banter. Patrice's sudden arrival puts an end to jokes. She takes her brother aside and reveals she might be pregnant. On his return to work, the razzing continues, with Louis taking the lead, but DeWayne's response is now subdued. Still, he is torn between his desire for sexual release and the realization of what fulfilling that desire can mean. At lunch, he sees his sister again, and there her own anger flares when he tries to talk to her about his dilemma. He's unable to get a sympathetic hearing anyplace. Back on the job, the teasing turns cruel, with Louis again taking the lead, implying some lack of virility on DeWayne's part, to the point the two almost come to blows.

You can see here, as the story approaches its key moment—DeWayne's date with Darlene—the conflict in the piece has been *modulated* so as to keep the reader involved. Scenes shift back and forth from public (the crew in the garage) to private (Patrice and DeWayne alone). The tones of these are different—raucous and jokey vs. intimate and frightened. Patrice and Louis represent two different courses DeWayne might take, and his choice is obviously going to be the crux of the story, its climax in not only the figurative but perhaps the most literal way.

In discussing these conflicts and complications, we are dealing with something that may have a more familiar ring to the average reader: *tension*. We all know what tension is, or at least think we do. It's that white-knuckled response to the time bomb ticking in the downtown restaurant or to the killer we know is hiding in the closet. Most all commentators on the subject find the remark of Russian short story master and playwright Anton Chekhov useful in the definition of tension. Chekhov said, essentially, if there is a loaded gun in act one, it must go off before the end of the play. Its simple presence onstage creates ongoing tension throughout the action.

In many popular texts, the origin of the tension is, broadly speaking, a thing—that loaded gun; the standard, central-casting psycho killer. The tension is created, however, less by *what* is in the narrative than by *how* that narrative is put together. Even when the origin of tension is the time bomb, an author doesn't (or at least shouldn't) simply sit us down in front of it and let us watch the timepiece on the detonator click down second by second from three hours, twenty-six minutes, fourteen seconds to "Bang!" Rather, though she may remind us from time to time of the descending numbers on the clock (time bombs these days having largely abandoned analog clocks in favor of digital ones), the writer will spend most of her time shuttling us back and forth among those innocent and unaware people in proximity to the bomb, those who have set it, and those who know it is "ticking" and are frantically trying to arrive in time to defuse it.

You can see even in this very simple example how tension and conflict are related. Let's assume, as is usually but not always the case (war, thriller and espionage heroes can virtuously blow things up), that our bombers are the bad guys (antagonists) and that the good guys (protagonists) are those who desire to foil the bad ones. To realize that desire, the latter have to overcome a series of obstacles. They have to find out the bomb exists, who planted it and why, when it will explode and where it is. They then have to literally race against the clock, overcoming skeptical higher officials, let's say, along with traffic jams, unreliable communications equipment and various bad guy attempts to throw them off the scent, in order to avoid a catastrophic result. The existence of the obstacles is a means by which the author creates tension. Imagine if there were no impediments to the fulfillment of the protagonist's desire.

> I picked up the ringing phone. It was 12:54.
>
> "There is a time bomb set to go off at 1:37 P.M. in the dishwasher of the Big Boy at the corner of 7th and Elm Street," said a voice in an unidentifiable foreign accent.
>
> I hung up immediately and called the bomb squad.
>
> I quickly explained the situation.

> "Lucky for us we happen to have a unit at 7th and Maple," the squad commander told me. "We can be there in three minutes."
>
> At 1:13, the phone rang again. "Well, we've defused the bomb."

A bit like watching grass grow.

In narratives centered on events like this, tension arguably *is* the story. For the most part, they are focused upon the character or characters who represent good, right and order, and our assumption is that these are the figures who will, in the end, prevail. In his James Bond novels, Ian Fleming had to come up with increasingly dastardly (and some would say, increasingly implausible) villains who possessed increasingly ingenious (some would say outlandish) ways of impeding 007's salvation of the world from their nefarious plots. The final outcome, however, is never in doubt. Indeed, when another famous author attempted to do away with a similar but rather more complex hero, the audience would have none of it. Arthur Conan Doyle sent Sherlock Holmes over a cliff with his nemesis, Dr. Moriarty, but was finally forced to miraculously bring Holmes back to life.

Nonetheless, it's important to note that in stories of this ilk, the antagonist at least approaches the protagonist in intelligence or strength or in some other key trait. Goldfinger can match MI-6's remarkable technology machine for machine. Moriarty is as cunning as Holmes—at least, almost. A struggle in which the opponents are unevenly matched cannot generate much tension. The bungling inspectors from Scotland Yard in Conan Doyle's mysteries exist not as rivals to Holmes, but as comic relief.

In a more serious vein, except in historical fantasies such as Philip Dick's *The Man in the High Castle* or Robert Harris' best-seller, *Fatherland*, both of which presume the victory of the Third Reich in World War II, we are often stuck with overarching and verifiable realities that the reader is aware of and that we cannot change. Hence, Beryl Bainbridge in *Every Man for Himself* cannot save the *Titanic*. We know the ship is going to sink. On the one hand this supplies ready-made tension in her story, but on the other, Bainbridge must rely on her own imaginative reconstruction of people and events that have been thoroughly documented in order to create new and distinctive tensions in her retelling of the famous disaster. What keeps the reader reading is not curiosity about what finally happens but rather a desire to know how and why things happen, and to whom.

To put this another way, what you attempt to do in a story is establish an unanswered question or questions ("How soon will DeWayne sleep with Darlene?"), which lead to other questions (after Patrice's visit to the garage, "*Will* DeWayne sleep with Darlene?"). Queries great and small should proliferate in the early development of a fiction, though remember that a reader anticipates that these questions will all be answered, at least tentatively, as your story reaches a conclusion. Those answers will be generated by processes throughout the story (e.g., DeWayne's inner struggle to reconcile his competing desires). If every mystery in your story is revealed in the paragraph following its postulation, there is no tension, and the reader will be bored.

What you do, once again, is withhold information; you manage or control it. Remember the discussion of the opening gesture in chapter four? In all of the cases discussed, we were given a striking image—such as Boyle's hero, Mungo Park, with his drawers around his ankles—and were then left with a raft of questions as to what was going on. By the time we reached the episode when Park dropped trou, of course, much else had transpired in the book and had generated a whole new series of questions.

García Márquez does much the same thing when he begins *One Hundred Years of Solitude*. We don't know how Aureliano Buendía ended up before a firing squad, or how he became a colonel, or why he didn't know what ice was. All these issues are ultimately cleared up in the course of the text. The author has piqued our curiosity and, in so doing, *foreshadowed* events that will only take on their full shape and significance later in the story. Foreshadowing is a useful means of creating tension, though it needs to be employed with some skill. It should be neither so subtle that the reader simply reads past it and never recognizes its import nor so blatant that the reader understands its entire import before the foreshadowed event occurs.

In *Jane Eyre*, Brontë establishes the facts of Rochester's dour temperament, his mysterious past that somehow involved the Caribbean and the presence of "ghosts" who rattle about in the dark in Thornhill Hall all before revealing the presence of his wife upstairs. Bertha's appearance surprises us, but not entirely. Brontë has injected a number of unexplained and suspenseful elements into her story, which achieve flesh and sense when the madwoman in the attic finally appears.

Ghosts, bombs, firing squads, liners plunging to the bottom of the sea—these are certainly enough to get a reader's pulse pounding. Tension, however, is often a quieter and more refined phenomenon than this. The obstacles confronted in a conventional romantic comedy tend to be quite quotidian, if often a bit broadly drawn. A difference in age, class, race or faith; familial disapproval; distinct goals and visions can create those strains we all recognize from our own adventures and misadventures in love. The clash between generations and their respective values (and their eventual reconciliation) has been a root of tension in stories since the parable of the Prodigal Son in the Gospel of Luke.

Tension can be communicated to your reader subtly. Where John and Marsha are concerned, what you try to capture is that uneasy feeling you had when you first observed John in the car as you were walking the dog, that sense that there was something off here. From the very first lines in the story, this feeling is quietly present: the man unmoving behind the wheel, the woman in the doorway who doesn't open the screen. Something is impending; these people are not relaxed; the rhythm of the everyday has somehow been interrupted. No one's screaming. No one's running. Nothing is blowing up. Don't forget that stillness can be a very effective tool. Remember all those old westerns and war movies: "It's quiet." "Yeah, too quiet."

Throughout a story, especially one of any length, the level of tension has to fluctuate without ever disappearing completely. This is necessary because unbroken tension begins to lose its effect, just as a persistent pain dulls over time. In life itself, the human animal is incapable of sustaining the heightened sensibility of tragedy or fear or panic indefinitely. This breaking or lessening of tension in the text can be achieved in various ways. Most commonly, the scene simply shifts to another that is occurring simultaneously. The psycho killer jimmies the window, slips into the intended victim's apartment, spies the closet and places his hand on the knob. Then, suddenly, we are with that intended victim as she lunches with a friend from work, chatting gaily about her new boyfriend. We feel relief on the one hand (we're not going to be witnessing a murder just yet), but at the same time our relief is tempered by that vague, ongoing itch of tension (the killer is now ensconced in his victim's house).

Characters themselves often take steps to alleviate the intensity of a particular moment. Marsha lights a cigarette, which allows for John's joshing and a racheting down of their nervousness with one another. This kind of breaking or varying of tension can be a means of demonstrating the extreme tension your characters are feeling. Chapter thirty-five of Wolfe's *Look Homeward, Angel*, in which Ben Gant succumbs to pneumonia, is arguably the most well-written death scene in American literature, and one of the finest in all of literature. One of the reasons for this evaluation is how effectively the author captures the family's fear and grief in all its bizarre manifestations. Ben's agony is the source of incredible sadness, but also brings to the surface the resentments and anger, the affection and real hatred the various family members feel toward one another. They whipsaw through an entire repertoire of emotions—terror, pity, rage, laughter; blaming and forgiving—as they sit the deathwatch. They speak brutal truths and invent elaborate rationalizations. They swing from despair to unjustifiable optimism.

This is the exchange outside the bedroom the day before Ben's final crisis. His siblings—Luke, Helen and Eugene—are there, along with their mother, Eliza.

> Luke was teetering about restlessly, breathing stertorously and smoking a cigarette, and Eliza, working her lips, stood with an attentive ear cocked to the door of the sick-room. She was holding a useless kettle of hot water.
>
> "Huh? Hah? What say?" asked Eliza, before any one had said anything. "How is he?" Her eyes darted about at them.
>
> "Get away! Get away! Get away!" Eugene muttered savagely. His voice rose. "Can't you get away?"
>
> He was infuriated by the sailor's loud nervous breathing, his large awkward feet. He was angered still more by Eliza's useless kettle, her futile hovering, her "huh?" and "hah?"
>
> "Can't you see he's fighting for his breath? Do you want to strangle him? It's messy! Messy! Do you hear?" His voice rose again.

This is son and mother again, the following morning.

> And Eugene, choked with exasperation at one moment, because
> of her heavy optimism, was blind with pity the next when he saw
> the terrible fear and pain in her dull black eyes. He rushed toward
> her suddenly, as she stood above the hot stove, and seized her
> rough worn hand, kissing it and babbling helplessly.
>
> "O Mama! Mama! It's all right! It's all right! It's all right."
>
> And Eliza, stripped suddenly of her pretenses, clung to him,
> burying her white face in his coat sleeve, weeping bitterly, help-
> lessly, grievously, for the sad waste of the irrevocable years—
> the immortal hours of love that might never be relived, the
> great evil of forgetfulness and indifference that could never be
> righted now. Like a child she was grateful for his caress, and
> his heart twisted in him like a wild and broken thing, and he
> kept mumbling:
>
> "It's all right! It's all right! It's all right!"—knowing that it
> was not, could never be, all right.
>
> "If I had known. Child, if I had known," she wept, as she had
> wept long before at Grover's death.
>
> "Brace up!" he said. "He'll pull through yet. The worst is
> over."
>
> "Well, I tell you," said Eliza, drying her eyes at once, "I be-
> lieve it is. I believe he passed the turning-point last night. I was
> saying to Bessie—"

Wolfe intensifies our own experience of Ben's death by showing
us the wild mood swings of the Gants as they confront their imminent
loss. They are furious one moment and embracing the next. We never
know exactly how Eugene or Helen or Eliza or the rest are going to
respond on the next page to a worsening in Ben's condition, and
hence, we push forward through the chapter with nerves on edge,
precisely as we would feel if we were actually present.

Tension, obviously, is one of the most significant elements in making
fiction compelling. As we've seen, it should be present at almost
every aspect of your story: the opening gesture, the organization of
scenes, foreshadowing, surprises, not to mention the emotional ebb and
flow of the tale in its conflict and complications. When we think of something suspenseful, we're inclined to go back to that gun in act one or

the ticking bomb. It should be obvious now, however, that the quality of tension is far more complex than we might assume and manifests itself in myriad ways we would not initially think of.

CLIMAX AND CONCLUSION

Climax. Now that's easy to explain. It's the culmination of action, the place all the tension finally and definitely breaks, the point toward which everything has been leading. That is, indeed, a perfectly correct definition of climax, though, in literature, it's slightly more complicated than that. We can use the term in two ways, and you should be aware of both.

What we just described is what the Greeks referred to as the catastrophe—literally "overturn" or "downturn." To use an example with which you're likely familiar, the duel between Hamlet and Laertes in the final scene of Shakespeare's *Hamlet* represents climax in this sense of catastrophe, and certainly, the corpse-littered stage at act five's conclusion is pretty catastrophic: Laertes—dead; King Claudius—dead; Queen Gertrude—dead; Prince Hamlet—dead. The poisoned cup and poisoned sword have done such a number on the royal court of Denmark that Shakespeare has to drag the Norwegian prince Fortinbras in at the end to speak the last lines of the play.

A sketch of *Hamlet*'s catastrophic climax would show an unbroken rising line up to that horrific final scene and then a sudden falling off.

I'll discuss this kind of climactic moment in greater detail later, but it's important that you as writer be aware there is a second definition of climax, one you need to be conscious of in structuring your fiction.

This different kind of climax would be diagrammed as a rising line that peaks much earlier and then falls more gradually.

In *Hamlet*, this occurs in the play's third act: (1) Thanks to the reenactment of the murder of Hamlet's father by Claudius that is staged by the traveling players, Hamlet's suspicions of his uncle's perfidity are confirmed; and (2) Hamlet, who up to this point in the play has not made any move to revenge his father's murder, kills Polonius on the mistaken assumption he is Claudius. The story *pivots* at this point: The action ceases to build and begins to fall toward inevitable disaster.

Much fiction possesses this kind of double climax—a pivot and a catastrophe—though they can occur so close together they are essentially the same thing. We could argue that, in the case of John and Marsha, they are notably distinct. When the couple kisses in our projected story, that's the pivot: What's been anticipated (the breakup) is not going to happen. The piece's catastrophe occurs later, with John alone and frustrated in the car.

A story by Greg Skwira, "Nightbirds," can serve to illustrate a simultaneous climax, that is, the one where the pivot of the action and the catastrophe are one and the same. The protagonist, an autoworker in Detroit, begins his tale by describing (none too enthusiastically) the court-ordered psychotherapy he's presently undergoing. The body of the story is taken up with how he came to this pass. Laid off in the midst of the industry's crisis around 1980, he has watched his life gradually unravel—losing job, savings, self-respect and finally his wife—and ultimately decides to move to Texas to begin anew.

After a couple too many at a favorite tavern on his way out of town, he stops on the bridge leading south from the city that crosses the River Rouge. There, overlooking the vast complex of mills, factories and coke ovens of the Ford Motor Company, he is overwhelmed by despair and begins to cast his few remaining worldly goods into the abyss, including, in the end, his collection of car magazines. Spinning like Frisbees into the night, they remind him of "flushed partridges," and as they flutter into the darkness like "nightbirds," a patrolman arrives to arrest him.

In the original draft, this moment was followed by a couple pages in which the protagonist describes his night in jail, his moving into his father's house, his continued joblessness and his legally mandated therapy. In revision, however, the story ends with the cherrytop pulling to the side of the road. We know, at that point, our hero is not going to join his kitchen table, dinner plates and magazines in the fetid waters of the Rouge, nor is he going to make it to Houston. The piece has pivoted. The character's despair has reached its height (or nadir, frankly), and, with his arrest, he will (we know from the opening paragraphs) survive. Too, he has suffered his catastrophe—the sacrifice of those magazines that represent everything he ever believed in. In the rough draft, the paragraphs following the incident on the bridge represented a far too gradual falling off, an accumulation of detail that is quite real but, insofar as the power of the story is concerned, is not only a bit beside the point but detrimental to its overall effect.

What this relates to is our sense of an ending, our need, as writers, to know when our tale is told. Here, given that the introductory passage indicates our protagonist's life has gone on, we really don't need information on where he is living, what he is or is not doing. Chronologically, it's the logical conclusion of the story. But this is a tale about despair, about someone whose life has been shattered by forces completely out of his control. The piece has much more impact if we leave the hero at that moment. Those magazines, glittering with the bechromed behemoths both he and the company he worked for thought would maintain their world indefinitely, become the emblem of his hopelessness. The action itself and the locale where it is taking place are much more intensely dramatic than those that follow.

The End

Just as Pound could tell Eliot "Start it here," you may need a friendly (or not so friendly) audience to tell you "End it here." Though certainly there are those instances in which you have moved confidently toward that conclusion you know is right (say, John sitting silently in his car as dusk slips into night), there may be others where you are not absolutely certain you have told too much or not enough. Should our last image of DeWayne be of him at dawn, asleep, holding Darlene in his arms? Him putting his arm around her and kissing her deeply? Perhaps even him arriving at her door? Any of these, properly prepared for, could indicate what his decision regarding having sex with her has been. It's once again a question of choice—your choice. Just as that opening sequence is your big chance to hook your reader on your story, your closing moment is your last word, the final opportunity to seal your fiction into the reader's memory, make it a little part of her life and, from a purely mercenary point of view, encourage her to recommend your work to others and keep an eye out for your next effort.

There is a conventionalism bordering on cliché that the difference between nineteenth- and twentieth-century novels is that the former "end" while the latter "stop." An analogy is often drawn to music, where, frankly, this notion may have greater credibility. Listening to the "William Tell Overture" (better known as the "Theme to the Lone Ranger"), it sometimes seems like it is nothing *but* ending, as Rossini piles one stirring and apparently conclusive passage on top of another. Compare that to Igor Stravinsky's groundbreaking ballet of 1912, "The Rite of Spring." There, the sacrificial victim of an ancient Scythian ceremony dances herself to death, and the music collapses on itself as if the orchestra as well had suffered sudden and massive heart failure.

It *is* generally true that novels of a hundred years ago conclude with "the world set right," a Rossinian flourish that lets us know we've come to the conclusion. A bit less charitably, it's sometimes said you know these stories are over because all the main characters are either married or dead. Readers of the nineteenth century anticipated a profound sense of closure, to the point that even as popular and powerful a writer as Charles Dickens altered the final pages of his *Great Expectations* so as to imply that his hero, Pip, and the somewhat difficult Estella would eventually and rather improbably marry. Fiction served a didactic, ideological, even philosophical master—a vision of human progress toward readily identifiable goals of stability and order. Even so, there were not infrequent exceptions to the rule. *Huckleberry Finn*, after all, leaves the door open for further adventures, as Huck threatens to "light off for the territory" if Aunt Sally continues with her schemes to "sivilize" him. Certainly, from all we've seen of "sivilization" in the novel, we can understand his reservations.

The conclusion that ties everything up with a nice, neat bow is still seen in some popular fiction, and especially in popular film. This may explain a common phenomenon in apprentice writing: the "big bang" ending—a murder, suicide, horrible accident or devastating diagnosis. I recently read a story in workshop in which, in five pages, a man discovers his wife in bed with his boss, goes through a divorce, is falsely accused of a hit-and-run and spends five days in jail. He ends up in his family's cabin where, on a walk in the woods, he observes two bear cubs at play and is then summarily dispatched by their mother.

Dramatic, yes, but death by marauding grizzly is, at best, an unusual finis for life's accumulated problems, even for that of this extraordinarily unlucky and put-upon protagonist. Though it's true that dying is in the contract for all of us from the very first, the fact is that life goes on. The betrayed spouse, the loyal employee out on his ear, the falsely accused, the evicted and so on usually do *not* turn murderous or suicidal. They make their peace, get along, survive.

It is perhaps an indication of our own uncertain times that we are more comfortable with the story that stops. This doesn't mean the book breaks off in midsentence with nothing resolved, but it does mean that those resolutions may be temporary or tentative. We're perhaps less likely these days to believe in "happily ever after," inclined to assume that relationships are fragile, that circumstances and people change, that what seems the fulfillment of our hearts' desires may, in a year or two or five, turn to ashes in our mouths. Arguably, we are not cynical, merely realistic, and our world-weary skepticism manifests itself in our fiction. One can imagine, fifty years earlier, the death of Gatsby in Fitzgerald's novel would have been so presented as to have some ennobling or humbling effect on all who knew him. Yet, in that preeminently "modern" novel, only Nick Carraway, our narrator, seems to see the larger significance of his death, and those indirectly responsible for it, Tom and Daisy Buchanan, retreat back into their money with hardly a second thought.

To return to that schema of conflict I discussed, your story is over, or so convention tells us, when the last obstacle is past and the protagonist does—or doesn't—achieve his desire. That's a good rule of thumb, but as indicated throughout this book, determining what that obstacle ought to be, what that desire really is, may require considerable exploration and thought. As with all the other issues discussed, it's you who has to make the choices.

CROSSING THE T

It may seem odd, after so many pages, that we finally get around to addressing the issue of theme. Since high school, most of us have been taught that it is a great theme that makes a great book, that the idea at the core of a story is what establishes it as something worth reading. This, as should be apparent by now, is at best half the truth, and probably less. Many is the novel that centers on a fine or moral or noble concept, or tells a tale of unquestionable transcendence, and falls flat on its face. To cite a famous example, take General Lew Wallace's *Ben Hur: A Story of the Christ*, one of America's greatest best-sellers and a book hopelessly weaker than the movie renditions of it. The life of Jesus has certainly given rise to great literature, and General Wallace may have been a sincere and devout believer. Unfortunately, he was a terrible writer: his prose, leaden; his characters, saltine thin; his plot, contrived.

So, a great theme does not a great book make. More than that, however, the theme of a story is probably its most unconscious element. In the fourth chapter, I mentioned I asked workshop members to tell me what a story was "about." I was looking for a synopsis of action and some notion of characters, not a statement of an overarching topic. It is not accidental that, in the first half of the century, when students were asked to write themes, it meant producing an essay.

Don't sit down to write about an issue—abortion, adolescent angst, the pain of growing old—if you are writing fiction. Wolfe didn't set out to craft "a classic tale of American youth," nor did Fitzgerald begin with the idea of painting "the definitive portrait of the Jazz Age." Each wanted to tell a story, that of Eugene Gant and his family, that of Jay Gatsby's impossible love, and in the process ended up with a book that would eventually bear the foregoing kind of encomiums on the dust jacket. The theme of a work emerges in the way a writer's voice emerges. Beyond this, a single book may have many themes, depending on who is reading it. A university colleague of mine can tell you at some length how my novel *The Professor of Aesthetics* fits into an entire American tradition of loss of innocence, of the conflict between the pastoral and the mechanical. He can quote you chapter and verse and, I can tell you, make a strong case for that reading. I can also tell you that this theme never crossed my mind when I was at work on the novel.

Does that mean my colleague is wrong? Not at all. The relations he has noted between my book and a larger tradition are ones he was likely inclined to look for from the first, given his interest in that tradition. However, with the story set in a small town during and after the First World War, perhaps it was inevitable that the collision of old and new, nature and machine would have to be significant elements in the text.

It is not that a story never begins with an abstract concept. Certainly, Atwood's *The Handmaid's Tale* arose from her unease before resurgent Protestant fundamentalism in the 1980s, as Orwell's *1984* resulted from the author's general perceptions of the monstrousness of both Fascism and Communism and his own disillusioning experiences with the Left during his service in the Spanish Civil War. The danger here is, first of all, topicality. Precisely what makes the book timely can, over the years, make it quaint. Certain stories avoid this fate—*Uncle Tom's Cabin, The Jungle*—but these survive from among hundreds if not thousands of abolitionist novels or labor novels. More than this, though, the problem resides in a story's falling captive to the idea that has motivated it. You sit down to write "a hard-hitting exposé of the problems of the aged in the inner city" but find that, rather than being interested in your senior citizen protagonist, you are really more attracted to the pregnant Dominican woman who lives across the hall. You conceive of DeWayne's story as one of "the difficult choices facing the young, African-American man of today," but Patrice seems to be demanding more and more of your attention.

It comes down to this: An emphasis on theme will tend to undermine the organic development of your narrative. It will define the story you tell from the outset, though that may not be the one you really *want* to tell. It works a bit like symbolism. Symbols, ideally anyway, are not something you put into your writing; they simply appear, bubbling up out of your unconscious and onto the page. That's probably the way it should be—the symbols coming from the realm of dreams. In later drafts, you may recognize these and make more conscious use of them, but initially, they are just there.

Likewise, the theme of your fiction is probably already present. You are writing this particular story because, in its heart, there is some issue that attracts or frightens or fascinates you, though you may not consciously be aware of what it is. Leave it to college professors and book reviewers and blurb writers to determine what your theme is. Your characters and plot and the prose itself will demand more than enough of your time, and if they are all working as they should, important ideas are sure to emerge as well.

EXERCISES

1. Take a favorite story by someone else and one of your own. See if you can trace the 5 Cs in each.

2. In one of your stories, alter the coordinates, ideally more than one, and then rewrite it. If you, like Phil, have one of those "boys on the beach" pieces, reset it in August of 1939, when World War II began in Europe, and see where that takes you. Other alternatives could be shifting the action from the Florida shore to Lake Mead, injecting a new character into the story or telling the tale from the point of view of what presently is one of its secondary figures.

3. Take three of your stories and three by writers you admire. Determine who is the subject, what is the object, etc., in each. Do your pieces manifest a particular pattern? Do those of the admired writers?

4. Using the same stories as in exercise three, try to determine if they possess both pivotal and catastrophic climaxes.

5. Look at the endings of a couple of your stories. Is there a way these pieces could be brought to a more striking conclusion by bringing them to a close sooner than you presently do? Try altering them to increase their power.

SIX

A CERTAIN AIR
OF REFINEMENT

I have spent a lot of time talking about plot. This is reasonable. With certain inevitable exceptions, a good plot is essential in fine fiction. But we know that a good plot is not all that's necessary. In chapter three, the role of language and its uses received considerable emphasis. In this and the following chapters, I turn to other elements you will want to keep in mind as you craft your work into something not merely able but memorable. Here, let's consider certain tactical and editorial questions that relate to your story's presentation, stylistic and structural techniques that can make for a more intense experience for the reader. You may take these into account in the conception of your story, though oftentimes, these come into play when you're refining a first draft.

DIALOGUE AND DOCUMENTATION

I have just, not quite arbitrarily, pulled two novels off the bookshelf. One is Edith Wharton's short novel of 1911, *Ethan Frome*; the other, Anne Finger's 1994 book, *Bone Truth*.

Wharton begins in this way.

> I had the story, bit by bit, from various people, and, as generally happens in such cases, each time it was a different story.
>
> If you know Starkfield, Massachusetts, you know the post-office. If you know the post-office you must have seen Ethan Frome drive up to it, drop the reins of his hollow-backed bay and drag himself across the brick pavement to the white colonnade: and you must have asked who he was.

It was there that, several years ago, I saw him for the first time and the sight pulled me up sharp. Even then he was the most striking figure in Starkfield, though he was but the ruin of a man. It was not so much his great height that marked him, for the "natives" were easily singled out by their lank longitude from the stockier foreign breed: it was the careless powerful look he had, in spite of a lameness checking each step like the jerk of a chain. . . .

Here is the opening passage of Finger's novel:

"I have the results from your test," she says. "And you are pregnant."

The prickle of artificial upholstery fabric against my bare elbows. The woman, who introduced herself to me a minute ago ("Hi, I'm Sherry, I'm one of the counselors here—"), sitting opposite me in a blond wood and brown fabric chair. The poster on the wall opposite, a bear balancing on a gaily painted circus ball, the word CYRK beneath it.

"Have you thought about what you're going to do?" she asks, leaning toward me. Her body language says, I'm open, I'm non-judgmental, you can share with me.

I consider saying, No, Sherry, I have never given it a moment's consideration. The subject of offspring has not crossed my mind before. Nope. No. Never.

I stiffen in my chair. I concede, "I've thought about it."

"Yes?" she asks, an indeterminate, open-ended "yes."

These are, of course, profoundly different books, written in profoundly different ways, eighty years apart. Their openings point out, in a very general way, how fiction has changed in the last century or so. Wharton's paragraphs are densely narrative, filled with information. We are in Massachusetts, in a town called Starkfield populated by both longtime New Englanders and recent immigrants. In front of a colonnaded post office, a man named Ethan Frome dismounts from a hollow-backed horse. Frome is very tall, striking, lame. There is a story to be told about him, one apparently mysterious in that it has come to our narrator only piece by piece in various versions.

Finger, on the other hand, drops us directly into a dramatic and overtly contemporary scene. There is an obviously unplanned pregnancy that can be tested for, a counselor who is nonjudgmental, artificial fabrics. We hear the conversation between the as yet nameless narrator and a social services provider. The description of their surroundings is terse, verbless, almost telegraphic, like a folder of snapshots flipped before us. The first-person narrator is ironic, tense, her voice edged by anger or, at the least, by wariness.

It has become cliché to note that the very "look" of texts has changed radically in the last hundred years or so. If you open a novel from the nineteenth century, almost inevitably you will encounter a page dark with print. The dominant techniques of storytelling in the previous century favored a kind of writing that featured elaborate description, formal (and sometimes rather windy) dialogue and complex evocation of place and historical moment. This was not merely an aesthetic decision. When Balzac or James spent page after page on cityscapes or interiors, on the layout of a Parisian café or that of an English country house, it was because a great many of their readers had never *seen* these things. Not only was travel more difficult then, but all the various means of visual and aural reproduction—photography and recording for example—were in their infancy or did not exist at all. People in the provinces had simply never seen the big city and its sights, even in photographs. They had never heard a symphony orchestra or the cacophonous roar of a steel mill. There were more intense class and gender divisions, so many places were simply off-limits to the less well-heeled, to respectable women, to sober and serious young men, while other places—the slums of the city, the mines, the stockyards—would not be familiar to the middle and upper classes. Even today, much historical fiction, as well as a great deal of popular fiction centering on "the rich and famous" (such as the millionaires of Danielle Steel) or "the mighty and powerful" (such as the admiral or chief petty officers of Tom Clancy), provide a great deal of detailed description, simply because most of us do not have access to the baccarat tables of Monte Carlo or the bridge of a nuclear submarine.

Still, most twentieth-century fiction, especially post–Second World War, looks very different from the novels of Émile Zola or Jane Austen. Rapid, colloquial dialogue leaves large white spaces in either margin; description is often minimal and woven throughout scenes that are dramatized.

Too much can be made of this. Certainly a glance at Faulkner, at Jack Kerouac or Thomas Pynchon is enough to convince anyone that density of narrative was not something completely abandoned in the twentieth century. Many short stories by Jorge Luis Borges have no dialogue in them at all. The young novelist David Foster Wallace, whose first book, *The Broom of the System*, was an immediate hit, relates that during his study at a well-known graduate writing program, his fellow students, firmly in the grip of then fashionable minimalism, moaned endlessly about his long, descriptive passages. On the whole though, most fiction in the last fifty years tends to balance dialogue, descriptions and documentation of place and time in ways different than in previous centuries.

At the outset, let's be clear that these balances are heavily determined by what kind of story you're telling. Tillie Olsen's short story "I Stand Here Ironing" is an interior monologue, a technique I'll discuss more fully in the next chapter. For our purposes now, I'll simply say that the character is "speaking" her story to us. Though there is not an inconsiderable amount of quotations of various characters, the text is tightly packed on the page, and it is, finally, the narrator's single voice we are "hearing."

> Now, when it is too late (as if she would let me hold and comfort her like I do the others) I get up and go to her at once at her moan or restless stirring, "Are you awake, Emily? Can I get you something?" And the answer is always the same: "No, I'm all right, go back to sleep, Mother."

Likewise, if the locale of the story is one foreign to most readers, a fair amount of physical description and social or historical information may have to be woven through the text in order to locate the audience within the world in which the action is occurring. This is obviously a given in a genre like science fiction. Even in more conventional texts, however, this may be necessary. Truman Capote, in *Other Voices, Other Rooms*, takes great pains to evoke the landscape and isolation of the rural bayou country in which his novel unfolds.

> Now a traveler must make his way to Noon City by the best means he can, for there are no buses or trains heading in that direction . . . this is lonesome country; and here in the swamp-

like hollows where tiger lilies bloom the size of man's head, there are luminous green logs that shine under the dark marsh water like drowned corpses; often the only movement on the landscape is winter smoke winding out the chimney of some sorry-looking farmhouse, or a wing-stiffened bird, silent and arrow-eyed, circling over the black deserted pinewoods.

If, as sometimes happens, the locale itself functions in the text almost as a character—the town and surrounding prairie in Larry McMurtry's novels of the American West, for instance—then the space given over to evocation of place will be considerably greater than in a story in which a general urban or suburban setting functions as a backdrop for a more intimate and personal tale. For an example of the latter, think of Phil's story about Gloria. When he planned the piece, he determined that New Hampshire itself, if not incidental to the central thrust of the story, was a secondary element. The specific state obviously establishes certain limits in the story's development. It's doubtful that Gloria's late husband, Mikey, took up surfing as a hobby late in life or that Gloria will be out tending her garden in the middle of February. Still, the "New Hampshireness" of the piece provides a background for the action and might be reworked only slightly, if Phil so chose, to become "Maineness" or even "Ohioness."

Form and Function

The motto for fiction as we enter the new millennium might well be that of the modernist architects of the fading century's youth: "Form follows function." In your initial draft of a story, simply write. Do whatever you have to do to get the text on paper, to get the story out of the realm of your imagination and into a real and tangible product you can hold in your hand. Then, as you read it, as you prepare for the writing of a second draft (or a third or fourth), one of the primary questions you should be asking yourself is, What "work" is every element of the piece performing to make the story successful and interesting? If, up to now, you've played God, you've now been transformed into the management consultant from Hell, brought in to streamline operations and turn your story into a smoothly running, almost organic, entity that accomplishes what it's supposed to with apparent effortlessness.

This brings us back to some issues discussed in a different context, elements such as dialogue and documentation. In measuring the efficiency of your narrative, a good place to start is with the dialogue. Recently, I read a young writer's story of the estrangement of mother and daughter. Their telephone conversations, largely taken up with trivialities, were rendered faithfully and at considerable length, whereas, in a key moment toward the tale's conclusion, their dialogue over the kitchen table, during which they achieved the beginnings of understanding, was summarized. This seemed an odd narrative choice, and, indeed, the author admitted that the telephone chitchat had been easy to write, but she was intimidated by the task of presenting the emotionally loaded face-to-face confrontation. One quick example of the superficial phone-talk would have more than sufficed to show us the distance extant between mother and daughter. Further phone conversations could simply be alluded to or summarized.

The "big moment," however, demands presentation. In many ways, it is the climax of the story, the place where the relationship between the two characters pivots. It's precisely there we should hear them speak, see them move, experience the act of communication—verbal and nonverbal—that will alter their lives.

Dialogue adds color and realism to a scene. It's possible, however, to overdo it. Much of what we say every day is not of any particular moment, and even conversations that are revelatory, significant, life-changing are bracketed or interspersed with talk that relates to quotidian matters. Where this latter is concerned, nine times out of ten, it is most effective to present it indirectly, narratively, in order to hurry the reader to what is truly important.

> "It sure has been a hot summer."
>
> "It sure has."
>
> "Hotter today than it was yesterday."
>
> "Uh-huh."
>
> "Did you see that old Steve McQueen movie on the late show last night?"
>
> "No, I missed it."
>
> "It was good. You should try to rent it at the video store."
>
> "I will." I couldn't take any more. "Mother, I think there are some things that need to be said."

It's possible—perhaps to increase tension, to give the reader the experience of the narrator's own frustration—you may want to present a conversation in this way.

Conversely, however, you may want to move the action forward more forcefully.

> She talked to me about how hot it was, how hot the whole summer had been. She asked if I'd seen the Steve McQueen movie on the late show.
>
> "You should try to rent it at the video store."
>
> "I will." I couldn't take any more. "Mother, I think there are some things that need to be said."

It's likely this latter configuration is a more powerful one. You cut to the chase, while at the same time indicating in your narration that some strained pleasantries have been exchanged beforehand, that there has been some avoidance on the part of one or both of the characters of taking up truly significant matters.

Be on guard for dialogue that is doing what it has no business doing, which is bearing too great a narrative burden in the story. "Oh, why don't you wear that favorite blue dress of yours your mother gave you? My brother, Bill, is in town with his roommate, Steve, and I'm sure he'd be happy to take you to the dance." People don't talk like this. The person these remarks are addressed to presumably knows where her blue dress came from and that it is her favorite; she knows her friend's brother's name is Bill.

Be wary of characters who speak in paragraphs. There are obviously instances where this is justified—those where someone is relating an anecdote or engaged in a political or philosophical discussion. It often indicates, however, that the dialogue is doing narrative work, which is usually inefficient. Conversations tend to be rapid, back-and-forth exchanges, not extended expostulations of concepts or events.

Details, Details

The kind of test you apply to your dialogues can apply to other elements of your writing as well. Is form following function? Are your descriptions and details working to clarify the piece and move your tale forward, or are they merely cluttering it up? Are they primarily demonstrating what you know about a particular landscape or what working conditions were like in a nineteenth-century brewery, rather than revealing to the audience aspects of the characters or the point of the tale you want to tell?

Again, answers here are not absolute. In Upton Sinclair's novel *The Jungle*, the horrific details of the unsanitary conditions of the meat-packing plants in which his characters labor, the long hours, the gruesome accidents on the job, the inadequate pay and flat-out exploitation of the workers all serve to explain their growing faith in unionism and socialism. On the other hand, in Georges Bizet's opera *Carmen*, based on a novel by Prosper Mérimée, we never even see the inside of the vast tobacco factory in Seville where our heroine spends most of her day. Neither Bizet nor Mérimée was particularly interested in exploring women's working conditions in Spain during the Napoleonic Wars. Rather, the story is that of the love triangle of the bullfighter, Escamillo, the soldier, Don José, and the passionate, independent and doomed Carmen. Her occupation is significant in terms of what it tells us about her position in society—a single woman with a job in protoindustrial manufacturing did not enjoy a lot of status in the Seville of that time—but the workaday details of cigar production have no particular place in the intense and romantic plot.

As stated before, you as author may indeed need to have an almost photographic vision of what the front of Marsha's house looks like; you may need to know, in some detail, precisely what Mikey's position was and in what kind of New Hampshire factory he worked before his death. The question is whether we, the readers, need to have that complete a picture to enter into the story you are going to tell us. Remember, we are your accomplices. We can fill in many details ourselves from what we know or imagine of a particular site or occupation. Apprentice authors often load their stories with a wealth of description and documentation—a true embarrassment of riches—that both slows the narrative and implies a certain distrust of the reader herself. This sometimes feels like an overt power play, a refusal to allow the reader to participate in the production of the story: "You're going to see this room exactly as I see it, even if I have to bore the socks off you!" This is the writer trying to be the movie director, controlling the image of that room as if it could be projected on a screen.

A workshop member a couple years back was writing a novel that, it appeared, would eventually rival *War and Peace* in length. Unfortu-

nately, it was not a vast historical epic covering two or three generations, but a rather intimate portrait of an ambitious and racially
conscious African-American woman (Catherine) coming to terms with
the death of her beloved aunt and the compromises made by her
cousin, her aunt's son (let's call him Walter), in his pursuit of success
in his career. The origin of the text's elephantiasis was the author's
insistence on describing absolutely everything. Hence, the text often
read something like this.

> Walter walked into the guest room, the first room on the left
> on the upstairs hall. There were the expensive reproductions
> he remembered of Watteau and Renoir in their gilt frames, hung
> on the robin's egg blue walls. The heavy, maple headboard,
> armoire and bureau gleamed with polish, and the beige wool
> carpeting looked good as new. On the bureau were Catherine's
> cosmetics—three lipsticks, eyeshadow, a bottle of Chanel #5—
> and her yellow scarf was slung carelessly across the back of
> the armchair upholstered in a floral pattern of daisies on a cobalt
> background. A Saks Fifth Avenue shopping bag sat on the chest
> under the window, a pile of books on the floor beside it: *Their
> Eyes Were Watching God* by Zora Neal Hurston, *Tar Baby* by
> Toni Morrison, a biography of Thurgood Marshall, among
> others. The heavy, tasseled curtains were closed, so none of
> the bright, October light pooled on the floor. Catherine lay on
> the bed with her eyes closed. She was wearing a taupe blouse
> made of silk and a chestnut skirt. One hand was draped over
> the edge of the bed, showing her fuchsia painted nails.
>   "Sorry to interrupt," he said softly in his soothing baritone.
> "I came to apologize."
>   She looked up at the six-feet, one hundred and eighty
> muscled pounds of him. He looked very handsome in his cream
> Armani shirt and crisply pressed gray Dockers, which broke
> over a pair of brown, Italian leather loafers. . . .

Arguably, there are details here that might reveal elements of character—such as social class or consciousness (the Chanel, a biography
of Justice Marshall rather than Justice Thomas)—an issue more fully
discussed in the next chapter. However, by this point in the manuscript,
these facets of Walter and Catherine had already been established. Do

we really need a description of the guest room (a room Walter is presumably familiar with); do we need to know that Catherine's nails are specifically painted fuchsia? Is Walter's outfit important, and, further, is it what the dozing Catherine would focus on as her eyes flutter open?

The idea is not that descriptions of place or person, documentation of income or geography are unimportant. Rather, it is a question of relevance. Are they appropriate in the scene evoked, or do they merely clog the movement of action, providing us with specifics we don't really need to know—for example, that the walls are blue, much less robin's egg blue.

It's apparent that setting the scene can be vitally important in your work, and certainly, there are times when stories cry out for greater concreteness, stronger grounding. As noted when discussing language and metaphor, color and smell and the tactile sensation of a surface can send a little electric thrill through a reader and imply a tremendous amount about a character—what he's like, what he values. The point for you as an artist is to determine the details that illuminate, those that draw forth other details that don't even have to be mentioned. Finger's synthetic upholstery and conventional "art" poster immediately cue our imaginations to fill in the other features of an institutional office—one furnished on the cheap that tries to be cheerful, despite the fact that much of what occurs there may be heartbreaking. She has selected those details from a myriad she might have chosen, achieved, presumably with much effort, what we might call the "Goldilockian mean," in which everything is "just right."

Pace

The balances I've been discussing are integral to that rather mysterious aspect of storytelling called *pace*: where the action speeds up and where it slows down; what is dispatched within a sentence or two and what is lingered over. You should be ever conscious of what should be narrated and what should be dramatized, what told and what shown. Again, this depends heavily on the kind of story you are writing. Nonetheless, there are two diametrically opposed problems that can afflict a text.

A frequent error of young writers is to present a story entirely in narrative so it reads not like a story but the *description* of a story. You've probably encountered these texts before. You always feel, as the reader, you are somehow at one remove from the action, not involved in it but obviously having it related to you. Concretely, think of reading a novel, and then of reading the Cliffs Notes or other study guides that deal with the novel. These synopsize the action, just as you did when you wrote a précis: They give you briefly the *who, what, where, when*; eliminate almost all the *how*s, and tell you the *why*s outright.

The converse of this is the draft in which virtually everything is dramatized, which reads not like a fiction but a *chronicle*. All events and information, whether significant or not, follow one another in a numbing parade, each given the same attention by the author. For example, should an equal amount of space be devoted to John's trip to Marsha's house as to the confrontation between the two of them? Probably not, though you might indeed be able to justify dramatizing the drive to Marsha's if it shows John picking up a few things at the pharmacy, stopping for a drink to build his courage, wandering aimlessly through her neighborhood, doing anything to avoid taking that long walk to her front porch.

Maintaining a proper pace in your work may require some painful decisions, the elimination of passages of considerable beauty, the summation of scenes that contain some passionate or amusing dialogue. Your own instincts about such moments are important. My advice on the matter runs as follows: In the first draft, if you question whether some description should be included, if some conversation should be related, put it in. It is almost always easier to eliminate excess in a text than to add to your story after it is on paper.

In subsequent drafts, however, as you streamline the piece for greater impact, if you question such passages, take them out. Like that "rev" at the opening, these are probably moments you needed to construct your story, scaffolding that allowed you to hammer together what is truly the edifice that is your tale. Don't destroy them! As said earlier, never throw anything way. You may later decide you were wrong to cut that paragraph and can then reinsert it. This happened to me with *Letting Loose*. The editors asked to see a previous draft of the novel, and we ended up integrating a half-dozen passages of varying length back into the book.

Trusting audience and editors on such matters is important. You should fight, as David Foster Wallace did in that workshop, to maintain what you think is essential to your text, but you should weigh suggestions with great care and try to make a truly objective case for retaining the material in question. This will save you from a moment I experienced with my first novel. My editor, again and again, expressed her reservations about a dense passage regarding the protagonist's emotional state. She felt it was about two times as long as it needed to be. I fought tooth and nail to maintain it, and she finally agreed with good grace, though unconvinced.

The novel was published, and I stood before an audience at my first public reading. I had chosen to present parts of the first chapter, which included the passage in question. As it rolled off my tongue, I delighted in the resonance of the language. On and on it went. And then, about halfway through that long paragraph, a red light went on in my head, and I could hear my editor's sympathetic but satisfied whisper: "This is going on too long."

FLASHBACKS AND FRAMING

Let's assume your story is sitting in front of you on the desk. You're satisfied you've centered it on the proper character; you feel its various narrative components are all in synch. The story whirs along from beginning to end without sputter or stall. And yet, there's something missing, or something that makes it less than you feel it should be— some spark, some dazzle that will lift it out of the run-of-the-mill, compel your reader to keep reading and make her remember it long after she's put it aside.

There are endless possible reasons for your dissatisfaction, and these will vary tremendously from text to text. Nonetheless, it's worth thinking about a couple of elements that can affect your fiction's impact and seeing if making certain adjustments with relation to these is what's needed to give your piece the oomph it's lacking.

First, have a look at your *backstory*. This is a term taken from film, meaning those events that have occurred before the present action takes place, and that are mentioned or alluded to in the course of a fiction's development. The standard way to communicate backstory is simple narrative.

> DeWayne remembered the time Patrice had come down to the
> garage to tell him about another argument with Luther, and

then ignored his advice. So, when she came in looking sad, he was wary, thinking maybe it was going to be the same thing all over again.

It had been four years since Mikey had gone into the hospital for his bypass. It had taken months for the shock to wear off after they came to tell her that afternoon that he'd died on the operating table. In the first months, Gloria would wake up and, finding the empty space beside her on the bed, wonder what Mikey was doing up so early, he who always loved his sleep. But those moments had gradually faded as she adjusted to the quiet house, to cooking for one, to that expanse of counterpane that stretched into the darkness. She still could never fall asleep unless she occupied only her side of the bed.

There is nothing wrong with this. It is an efficient, sometimes elegant, way to communicate necessary information to the reader without sacrificing the pace of what is truly in play, which is your story of the here and now.

There are times, however, when rather than merely telling the reader about an event in the past, it is more effective to actually show it to him. This is what we usually call *flashback*, dramatizing a past event in the midst of our present narrative. Flashbacks were once considered a daring innovation, though now they are simply yet another implement in the writer's toolbox. Indeed, in many workshops, textbooks and so on, there are warnings against the overuse of this technique, which is suspect for being showy, confusing or unnecessary.

This advice is well-taken, though with some reservations. A flashback can badly throw off the pace of a story. Suddenly shifting the time frame may trip the reader, lead to an at least momentary sense of being lost that breaks the story's spell, interrupting that collusive imaginative act of author and audience. Perhaps, as noted regarding other details, it may be that you need to actually imagine a particular scene in your character's past, but, in the end, its full-scale dramatization is unnecessary in the text, as effectively put over in a paragraph or a couple of sentences as in a page or two.

Nonetheless, the flashback can be a handy tool, especially if that "flash from the past" is key in understanding why a character acts in a particular way. In our tale of John and Marsha, if indeed John's reticence about breaking up has to do with that traumatic experience with Sally and her boxcutter, we need to see that moment, feel John's horror and fear, which will eventually culminate in guilt and help us understand why he fails to carry out his intentions where Marsha is concerned. A paragraph of narration will not have the same impact on the reader, cannot allow for the same intimacy, as a flashback will.

That said, remember the balances. As the conventional advice would indicate, a five-page story containing three flashbacks is likely to be confusing. Likewise, if the scene with Sally constitutes a third of the tale told, the question arises as to precisely what the story is about and whether the action with Marsha—inherently less dramatic—should be there at all. One of the advantages of this particular technique is that it allows you to "get in and get out fast" and permits the reader to experience that moment of the past's intrusion as the character does—as that sudden memory, that feeling of déjà vu.

Let's rough out that moment of John's. When he goes to Marsha's, he's driving a black Toyota that he parks at the curb in front of her house. It is late spring. Her house is red brick with white shutters. He sits for a minute, gets out and comes around the back of the car to head up the flagstone walk to the porch. All this is established in the present narrative.

> There was the whir of a cicada, and two boys whipped by on Rollerblades behind him on the street. Across the green expanse of the lawn, he could see Marsha, indistinct behind the screen.
>
> As his feet hit the first flagstone, he felt the October chill. The dead leaves were slick with frost beneath his feet. He wished he were somewhere else; could slip back in that blue Chevette, the first car he had ever owned, and drive back home. But he kept going, step-by-step, seeing her push the screen, step across the threshold, stand stiff before the clapboards— Sally, whom he had known since he was fifteen; Sally, the first girl he had slept with; Sally, the only one he had really made love to.
>
> She stood there, not speaking, her hands awkwardly before her. In the glum, autumnal light that evening, he could not distinguish what she gripped in her palm. Then, in an instant,

fear and panic mingled, then washed through him in a hot wave that almost made him faint.

Just a sliver glinting from the dull gray of the handle. He could see the razor's edge against the white of her skin.

Sally remained still, motionless, a boxcutter in her hand.

At the foot of the steps, John stopped, suddenly breathless, sweat burning his upper lip.

Marsha looked down at him, a look of honest concern on her face. "Are you all right?" she asked.

You can see how the flashback works in this instance. There is the image of Marsha behind the screen door. Then, as John begins up the walk to the porch, the memory of his earlier experience begins. The incident with Sally is brought back in sensory details ("the October chill," "slick with frost beneath his feet") that contrast sharply with those of the paragraph immediately preceding (the green lawn and boys on Rollerblades), cuing the reader that in this realistically narrated tale, something is going on, even if that something is not immediately apparent. The two scenes continue to be differentiated (John's blue Chevette versus his black Toyota; the clapboards versus Marsha's red bricks), up to the point of the introduction of Sally, whose name and status ("whom he had known since he was fifteen," etc.) give us the necessary information to comprehend and put in context what we have previously read in the paragraph.

We then get the traumatic moment, the recognition of the boxcutter and Sally's unspoken threat of suicide. The penultimate paragraph, with a breathless, sweaty John, bridges the story back to the present. It is a moment that might be occurring either at the foot of Sally's steps or of Marsha's. The final paragraph then locates the reader, who is back once again in that May evening at Marsha's front door.

Flashbacks can occur at virtually any point in a story, though they most frequently fall, as is true of most elements of backstory, during what we might call dead time—that is, when a character is involved in a quotidian activity (taking a shower, driving to work, getting ready for bed) or an activity that is merely functional, in the sense of moving the action forward. John has to get from the street to the porch; there is a period of seconds when he is simply going from one place to another. That innocuous moment, however, is an attractive place to inject what will, in a sense, be the key to comprehending how the story of John and Marsha plays out.

This, of course, like all generalizations we've made, isn't always true. It might be appropriate to inject a flashback at a moment of considerable dramatic tension. In my novel *Letting Loose*, a fight between one of the protagonists and his parents, which has been alluded to various times in the text, is finally narrated only when mother, father and son are reunited after more than twenty years of estrangement. The son recognizes that, with the years, his parents have changed as he has.

> They were not the same as they had been when he last confronted them, directly below where they were sitting now, in that furious and final standoff.
>
> *"Barry. Barry! That cannot be. It is disgusting . . ."*
>
> *"It is not disgusting . . ."*
>
> *"It is disgusting . . . and sick . . . and, and shameful." His father's voice, his whole body, shuddering, scared and appalled. "How could you"—small and soft—"How could you"—almost a whisper—"even begin to admit to something that"—searching for the word that would somehow capture what he felt—"vile."*
>
> "The tables do look terrific," Barry agreed. "Did they use one of those polyurethane sealants?"
>
> "Verathane. It makes them so easy to keep," his mother said.

The interpolated flashback—full of shouting and accusation—contrasts sharply with the strained politeness and reserve of the family brought together again, which is, of course, the point. This was the justification I found for employing the technique at this juncture. It seemed to me more powerful than simply including the argument where it would have fallen chronologically in the action. You can see in that decision a number of the points I've made earlier in this book: Information has been withheld; a certain suspense has been created; the reader's curiosity, previously piqued ("What exactly got said in the basement that night in 1970?"), has finally been satisfied. The argument, a key manifestation of one of the central conflicts in the novel, has "haunted" it. Once again, form has fulfilled a number of functions.

Frames

Earlier, I made the suggestion that, perhaps, the story of John and Sally was a more striking one than the subtler episode of John and Marsha. Looking at that imaginary piece before you, maybe you conclude that, actually, that dark tale of the boxcutter is the one that ought to be front and center. Yet, cognizant that one of the key elements of fiction is the notion of actions or events with consequences, you still want to show how the breakup of Sally and John resonated into the future. Searching for a way to salvage your story, you come up with the idea of opening and closing with brief scenes involving John and Marsha, but spending the bulk of the narrative focused on that day in October when Sally nearly went over the edge.

This structure is called the *frame narrative*. In its most primitive form, this is the kind of story that begins with something like "Back when I was young and a sailor, one of my shipmates told me about his first voyage to the Pacific . . ." and ends "I didn't believe it at the time, but that's what he told me, and the more I've thought about it, the more it makes sense." *Primitive*, incidentally, does not translate as "bad," in that, arguably, this is a form chosen by a number of great novelists, including such masters as Joseph Conrad. In our own story, parallel incidents constitute the frame. A story could also be framed by action in the present that then allows for an extended explanation of how a particular character came to be where she is today.

Michael Martone has an often anthologized piece called "It's Time." It begins with this sentence: "I remember the time each year when my husband cut back the raspberry bushes." The paragraph continues with a description of that chore, filled with an odd violence. The second paragraph then takes the image of raspberries and transforms it from the literal fruit to the noise, the blatting sound made in derision but here used to describe the noise made, years before (in the "remembered" time), by the narrator's baby daughter, which allows for a description of the child in her crib.

> Does it count as a first word? The other raspberry, the sound my daughter made, her tongue belting into slobber between her lips, stirring before dawn in the tiny bedroom down the hall. It was dark, and the wet blasts helped me navigate, the floors covered with her blocks and toys. Her room was pitch,

the only light the daubs of radium I swiped from the factory outlining the rails and bars of her crib.

With this, we segue into the central action, which takes place just after the Second World War. Our narrator has worked painting the faces of watches and clocks with paint laced with luminescent radium, unaware, as she hones "a point sharp enough to jewel each second" by placing her brush in her mouth, that she is exposing herself to radiation poisoning. She and her co-workers eventually begin to suffer the effects: hair loss, bruising, brittle bones, deterioration of their flesh. This leads to a trial of their employer, during which the women "couldn't blot our lipstick, since our skin was so tender." The bosses are convicted of negligence, but, of course, this will not save the women they have exploited and exposed to radium. At story's end, the narrator—unable to speak now, capable only of "the same sounds the baby made," is in her back yard, picking raspberries.

> . . . I reached out for another berry and then another, dumped them into the pint baskets squashed and ruptured, and rushed them into the house. I found a pencil and a piece of paper to write this down. Each word fell on the page, a burning tongue.

The story is incredibly rich in its resonance and nuances, but our point here is to note how Martone frames the tale with a domestic image, that of the berries, which come to symbolize so much in the story itself: innocence and nature itself on the one hand; the results of this woman's poisoning—her battered flesh, her speechlessness—on the other.

As in this example, framing tends to throw our attention toward the consequences of the central action. The story begins and ends with how the main action has resonated across time. Wharton does the same thing in *Ethan Frome*: The bleak chronicle of the love triangle among Ethan, his wife, Zeena, and her cousin, Mattie, is bracketed by the narrator's discovery of the truth. Employing this model and framing the tale of Sally with that of John and Marsha, you can see how, as a result of his experience with Sally, John is unable to act decisively. Sally's despair resonates in his relationship with Marsha. He is unable to do what he wants because of what occurred before. Even in that earlier example of the most primitive form of frame—

that of the sailor who sits his audience down, tells a tale and then delivers some final remark on what has been told—there is this same kind of emphasis on the impact of an event over the years.

As you might imagine, there are variations in the ways flashbacks and frames can be structured. Previously, I demonstrated a single-scene flashback, but such a scene can be scattered piecemeal throughout the main text, as those I described with relation to my own novel. In "Nightbirds," described near the end of the previous chapter, you can see an example of a half-frame, one that opens but does not close. You should not feel you are obligated to apply these techniques in your fiction, that writing a straightforward, chronological narrative is somehow dull and unsophisticated. These and other techniques are simply a way you can, perhaps, condense, intensify or clarify your story in the most economic and compelling manner.

SORTING, SHIFTING, SHAPING
So you're all set, right?

Not quite. In the physical act of writing, all kinds of other questions, issues and problems emerge. You make decision after decision, many of these quite unconsciously. Some, however, will require a great deal of thought, agonizing, consideration of suicide and so on. This will vary from story to story, but I'd like to turn to a few of the glitches that may arise as you go about writing, then rewriting, then rewriting yet again the story of John and Marsha.

For many of you apprentice writers, rewriting, editing, buffing and polishing seem like hell itself. Yet, they're simply parts of the process to which you're not entirely unaccustomed. Think of redecorating a room in your house. You shift the furniture here, then shift it there. You hold a picture up against one wall, and then realize you've placed it directly in line with the afternoon sun, which will fade the print to nothing before the summer's out. You buy a green throw rug, only to see, when you get it home, that the heavy, wooden furniture you have makes the green look muddy. There is a panoply of tasks you undertake that require precisely the same skills as revision, and many times, an author finds this step in writing is no more painful—and often considerably less so—than the hard work of getting the first draft on paper.

In this age of computers, I have suggested to students that after they have written a rough draft, they print a hard copy and edit it by hand. Then, they should go back to the machine, open a new file and retype the entire manuscript into the computer again. This may seem outrageous, though even twenty years ago it would simply have been part of the game. The personal computer has given us tremendous flexibility, but it has also, in some ways, profoundly altered the editorial process. I'd argue that, after a hand-edit on hard copy, physically reproducing the manuscript represents a kind of third, fine edit, a *tactile* edit. I remember when I was retyping a story on my old portable typewriter, I would catch run-on sentences, repetitions and so on I hadn't noticed. My fingers would *feel* that word I had just typed two lines before.

I realize most of my students don't do as I suggest, and I must admit, with the ease and speed word processing offers, I rarely do it either. But it is something you might at least try.

I should clarify here that when I say edit, I am talking about a number of different issues. First, there is line emendation—striking a sentence here, adding a word there, rephrasing a passage slightly and so on. It is extremely rare that your first draft will entirely satisfy you. You've done what a sculptor does when she hacks out the first rough outline of what will be her statue. Next comes the meticulous work that makes marble lifelike or convinces us of the unique significance of Marsha and John.

Where language is concerned, I've already addressed various issues in chapter three. All writers are in an endless and finally futile quest for "all" the right words. Even the masters can slip up. Hemingway can write a sentence like "They got right up in the car the minute I motioned to them," which seems less a brilliant mixing of codes than a clumsy one: the colloquial "got right up" clashing with the rather stiff "motioned to them," as opposed to "waved at them" or "called them." In his *Lady Chatterley's Lover*, D.H. Lawrence can sometimes sound decidedly cutesy rather than daring, as when the lovers Mellors and Constance dub their respective genitals "John Thomas" and "Lady Jane." Constance seems more the breathless schoolgirl than a mature, married woman when Lawrence tries to describe her rapture at making love with her groundskeeper: "And now in her heart the queer wonder of him was awakened. A man! The strange potency of manhood upon her!"

Strike out. Caret in. Reverse phrases. Read aloud. Your ear often will tell you when a phrase is exactly right and when it could use further refining. Be on the lookout for repeated structures. Do your adverbs always immediately precede the verb? Could some of them go elsewhere in their sentences? Or do they have to be there at all? As with my final line in *Mean Time*, would a verbless fragment be more powerful than a complete sentence, or, conversely, is this a technique you use all too frequently?

With this kind of fine editing, once again, let pieces sit. You will see both the virtues and shortcomings of a story more easily if you have not looked at it so constantly that you can virtually recite it without benefit of text. Work intensely for a day, then put your prose aside for a weekend or a week, then go back to it again. You'll come to it with fresh eyes, in part because, unconsciously, you've been turning certain elements over in your head all the while. Give yourself some "time in the hammock," time to do that work you're accomplishing unawares.

As you can see, the questions never end. Don't worry. You should not expect them to. Even on that happy day when you see your text in cold, black type, there will be instances when you will wince. The story you imagined is never quite the story you set down. That is why, years after their initial publications, Henry James published the "New York Editions" of his novels, why W.H. Auden constantly revised his poems for each collection of his works, why Gore Vidal's *The City and the Pillar* of 1964 is considerably different from the original version of 1948. A writer loves to think that with only one more draft, one final edit, the story or book will somehow be the Platonic ideal of it she carries around in her head.

It doesn't work that way.

You must learn, among other lessons, to know when a work is ripe, ready to be shown around. Listen carefully to the advice of those who read it—those Ezra Pounds to your T.S. Eliot. But recognize, too, that there comes a point when you're finished, when the story you've written—like a child who leaves home—is on its own. You can do no more. It's time to make another baby.

EXERCISES

1. Write a narrative passage of a page or so. Then, go back and recast it, employing dialogue at key moments to heighten the effect of the scene.

2. Write a description of the room where you are sitting, including as much detail as possible. Set the work aside. Return to it tomorrow and determine which, of all the details you've included, would best give a reader an idea of who you are. Next, pick details that would appropriately define a character who is very different from you.

3. Find an instance of narrative backstory in one of your works. Try transforming it into a flashback. If you've employed flashback at some point, rewrite it as a simple narrative paragraph.

4. Take one of your stories and build a frame around it. For example, if you have a tale of childhood experience, bracket it with your protagonist's reflections ten or twenty years later.

5. Retype a page or two of a draft of a story you have in your drawer to see if you experience that tactile editing I discussed.

6. Go through one of your finished pieces and strike every word you feel is not absolutely necessary to the narrative. Cut the story to the bone, then compare it with the original. What that's valuable has been lost? What, if anything, has been gained? Prepare a new version of the story integrating the best of the two different versions.

SEVEN

CRAFTING CHARACTERS

In the chapters thus far, I have often used metaphors drawn from construction to talk about writing: architecture, building blocks, edifice. All this is defensible, but I need to turn now to what may be the most central element of any story told. Plot and language give fiction its form, much of its color and heft.

But characters are what give it a spirit.

Arguably, fiction communicates the complexities and vagaries of the human animal more effectively than any other medium. Theater, surely, can stir us with a fine actor's delivery, film can overwhelm us with spectacular visual effects, but neither can deliver the shadings and depth of character the written word can. Neither can move with such ease and precision from without to within, capture not only action but the nuances of motivation as we can in fiction. In a novel or story, a reader actually hears a character think, is privy to his rationales and excuses and can judge whether these are legitimate or self-deceptive. Fiction allows a character to "speak for himself"—aloud and in the most private recesses of his mind—in a way other genres can only dream of.

This is not entirely surprising. Modern fiction—which has increasingly centered on distinctive and strongly delineated characters—was largely an invention of the eighteenth century, the era of the dawn of "the individual" in the contemporary sense of the word. If people have always been interested in other people, as time passed we grew ever more curious about our fellows, what makes them tick, why they do the things they do. *Novel*, after all, means "new," and fiction, over the last couple hundred years, has been one of the primary if not *the* primary way through which new consciousnesses, new moralities, new fashions, new attitudes and new ideas have been transmitted. Today, if we seek a real sense of the mores of the English gentry of the Georgian era, we turn to Jane Austen; for the quintessence of the Jazz Age of the 1920s, to F. Scott Fitzgerald; for the confusion and contradictions of the 1950s, to J.D. Salinger. And at the center of all these works, and so many others, there is a compelling character, an Emma, a Gatsby, a Seymour Glass, who serves as our entrance to or image of a particular chapter in human experience.

But whence do great characters arise? Where do we find them, and how, in our own work, can we take what may be an entirely conventional creation and make her distinct, alive, real, someone who, a year down the road, the reader will recall vividly, more vividly perhaps than many of the actual people who have crossed his path over those twelve months? How do we, in what is perhaps the most godlike of all of a writer's tasks, breathe life not into a handful of dust, but a handful of words?

OBSERVATION

The place to begin, as I have said time and time again in this book, is in real life. Settle back and simply observe the people you come in contact with day to day, those at the market, those at the mall, your neighbors and co-workers. We have a tendency, particularly with those we know, to stereotype them, or at least to pigeonhole their personalities with a kind of psychological shorthand: "Mary's passive-aggressive," "Bart's the original good-time guy," "Rodney is a Momma's boy," and so on. It's interesting to see how often these thumbnail sketches are shared among a group of friends or acquaintances. But what do they really mean? If, indeed, everyone agrees that Mary seems passive-aggressive, what are we saying and how does this manifest itself? In these post-Freudian times, we tend to bandy about psychiatric terms—manic-depressive, schizophrenic, paranoid—with tremendous abandon and only the vaguest sense of what their true, clinical definitions are.

For example, as you observe Mary's "passive aggression," you will probably find it is composed of a range of idiosyncratic characteristics and behaviors. She is a bit shy, more than a little unsure of herself. Perhaps she's a tad younger than most of the people she associates with. She seems to want to be liked, to fit in, and hence avoids expressing an opinion, even in cases where assenting to a majority view goes against what you suspect are her own real desires or deeply held beliefs. Repressing what she really feels, however, leads her to various strategies of manipulation or sudden episodes of anger or surliness that encourage others to see her as passive-aggressive.

As you can see, this analysis of Mary exposes a far richer individual than two words can communicate. As you pause and consider those around you, you will find this holds true with most such labeling. The good-time guy, the Momma's boy, the bully and the martyr all have histories and probably live in circumstances beyond those in which you know them and that provide dimension to the role you conceive them playing. Bart, always ready to party, may still be acting out a youthful rebellion against a constrained and repressive childhood. Rodney may crave a kind of approval he's never received in his growing up or in his marriage. Bullies are often, at base, motivated by fear and a sense of inadequacy; martyrs, ironically, by a peculiar sense of moral superiority. Typing those around us is easy. Understanding who they are and why they are that way is hard.

But hold on, you may once again object, I simply don't have much information on Bart's growing up or Rodney's home life. I don't plan to pry. Even if I were to do so, I'm not a shrink or a social worker, and besides, Bart and Rodney might not be too crazy about being quizzed on their private affairs.

Fair enough. As an exercise, though, jot down the names of four of your associates. Choose a range of individuals, from someone you feel you know pretty well to someone you would define as an acquaintance. Beside each one, note the tag you and others would attach to each individual. Next, list things you know or have observed about these people—histories, religions, modes of speech, eccentricities, what they eat at lunch, educational backgrounds, family ties and so on. Then write a character sketch of each one.

Remember, you are a fiction writer, not a journalist, psychiatrist or biographer. What this means is that you can "fill in the blanks." In writing about these people, you will reach certain impasses, points where you indeed don't have enough real information. You've heard that passive-aggressive Mary comes from a large family, but how large? Four children? Five? Eight? Is she the youngest? The eldest? How many boys and how many girls? Given what you do know of her, make a guess. Do this with the various dead ends you reach.

Though you may not end up with a veridical sketch of the real Mary of your acquaintance, you will end up with a sketch of *a* Mary, a *different* Mary, one who resembles in certain ways the one you know, one who has a past and present, one whose behaviors follow a particular, logical pattern and who is not just passive-aggressive, but a person whose actions and mode of being make sense to you and, you hope, to a reader as well. Try the same exercise with Bart and Rodney. Once you're finished, don't go around explaining to everyone why your co-workers act as they do. You haven't nailed down the origins of the behavior of the Mary at the office. What you have done is come up with a reasonable history that can illuminate why people *like* Mary, Bart and Rodney are the way they are.

Now that you've experimented with individuals you know, give it a shot with people you don't, the ones in the market or the mall, the guy who delivered the package from UPS, the person whose face you noted in a photograph in the paper. Just as an image can spark a whole novel, a stranger or strangers can catalyze a character. If you're a retired sheet metal worker on Social Security and you have an idea for a story that includes a boomer yuppie, seek some out in their natural habitat—the office complex down the block or some upscale restaurant downtown—and simply watch them. Need a college student character? Go wander around campus for a day or two. Listen to voices and take note of haircuts and what people seem to be reading or watching on TV. Are bikes or skateboards the preferred mode of transport? Does smoking seem to be making a comeback? Loitering around schoolyards or too many nights of "research" at the local watering hole can get you in trouble, but, when you're unfamiliar with the externals of a particular kind of character, there's nothing wrong with undertaking some field work. To help in his writing of *The Cider House Rules*, John Irving managed to get attached to the maternity ward of a university hospital. Russell Banks hung out with mall rats when preparing *Rule of the Bone*. Novelists have gone undercover at construction sites and offices and retirement communities to accumulate material.

Most often though, your fiction will not demand such elaborate undertakings. After a few hours of observation, go home, ruminate a bit, sit down with a cup of tea and sketch your boomer or college student just as you did Bart and Rodney. What you have observed can be a great help in giving you insight, both into a particular class of people and into the particular individual you want to create. You may want your yuppie to be an anomalous one, but you then need to know something about the standard-issue young urban professional in order to make your own stand out.

Be aware as you create this individual who is different from you that, in many particulars, she may *not* be so different. In introductory workshops, I often ask that members write stories that take place in a different historical period or that are narrated by characters of a different gender, sexual orientation, ethnicity, nationality or race than that of the writer. This often creates great consternation, and yet, many times the results are good. We should always be aware of difference, of what makes people distinct, at the same time we recognize that much about people's desires and emotions is similar. We all have childhoods, we all need love, we all have weaknesses, we all die. Even your creations who are intended to be thoroughly irredeemable should have motives and traits that are universal, that are understandable and human. Remember, as we remarked chapters back in relation to Adolf Eichmann, the Nazi deathmaster, that he seems all the more monstrous because his ambitions to finally make a success of himself at *something* led him to ship human beings to slaughter as if he were shipping produce to market.

Let's admit, however, that writing individual histories is something rather different from integrating characters into a story. Action can't simply stop while we get in-depth profiles of DeWayne and Patrice or John and Marsha. You may find it useful to sit down even before you begin a story and sketch out the characters, or to pause in its composition and analyze your protagonist and a couple other members of your cast, just as you've done with Mary or the students at Evertrue State. Still, it's unlikely you will employ all you know about these characters in the story itself. The sketch serves as your guide to how your characters will comport themselves. At this point, let's turn to various ways character can be presented within the context of a larger fiction.

OUTSIDE

A couple of chapters back, we used the 5 Cs to talk about how to put a story together start to finish. You could argue that I've just slipped in an overarching sixth C to go with the previous five, this one being *character*. Now, I'll appropriate the next letter of the alphabet for a mnemonic device for methods I'll call the 7 Ds, which have to do with various means you can employ to bring your characters to life *externally*. In what follows, you're going to encounter some old friends, various techniques I've discussed in other contexts. Here, however, I'm considering specifically how they can be used in illuminating character. I'll talk subsequently about some of the means by which your characters' inner lives can be put over on the page.

Description and Declaration

The most obvious way to characterize someone is bald *description*. This is an efficient way to immediately let the reader know important information.

> DeWayne was an energetic black sixteen-year-old, slender and of middling height, with many friends and a certain competitive streak.

This tells us a lot about DeWayne, but it's frankly a shade dull: journalistic, flat, packed with data, but distancing. Here we are presented with DeWayne rather than discovering him. The picture we form in our minds is generic and contextless. Let's step back, still employing a omniscient stance, and try it again.

> In the half-dark of the garage, DeWayne's bare chest shone like fine honey as he and Louis wrestled the engine onto the makeshift cinderblock stand. Puffing from exertion, Louis draped his massive arm across DeWayne's shoulders. "Whew! Had me scared there, homey."
>
> Dwarfed by the left tackle of the football team, DeWayne huffed a laugh, "Get on."

Admittedly, this is less succinct. Yet I would argue that we see DeWayne more *vividly* in the second example. We get a notion of his skin tone, of bodily strength, of his physical size in comparison to someone else, of the way he relates to his fellows. His competitive streak is implied in his exchange with Louis; that laugh is "huffed," after all. Here, he's engaged in a specific activity—working on a car rather than hanging on the corner or playing the violin. We sense a person, a body with a personality and a voice.

Beware the temptation of descriptions that are meant to reveal something and reveal little. To say DeWayne is "not that tall, but dark and handsome" tells us virtually nothing about him, nor, frankly, does saying he was "five-foot nine, with a brown complexion and a strong chin." As in other contexts, physical description in and of itself often merely takes up space. Especially in short stories, a few details allow the collusive reader to form an image of the character in her mind. In Hemingway's "The Light of the World," most of which occurs in a train station in Michigan, there are "five whores . . . and six white men and three Indians" along with the narrator and his friend, Tom. Yet, most of these people are not described at all, and about those who are, we are given only a detail or two. We know, for example, that the one prostitute, Alice, weighs far too much and has a "sweet lovely voice." That's more than we know about Tom, while the narrator, who is presumably Nick Adams, is never even named in the piece!

Appearance should reveal something, cue us as to some larger element of the character's self.

> DeWayne's body was angular, almost mismatched: his torso too long and his legs too short. But he moved gracefully—a grace that was calculated—and that, with his honey-colored complexion and strong chin, the small, pale scar on his brow, made him the center of attention wherever he went.

The details here give us some clue as to what this person might be like. That his grace is "calculated" could indicate that DeWayne is aware of his imperfections, has worked to compensate for his lack of classic proportions. The old scar might indicate a certain rambunctiousness in boyhood, or perhaps a bent toward violence. His beauty is more than that of "just another pretty face." It is unusual, striking, so that people don't merely notice him but actually take note of him.

As you can see in all the foregoing examples, language is key. Language itself can characterize. In your descriptions of the body, for example, you send messages about an individual merely by the words you choose to describe a particular attribute. Compare the impression made by these two, theoretically synonymous pairings.

> He was a thin, sharp-featured man.
> He was a lean man with chiseled features.

> She was a fat, lazy-looking blonde.
> She was an ample, languorous blonde.

You can doubtless come up with endless such doublets. *Fair* and *pale*, which "mean" the same thing, have very different resonances in our imaginations. *Tart-tongued/shrewish, quick-witted/smart-alecky, slow/deliberate*—your election of one of these rather than the other automatically transmits something about your character. *Thin* and *sharp-featured* imply someone underweight, unattractive, rodentlike, perhaps shifty and mean-spirited. *Lean with chiseled features*, on the other hand, evokes a kind of hard-bodied health and a striking, aesthetically pleasing countenance, an intelligent if possibly dangerous animal such as a leopard or a wolf, someone with the potential for heroic action. *Fat* and *lazy* take us right back to two of the seven deadly sins: gluttony and sloth. *Ample* and *languorous*, on the other hand, are words of abundance and luxury, here promising a wise, Rubenesque femininity.

A subset of description is *declaration*. This is the simplest of devices, in which the author overtly states an essential quality of a particular figure. "Tim McManus was the meanest man ever to walk the earth of Fulton County." "Lurleen was the prettiest of the Cathcart girls." "Nobody could hold his liquor like Billy O'Reilly." While such bald-faced assertion can seem a trifle clumsy, its telegraphic brevity has unquestionable impact and can be particularly useful in a story in which the space available for more leisurely characterization is limited, or in sketching secondary or tertiary characters upon whom the author does not want to lavish too much time.

Note, however, and this applies to all the various techniques I will be discussing, that precisely *who* is characterized by a particular declaration depends, in part, on *who* is doing the declaring. "My momma told me that Tim McManus was the meanest man." "I always thought that Lurleen was the prettiest girl." "His little brother, Tommy, was certain that nobody could hold his liquor like Billy O'Reilly." Those introductory, attributive phrases shade the meaning of the descriptive characterizations. My momma may have particular reasons for defining Tim McManus as so utterly unredeemable. Though "I" preferred Lurleen's looks, someone else might be more impressed with those of one of her sisters. Tommy's perspective on Billy may be skewed by the natural hero worship (or rivalry) of younger sibling for older, or by a lack of exposure to the consumption of hard liquor. In the end, these subjective evaluations may tell us more about the person who makes them than the person they are made about. Even without direct attribution, unless yours is omniscient narrative, such declarations can be a means of characterizing the narrator. A look at some classic stories—Joyce's "The Dead," Eudora Welty's "Why I Live at the P.O."—can provide object lessons in how, through the "indirection" of the protagonist's judgments and descriptions of others, an author can reveal that central character's inner self to us.

Dressing

Revelation awaits, of course, not only in the presentation of the physical body, but in what I'll refer to as the *dressing* of a character. What a person wears, how she cuts her hair, how she uses makeup—all these can tell us a great deal about an individual's larger self. In the 1950s, a friend's mother met Albert Einstein at Princeton. With his famously unruly shock of hair, the great scientist stood there, turned out in chinos, a Mickey Mouse sweatshirt and sneakers. What better image of a man whose concerns ran more to the secrets of the birth of the universe than sartorial splendor? His "gray-flannel-suited" contemporaries accepted a little lack of conformity in dress for a chance to hear his thoughts on unified field theory.

Employing our own examples, what Marsha is wearing when she steps out that screen door can tell us much about what she is like, and what she is anticipating from the upcoming encounter with John. Is her outfit girlish? Sexy? Severe? How will DeWayne be dressed when we finally get him to Darlene's house? Casually? In a suit? Like an extra in a rap video? A great deal of information can be telegraphed rapidly in this type of detail. DeWayne's decision about how to proceed with Darlene can be foreshadowed by the way he decks himself out for his meeting with her.

The character's dressing also includes those things with which he chooses to surround himself—home decor, books, videotapes, compact discs, the kind of food he likes and the kind of car he drives. In Armistead Maupin's *Tales of the City*, this passage deals with Mary Anne Singleton, a recently transplanted Midwesterner, dining alone in her San Francisco apartment.

> She quick-thawed a pork chop under the faucet, wondering if it was sacrilegious to Shake 'n Bake meat from Marcel and Henri.
>
> Lighting a spice candle on the parsons table in the living room, she dug out her Design Research cloth napkins, her wood-handled stainless flatware, her imitation Dansk china, and her ceramic creamer shaped like a cow. . . .
>
> She supped by candlelight, bent over a *Ms.* article entitled "The Quest for Multiple Orgasms." Music was provided by KCBS-FM, the mellow station.

On the one hand, all the "cultural markers" of a single, urban woman of the mid-1970s are here: *Ms.*, the imitation Dansk, a spice candle. However, we see certain remnants of Mary Anne's Midwestern past (the creamer shaped like a cow) and, as well, can sense a discomfort or dislocation on her part with the modalities of the new life she's adopted. She frets about using Shake 'n Bake on the meat from that expensive market, though the butcher there would probably already be appalled by her thawing it under running water. Her possessing all the "right" objects for someone of her age and station, along with her solitary stewing about whether she is doing something "wrong," reveals someone not entirely at home with her reinvented self.

Maupin doesn't overdo it here. Remember that workshop piece I cited, the one featuring Walter and Catherine in which we got an all-out, living-color *House Beautiful* tour of the guest room, along with the shade of Catherine's nail polish and the brand of Walter's slacks? That author could have learned from this passage regarding Mary Anne. The details here are carefully chosen to reveal who Mary Anne is and what she's feeling. They are integrated into the action. She is cooking, setting the table, eating, reading as those cultural markers pass before us. The story doesn't stop. Maupin's descriptions of things are such that they are not simply signs of Mary Anne's self, but parts of that self.

Likewise, if our sixtyish New Hampshire widow, Gloria, returns from the grocery store in a spanking new Ford Taurus, as opposed to the Buick—the last in a long line—she bought with Mikey, this may tell us a great deal about her own feelings about her loss. Does DeWayne have posters of Dr. Dre or Boyz-II-Men on the walls of his bedroom? Does he favor Spike Lee films or those of Keenen Ivory Wayans? Is that a German textbook on his desk? These kinds of small facts about a person can help the reader form a notion of his character even before she's had a chance to know him very well.

Dialogue

Where *dialogue* and dialogic characterization are concerned, bear in mind that, just as in real life, the first words out of a character's mouth have particular import. It's that first impression your mother warned you about. If, when we meet a character, the first thing he does is curse, we are going to make certain assumptions. Or consider what kind of image I was trying to create in the following phone conversation from my own novel, *The Book of Marvels*.

> Lila Mae splayed her fingers and waved her hand gently in the air.
>
> "That's a fact, Momma. Hotter than the blue blazes. It is."
>
> She set the heel of her palm on the edge of the table, surveying her nails critically.
>
> "Uh-huh. My land. And on national television! Uh-huh!"

I hope, at least, that she comes over as agreeable, a bit distracted, obviously accustomed to chatting on the phone with her mother, a bit of a "Momma's girl," concerned about her appearance. She's young enough to still have a mother to talk to, probably either working class or Southern or Southwestern, if the clichés she uses are anything to go by. If two or three of those flashed through your mind as you read the passage, then I've succeeded. The other elements that didn't occur to you will, presumably, fall into place soon enough.

Though I earlier warned that dialogue should not, on the whole, be called on to handle narrative tasks, it can be useful in emphasizing or foreshadowing aspects of character. The reptilian unctuousness of

Eddie Haskell of *Leave It to Beaver* fame ("I hope you are well today, Mrs. Cleaver") cues us before we see further evidence to the smart aleck and bully he truly is. An obsessive loquaciousness can sign a character who is utterly self-centered or, conversely, ill at ease. A radical change in the way a character speaks—remember that long-ago example of Patrice swearing?—can be a far more effective way of indicating what she is thinking or how she is feeling than a long narrative intrusion.

What people say and how they say it provides insight into who they are. Certain language, specific metaphors and allusions can point the reader toward particular assumptions about particular characters. If a woman remarks, "What a nice little bourgeois dress," what is a reader likely to conclude? College educated? Left of center? A snob? Whereas, if she says, "Why, I haven't seen a dress that pretty since that party at the VFW," what is implied? Working class? Rural or ethnic roots? A more conservative world view? As I said chapters back when discussing voice, the one you want to be hearing most of the time is not yours as a writer, but those of your characters.

Demeanor and Dramatics

In describing a character's "externals," you are not merely presenting her at rest, but also in motion. You are dealing with *demeanor* and *dramatics*. You are concerned with her carriage, her gestures and table manners. As Gershwin put it, "The way you hold your knife, / the way you sip your tea. . . ." We absorb a great deal of information about people in daily life by their body language rather than through what they do or say, and the same is true on the page. "Gloria strode up the walk" conveys something very different from "Gloria shuffled up the walk"—if not about Gloria's most profound self, then at least about her present state of mind. And if I were to add a few words here and there, I could indeed indicate certain constants about the character: "Gloria strode up the walk with her usual confidence." "As ever, Gloria came shuffling up the walk."

Likewise, how people move when they speak can not only provide a means to break up the phenomenon of "talking heads" in dialogue, but a way to indicate larger truths about the characters conversing. If someone is persistently avoiding eye contact, this signs to us some kind of discomfort, distrust, embarrassment. Extravagant gesturing can indicate frivolousness, or enthusiasm, or simply a particular cultural formation. Such elements enhance the realism of the exchange. Watch people on the telephone. They are in dialogue with disembodied voices, and yet, usually, both parties—though they can't see each other—change expressions, make faces, move their hands, shift from foot to foot.

Let's imagine that moment when Marsha smokes.

> Marsha lit a cigarette.
> "You know, you shouldn't smoke those things," John said.
> "Maybe I do it just to get a rise out of you. You used to smoke."
> "Once upon a time. But never very much. And that was before we all knew how bad it was for you."
> "There are lots of things that are bad for you."

Compare that exchange to this one.

> Marsha lit a cigarette.
> "You know,"—something like relief passed across John's face—"you shouldn't smoke those things."
> "Maybe I do it just to get a rise out of you," she smiled playfully. "You used to smoke."
> "Once upon a time. But never very much. And that was before we all knew how bad it was for you."
> She took a step back, looking him up and down wryly. She took a deep, luxurious drag, then turned away to exhale the smoke into the evening. Her voice was clipped when she finally spoke. "There are lots of things that are bad for you."

Note how the descriptions of facial expression, Marsha's use of the cigarette as a kind of prop and the movements she makes emphasize and refine the scene's emotions, telegraphing to us the characters' emotional states.

The very sound of a voice can serve as a marker of the kind of person who possesses it. If someone growls, barks, snaps and whines, it's likely to be a character who has a rather dog-eat-dog view of the universe, while someone who croons, purrs, murmurs and hisses is perhaps more refined, though not necessarily more trustworthy. Note, incidentally, that while these kinds of "verbs of speech" can be overused, they are a legitimate weapon in your arsenal of characterization. Some take the position—one supposedly originating with Hemingway—that the only verb you need to indicate speech is *said*, on the theory that *how* something is voiced should be apparent in *what* is voiced. While there's obviously some truth to this, to make it a hard-and-fast rule, I'd assert, is a bit like demanding unity of time, place and action—a needless crimp in an author's style. More colorful verbs of speech carry a particular weight and no doubt should be used sparingly, but it's not necessary to cast them out entirely.

Deeds

So far, we have come up with 6 Ds useful in developing a character: *description, declaration, dressing, dialogue, demeanor, dramatics*. To these, let's add one more, perhaps the most important of all: *deeds*. As Ben Franklin put it: "Well done is better than well said." Again, as in daily life, more than what someone says, more than what we are told about her, more than how she dresses or what she drives, our ultimate judgment of her will be based on what she does. Or doesn't do. The character who talks big but whose acts never quite measure up is a fixture in Western literature, going at least as far back as the figure of Ajax in Homer's *Iliad*, the resident blowhard of the Greek Expeditionary Force. Too, acts often speak realities of which the actor is only vaguely aware. In Andrea Barrett's award-winning novella, *Ship Fever*, Lauchlin Grant decides to leave his comfortable if dull life as a Quebec physician to go to the immigrant quarantine station at Grosse Isle to care for the typhus-ridden Irish fleeing the potato famine. This admirable act, however, has as much to do with his desire to impress his now married childhood sweetheart, Susanna, as with his desire to help the sick. Though he himself cannot exactly admit it, we as readers can recognize that his motivations are at least as personal as they are humanitarian.

Elsewhere, we can see how one character's deeds, though they may run counter to the prevailing notions of morality (not only of society but of the character himself), nonetheless can raise him above all his fellows in the eyes of the reader. No better example of this can be found than Huckleberry Finn. By the standards of mid-nineteenth-century Hannibal, the orphaned and renegade Huck is bad news. But our response is entirely different. The boy who is willing to "go to hell" rather than betray or abandon his companion, the runaway slave, Jim, represents a heroic figure morally superior to those who embrace the prevailing standards of the day.

It all goes back, of course, to the adage that "actions speak louder than words." What your characters do will be the ultimate measure your readers use to determine who they are.

INSIDE

To this point, all the means of characterization I have discussed have been external and are, on some level, as available to practitioners of other arts as they are to a writer. The costuming in a film, the set design of a play, the mode in which a comic monologue is delivered, the actions a protagonist on screen undertakes all employ techniques already described. As I noted at the beginning of this chapter, however, writers have unique access into the minds of their characters. Joyce can tell us what Molly Bloom is thinking in *Ulysses* for page after page. However, a playwright—at least a conventional one—cannot have a character in monologue for five or ten minutes. Admittedly, some great dramatists, such as Beckett and O'Neill and George Bernard Shaw, undertake this, but other equally important ones, Tennessee Williams, Arthur Miller and Shakespeare, for that matter, don't even try. And in the end, the work of the latter is probably more popular and often produced than that of the former trio.

What you as fiction writer can do for your reader is give him access to your character's "secret life." E.M. Forster, in coining this term, restricts its meaning to "happiness and misery" that are never externalized, but I'm inclined (though Forster sees this as "vulgar") to take the broader view that the character's secret life is the sum of those things you communicate to readers that are not ever overtly communicated to other characters in your story.

Even this represents, frankly, a remarkable intimacy. We can know characters in a novel in a way we can never really know anyone. The depth of your insight into your characters will vary in accord with their importance in your story, of course, and also with the story itself. Nonetheless, in a novel, for example, your awareness of a number of your characters' interior lives—thoughts, emotions, pains, resentments, joys and so on—will not only be greater than that you have of your parents or siblings or children or the person there next to you in bed, but greater—or at least clearer—than your awareness of your own interior life.

A practical question is how that inner life, those conceivings and emotions, are transmitted. Probably the most famous technique is *stream of consciousness*, a kind of narrative in great vogue earlier in this century during the era of high Modernism, though now used much less frequently. In stream of consciousness, we literally "hear" what is going through the character's head, often without benefit of punctuation or logic. The "stream" is filled with the kinds of associative loops and swirls that frequently characterize thoughts, though these are usually edited out before we voice them. Stream of consciousness is often dreamlike, with the mind wandering between the conscious and the unconscious, negating time and distance. It is sometimes thought of (a bit confusingly) as preverbal, intended to tap into our most primitive selves. Here, for example, is a passage from what has come to be called "Benjy's Book" from Faulkner's *The Sound and the Fury*. Benjy is, literally, an "idiot" in the culture of Mississippi circa 1910, a severely retarded boy for whom all moments not immediately present blend together into a single, orderless "time before."

> "All right." Versh said. "I aint going out in that cold for no fun." He went on and we stopped in the hall and Caddy knelt and put her arms around me and her cold bright face against mine. She smelled like trees.
>
> "You're not a poor baby. Are you. You've got your Caddy. Haven't you got your Caddy."
>
> *Can't you shut up that moaning and slobbering, Luster said. Aint you shamed of yourself, making all this racket. We passed the carriage house, where the carriage was. It had a new wheel.*
>
> "Git in, now, and set still until your maw come." Dilsey said. She shoved me into the carriage. T.P. held the reins. "Clare I don't see how come Jason wont get a new surrey." Dilsey said. "This thing going to fall to pieces under you all some day. Look at them wheels."

Here, Benjy is recalling three separate incidents, but all, in his mind, seem to occur simultaneously, one bleeding into another bleeding into another. The sign of the distinct times is the difference in the black retainers—Versh, Luster, T.P. and Dilsey—who, throughout the text, somehow hold the crumbling Compson family together as they hold Benjy's fractured discourse together.

This is admittedly an extreme example of this technique, but in most all instances, stream of consciousness can prove challenging for the reader. Many times, to get into a character's thoughts, authors opt for a less extreme form of narration—*interior monologue*. This is where a character talks to himself, remembers a different moment, recalls a dream or conversation, but expresses himself in a somewhat more conventional manner. It features events, but also the character's comments upon and evaluations of the events. It is a product of consciousness as opposed to the unconscious.

In *The Sound and the Fury*, the first two sections of the novel, "Benjy's Book" and "Quentin's Book" (narrated by Benjy's eldest brother) are stream of consciousness narratives, while the third of four, "Jason's Book," is an interior monologue. You'll note the difference in the sound and structure of Jason's voice immediately.

> Once a bitch always a bitch, what I say. I says you're lucky if her playing out of school is all that worries you. I says she ought to be down there in that kitchen right now, instead of up there in her room, gobbing paint on her face and waiting for six niggers that can't even stand up out of a chair unless they've got a pan full of bread and meat to balance them, to fix breakfast for her. . . .

Stream of consciousness can be construed as a kind of subset of interior monologue, one that tries harder to recreate the actual, unedited mental process, though it often sacrifices clarity for the sake of psychic realism. Likewise, interior monologue itself is a variation on a very conventional narrative technique, which is simple reportage of the character's thoughts and emotions.

Using our own material, let's attempt to make a distinction among these three, starting with the most straightforward and ending with stream of consciousness. Let's imagine John in that car out in front of Marsha's house, his attempt to break things off in shambles.

> He sat in the car, stock still, unblinking. He thought about how he had failed, how from the moment the memory of Sally had returned, he should have known he could not go through with

it. A boxcutter would haunt him always, etch the limits of his actions, and in that instant, he had no idea what he would do.

There in the car. Still. Unblinking. Failure. Just a numbing sense of failure. And it's all Sally's fault. Sally and that damned boxcutter, there against her wrist. Sally. Marsha. Both the same. And would they all be from now on out? All the same over all the years? And nothing to be done. Not now. Not ever.

It's the car. In the car now. I fail, failed, will fail. Sally, Sally, what are you do— Honey. No. Put it down. Down! Don't be silly. Yes. I love you, Sally. Marsha. I love . . . love Marsha I want to say Sally . . . Marsha. I want. I mean. I can't. Will I ever ever?

As with so much else I've talked about, the choice among these three options is yours. None is inherently superior to the other two. They are expressing to the reader the same ideas and emotions but in different ways. The initial reportage is clearer, but may lack the immediacy and intensity that actually entering into John's head affords. You need to determine which seems, for your text, to best communicate who John is at story's end and what his emotions and mental state are.

In your delvings into your characters' minds, remember they are not omniscient and need not be either honest or, more charitably, entirely self-aware. As noted when I discussed the question of narrative stance, your literary creations, just like you and all us other poor creatures of clay, can be vain, deceptive, insecure, unhappy, bitter and the victims of forces and desires of which we are only vaguely conscious. Rodney, that "Momma's boy" you know, probably does not see himself as others see him. Dickens' broadly drawn Ebenezer Scrooge certainly does not recognize himself as a snarling, narrow, mean-hearted and self-centered skinflint until the visitations of Marley and the various Spirits of Christmas. Rather—and surely this was Dickens' point—he sees himself as an example of mid-nineteenth-century English capitalist virtue: thrifty, hard-working, confident in the ultimate justice of the world of which he is a part.

You, your reader and the character himself are the ones privy to the crabbed recesses of the latter's consciousness. But it is you—and through you, your reader—who has an awareness of that consciousness your very character may lack. Dostoevsky traces the gradual collapse of Raskolnikov's justifications for murder in *Crime and Punishment*, but we are aware of the depth of his self-deception long before he is. In our own tale of John and Marsha, if we work it right, the reader will intuit the likely failure of John's intentions before the actual event. There is, in the successful evocation of character, a kind of terrible voyeurism. Once again, the writer and reader collude, this time in the discovery of what the character himself is in the act of comprehending.

Employing a variety of the techniques I've discussed should allow you to create a viable figure around which your story can grow. Still, that final, literally "vital" element in characterization is one over which you have no control. As you describe and dress a character, comprehend his history and delve into his emotions, if he is finally to be successful, there will come a point in his creation when you can feel him move, when he begins to assume a reality separate from the mere construct you've been working on.

Among our ancestors, there was a moment in pregnancy that was referred to as "the quickening," the point at which the unborn child began to shift and kick of her own accord within the womb. If not quite so transcendent or miraculous, when you feel that character begin to kick, when you cannot write a particular incident in the story because the character won't let you, when you choke up at his downfall or smile at his delight, when you know that this character is someone who is not you and has acquired a reality beyond you, that is the moment you know you have succeeded.

EXERCISES

1. Write some character sketches. First, as suggested, deal with real people you know. Then, try doing the same with characters in a short story or novel you admire. Finally, take a couple of the characters you've invented in stories you've written and write their "case histories."

2. Do some field work. Visit a site you are unfamiliar with. Sit around for an hour or so and watch the comings and goings of those who frequent it. Then, go home and write character sketches of three

or four of the people you observed. Start a story involving at least two of them.

3. As an experiment, write a vignette in which *all* characterization is communicated via externals, employing the 7 Ds.

4. Undertake a short narrative in which the protagonist is largely characterized by his responses to other figures in the story.

5. Write a stream of consciousness monologue of a page or two. Then, recast the piece as an interior monologue and then as reportage.

EIGHT

THE CONTENT OF
YOUR CHARACTERS

Talking about methodologies of characterization, as I did in the last chapter, is relatively easy. But character as a topic is more complex and elusive. Plot we could consider from a variety of different and concrete angles. Character, on the other hand, is harder to conceive. "Building," perhaps, is more easily dealt with than "spirit."

In the next few pages, we'll approach character in broader and rather more abstract terms than we have so far. What are the different kinds of characters we create? How can they interact with one another, and how do we increase their resonance for the reader? What can a writer do to present characters who are, indeed, compelling, who will remain with her reader after the text has been put aside?

THE ICON
Once upon a time in fiction, the world seemed a somewhat easier place than it is now, and in some popular fiction, things haven't changed much. In that realm, humankind divides neatly into white hats and black hats, good and bad, virtuous and corrupt, saved and damned. Samuel Richardson's eighteenth-century heroines battled to keep their virginity against the assaults of various lechers in the same way that, in much contemporary romance, the protagonist must fight to maintain her virtue against a horde of seductive philanderers till she is finally rewarded with her true love. This characteristic dualism is certainly not limited to books directed at women. Many westerns and thrillers and war stories, much crime fiction as well, maintain a similarly Manichean view of things: good guys battle bad guys and usually (though not always) win.

The protagonists of such stories tend to be what I call *iconic*. These figures, in the end, evoke an image, not a person. Like the Orthodox icon, they can be dazzling, but they lack dimension. They have no depth. And literary characters, without the palpable substance of the beautiful object that is a painting in the tradition of the Eastern Church, are always in danger of vanishing behind a yet newer icon that better represents certain fleeting temporal realities, larger cultural notions of what it means to be feminine or brave or moral.

Take the example of Mickey Spillane's Mike Hammer (names mentioned before that may mean absolutely nothing to those of you born after 1960). This was the quintessential man's man of popular literature in the 1950s—a hard-drinking, crewcutted detective who took no guff, was quick with his fists and his gun and, where women were concerned, loved them and left them. By the mid-sixties, however, Hammer had been dethroned by James Bond, an altogether more suave and genial figure. He insisted his martinis be shaken not stirred, was outfitted with technical marvels far beyond a mere revolver and if he still loved and left, usually did so with an insouciant smile. Though Ian Fleming's hero still enjoys apparently endless filmic avatars, they tend toward the parodic, while the iconic status he enjoyed has been inherited by—whom? Given the demographics of the audience for such novels—men from their twenties into their forties—the answer may well be Tom Clancy's Jack Ryan. Not much of a drinker, middle-aged and *married*. With children!

See how the mighty are fallen!

Let's be frank. All writers, even the most self-consciously literary, dream of creating an iconic character who will assure us royalties in six or seven figures. The truth is, though, the icon is the product not of the author's will, but of history and social trends and the vagaries of public taste. There is no way to instruct anyone on how to put the next James Bond together. It is possible, though, to discuss some specific elements of characters who, in the end, move and inhabit us in a way the icon doesn't.

This is the key issue. A compelling character is one we *care* about, one with whom we connect on an emotional level more complex than we can with an icon. The latter tends merely to reaffirm certain conventional notions of whatever the character is intended to represent. As readers, we can collude only in a very limited way with Ian Fleming in the creation of James Bond because we have so little insight into 007's humanness. The counter to the figure of Bond in his heyday of the 1960s was perhaps John le Carré's Alex Lemas, "the spy who came in from the cold." Here was a man involved in espionage, a job dull and gray and dangerous, a man who drank too much and was liable to the temptations of desire and loneliness and love in a way that readers who had never set foot out of Oswego, much less penetrated the Iron Curtain, could comprehend and identify with. His grim fate serves as a reminder of the real, human cost of the Cold War.

In sum, what we should concentrate on is not making characters who infiltrate a mass consciousness only to be replaced by another figure in one year or three years or five. Rather, we should strive to create those who infiltrate individual consciousnesses, one by one by one, and remain there, a living part of a lived life.

THE GEOMETRY OF CHARACTERS

What makes a character particularly interesting, one who remains with the reader after the story is over and done with? E.M. Forster, whose *Aspects of the Novel* we've invoked before, suggests that there are two kinds of characters: *rounded* and *flat*. To these, I'm inclined to add a third, intermediate category, which I'll call *angled*. This is not, as you'll see, merely so I can invent yet another mnemonic device (RAF, like the Royal Air Force), but because there really does seem to be a need for it.

Flat Characters

A *flat* character, in Forster's scheme, is one who represents a single idea or quality. He is consistent, and hence, static. Obviously, merely functional characters in a story are flat—the kids rollerblading past John as he sits in his car, the checker at the grocery store who tells Phil's Gloria to "have a nice day." Likewise, stock or stereotypical characters are flat: the tart-tongued drag queen, the kvetching mother-in-law, the office Lothario are one-dimensional creations predictable in their actions and reactions. This is not to say, incidentally, that they are bad or unsuccessful or unimportant or forgettable. Dickens' novels, for example, brim with great, flat characters like Uriah Heep or Bob Crachit, and the theater is filled with them: Richard Sheridan's Mrs. Malaprop in *The Rivals*; Oscar Wilde's Lady Bracknell in *The*

Importance of Being Earnest. Such figures embody a concept, or they are possessed of particular quirks or characteristics that overwhelm all other elements of their personalities. Lady Bracknell is the personification of the popular view of aristocratic artifice at the turn of the century, Queen Victoria "not being amused." Mrs. Malaprop is the sum and substance of her problems with the English language, the source of our word *malapropism.* In our own invented canon, Sally, John's ex-girlfriend, is overtly and intentionally flat. Her function in the story is certainly significant, but she is meant specifically to give shape and form to the image of the spurned and suicidal lover. A great deal of humorous writing depends upon readily identifiable types who can fill particular roles within comic conventions. A satirical novel such as Tom Wolfe's *The Bonfire of the Vanities*—with its sharky, stockbroking "masters of the universe," self-serving public servants and so on—trades heavily upon these kinds of figures.

Beyond this, a great deal of the literature, broadly speaking, that we consume day to day is populated by flat characters. Television serials, action films, many popular novels feature supporting casts made up of flat characters, and their protagonists are comparatively flat as well. The unflappable Joe Friday or the invincible John Rambo motor along through their stories as reliably as well-tuned Chevrolets. These are those iconic figures just discussed. They stand for truth, justice and the American way and suffer nary a shade of self-doubt. They are comforting: stolid and predictable and constant. They are also fantasy figures—fun to cheer for—but creatures of a world very different from the one we inhabit.

Angled Characters

My new category, *angled*, describes a character who, if not fully drawn, nonetheless manifests a complexity of personality her flat counterpart does not. In stories, in particular, it seems to me there are often figures of this type. A novel allows the space for the elaborate development of a range of characters beyond its protagonist. Indeed, a novel may have multiple protagonists. In the works of writers like James or Faulkner, critics can make a case for any one of a number of figures as absolutely central to the fiction. Is *Light in August* Joe Christmas' story or Joanna Burden's or Gail Hightower's or Lena Grove's? All of them, in Faulkner's baroque plot, are indispensable.

The story, though, usually offers space to fully explore only one or two figures. Nonetheless, there are others—usually the major secondary characters—who demonstrate more than mere stock responses to the protagonist or have an impact upon her greater than a mere stock character. In Hemingway's "The Light of the World," Alice, the whore with the sweet voice, has a presence the other prostitutes in the railroad station do not. She has a past (even if her memories of it are questionable); she reaches out to and moves the narrator in a way the others fail to. Presumably, in Gloria's story, though she would be the character we truly "know," both her late husband, Mikey, and their old friend, Tom Frankel, would make an impression upon us, have a specific life within our imaginations that a flat character would not. DeWayne's friend Louis would have to be angled for that story to be successful. Though probably not as complex and solid as Patrice or DeWayne, he would need to have some kind of faceted personality. As noted in chapter five, if DeWayne's struggle of conscience is to have meaning for him and for us, the representatives of both of his alternatives have to have sufficient substance to make the positions they embody seem attractive and reasonable. We perhaps need a clue as to why Louis is such a cheerleader for DeWayne's bedding of Darlene. Has he gotten a girl pregnant in the past? Is he shy around women, and so a vicarious romancer?

Rounded Characters

Forster's final category is a *rounded* character. This, of course, is one with a *complete* personality, one able, as it were, to hold two contradictory opinions at the same time. Rounded characters have the richness of real people. They present a range of emotions and represent a range of ideas. Our Marsha, for example, is both vulnerable and assertive; DeWayne is both lusty and love-struck.

For Forster, the key to a rounded character was that he was "capable of surprising us in a convincing way." This ability to do something unexpected that is nonetheless consonant with what we have seen of someone is not always easy for the writer to bring off. Think of it in terms of a logical extension of a character's established behavior, though one that the reader would not particularly anticipate.

For example, a few years ago, a student in an advanced workshop was deep into an elaborate fantasy novel. The world he created was populated by three different species of beings: a dwarfish, agrarian race; muscle-bound, nomadic warriors; and ethereal, forest-dwelling magicians. The three are forced to cooperate due to the appearance of a horde of demonic invaders. As we discussed the draft of the novel—one quite competently and suspensefully written—the most significant objection seemed to be that each of the three races comported itself in precisely the way we would anticipate, in a way we had seen before in other fantasy stories.

The audience reviewed the text and began to search for ways we could be surprised. What if, someone suggested, the warrior race were homosexual? Look at the way they care for their wounded, look at the dynamics of their ritual mock battles, look at their absolute lionization of all things masculine. Think of the Thracian Band, somebody said, the army of lovers in ancient Greece. Think of all the displaced eroticism in fraternity initiations, the military, sports, others suggested. The point was that we would not *predict* the warriors would be homosexual, but that when they ultimately engaged in homosexual acts, our surprise would be accompanied by a whispered, "Of course."

The same held true when we discussed the forest-dwellers, so intimately in touch with nature, so in tune with seasonal change, so conscious of the interrelation of all things animate and inanimate—spiritual, mystical, magical. How did the workshop suspect they might surprise us? Human sacrifice. Cannibalism.

How on earth! you might say, but again, one can connect their oneness with all that surrounds them, their emphasis on life's continuity in all things, their sense of themselves as part of larger cycles, to ancient mystery cults that indulged in precisely the kind of acts we would now think of as unspeakable. Likewise, of course, it gave these mythical ecologists a certain, spectacular otherness, just in case we might confuse them with a band of latter-day hippies inexplicably transported from northern Marin County to a planet with two suns.

On a more earthbound level, let's consider our Patrice. Here is a woman who has always deferred to men and has been ill-used in love. When she swears at her brother for his designs on Darlene, he and we are surprised. But her vehemence arises logically from her character and experience. She can put herself in the place of Darlene, see the potential for her brother's girlfriend finding herself in a situation not unlike the one Patrice found herself in with Luther. The fact that

DeWayne may play a part similar to that of her own inconstant lover pushes her to act in a way that is not like her everyday self, but is a reasonable manifestation of her own hurt, her determination to prevent someone else from being hurt as she has been, *and*, finally, an expression of her love for DeWayne.

To use a critical commonplace, what Patrice does is "violate our expectations," while not violating the character she is. Obviously, were she to pull out an Uzi and obliterate Louis and the whole garage crew, we'd have more than a little trouble accepting her actions. A reader likes, however, to discover layers in a character, strengths and weaknesses. A degree of complexity and contradiction invites a reader's engagement: It implies a lack of certitude within the character herself, a nuance and fluidity that we recognize as human and that allows us to identify with her in a way we cannot with flat characters, and to a greater and deeper extent than we can with angled characters. Holden Caulfield's obnoxiousness and adolescent posturing give shape and substance to his final youthful vulnerability and thus provide him a poignancy that, arguably, few of his nineteenth-century counterparts (Huck being the obvious exception) ever attain. One can go overboard on this, inventing those who are such an amalgamation of quirks and complexes and neuroses and types and troubles they merely confuse us. Yet, it is generally true that, the more rounded a character, the more shaded his personality, the more easily the reader sympathizes with him.

This identification goes beyond just rooting for the hero, beyond something that will last just as long as it takes for another book to be opened and another hero to make his appearance. Too, it should not be seen merely as our finding our own persona within a particular story. This is not about middle-aged men finding middle-aged male characters whose quandaries they can parallel to their own. Rather, this is a deeper, human level of identification, in which the character's doubleness and doubt remind us of our own, even if the particulars of the situation are ones we ourselves have never felt or confronted. Japanese teenage girls, it turns out, find the swoony despair of impossible love in the experiences of Edmund White's gay teenager in *A Boy's Own Story*. Our middle-aged man can encounter in Faulkner's Dilsey—the African-American domestic servant of radically segregated Mississippi—a strength and endurance that evokes his admiration and empathy.

THE COMMUNITY OF CHARACTERS

In most all stories you write, you will employ all three types of characters, and, indeed, almost have to. Characters, like their human counterparts, generally live in communities, and just as we come to know and understand those around us by watching them in social interaction, we come to know and understand the figures in our tales by watching them deal with one another. We are more likely to accept the notion that Louis is an old and true friend of DeWayne's if we actually see some example of this rather than if we are merely told it. At the same time, though, remember that in any community we have a deeper knowledge of some members than of others. All your figures cannot be of equal valence. They cannot all be rounded and memorable. Interesting as Jordan Baker or Tom Buchanan may be in *The Great Gatsby*, these angled characters can take up only a limited amount of space in a novel whose focus lies elsewhere. Recall the earlier warnings about character clutter, getting too many people on stage, spending too much time trying to provide space for each of them. But as in the other arts, you need that supporting cast to foreground those figures about whom you expect your audience to truly care.

Interaction among characters can take a variety of forms, and different kinds of interaction are often present within the same story and often evolve throughout a story. The kind that comes to mind most easily is the *combative* relationship, the traditional face-off between protagonist and antagonist. These are inherently dramatic, though they can invite simplification that leads to two flat figures—the true-blue hero and the moustache-twirling villain—pounding on each other with the outcome of the combat never in doubt. These kinds of interactions can be a lot of fun, but often don't stick with us over time. You ought to see if this is a pattern in your stories, in which case you might consider "rounding" your protagonist or "angling" your antagonist a bit.

In giving your antagonist a deeper personality or discovering further complexities in your protagonist, their relationship may move toward one that is more *conflictive*, one more fraught with ambiguity and uncertainty. I have already talked about how conflict is at the center of many plots, and the representation of the central conflict in complex characters pulls a reader more profoundly into a story. This holds true even in what we might think of as genre fiction. Are your policeman hero's motives in confronting his cop-killing nemesis, for example, purely selfless? Or are they overdetermined by something in his own past—a desire to prove his own bravery or some old sibling rivalry or the memory of a past assault? Is his determination tainted by some racial or ethnic fury? Likewise, does that villain who blew away a man in blue have at least some reason to fear or hate the police?

This kind of interaction may be more powerful for us because in our real lives, we are much more likely to be in conflict rather than combat with those around us. At school, at work, especially within the family, the collision of different roles and worldviews places us in situations where we try to fight for our own particular positions without slaughtering our opponents. Stories of parents and children almost inevitably partake of this kind of interaction, crackling with the ambivalences running through such relationships. Certainly, in the example in chapter five, we can see how Thomas Wolfe's Eugene Gant is at odds with his entire family, most especially his mother, but at the same time he obviously loves them all fiercely.

Another useful strategy within a story is the use of *contrasting* characters. This often involves a major secondary figure whose role, at least in part, is to ultimately point up the significance for good or ill of the protagonist and his actions. In comedy, this is traditionally the straight man; in more serious fiction, the foil. A classic if controversial example of this in American literature is Tom Sawyer's appearance at the end of *Huckleberry Finn*. Many critics have lambasted Twain about the concluding episodes of his novel, which seem to descend into a kind of racist slapstick. A second look, however, may incline the reader to see Twain emphasizing the moral difference, and moral superiority, of his orphaned outsider over the ultimately conventional Tom. Tom is not wicked, but the contrast between his fantasies and pretense and the real and serious choices that Huck has made in his travels with Jim represent in human terms the grand significance and also the possible transience of Huck's rebellion against the "sivilization" Tom ultimately embodies, a civilization that embraces the concrete evil of slavery and has been shown again and again to be mean-spirited and corrupt.

My list could go on indefinitely. *Complementary* characters, for example, often prove useful, as in Alcott's *Little Women*. Even if the author herself is overtly partial to Jo, the four sisters represent four distinct approaches to womanhood, each legitimate but replete with its own problems and limitations. This is, likely, one of the strongest reasons for the novel's continued life, for different readers can find different entrances into the world of the book through any one of the March girls. The point is that characters can interact in as many ways as real people can. Again, it may prove useful to go through your own work and see if your created individuals, though they differ from one another, *relate* to one another in virtually identical ways. If that is the case, you may want to try varying this particular element in your work. In the face of some adversity, are your groups of friends always complementary? A little conflictive tension among them might liven up the proceedings a bit. If you always write about siblings butting heads with one another, perhaps it's time to try a story in which they are possessed of an almost incestuous solidarity. The permutations of human interaction are theoretically limitless, if not in their general outlines, in their idiosyncratic particulars. Nuancing your characters' relationships is yet another means by which your reader may be pleasantly surprised in your story.

FLAWS

The idea of the flawed character, an imperfect one, is very old, arising in part from our religious traditions. Humankind is, after all, "fallen," degraded, conceived in sin and incapable of perfection. Even in the Old Testament, such a magnificent figure as King David lusts after Bathsheba, arranges for the death of her husband, Uriah the Hittite, and must suffer the loss of his baby son and heir as punishment. Saint Peter, the "Rock" upon which Christianity was built, three times denies Jesus. Lucifer himself was God's favorite, the most beautiful of the angels, but was brought low by his pride.

Indeed, the tragic flaw has become something of a cliché. We are accustomed to the old saws that Othello is destroyed by his jealousy; Macbeth, by his ambition; and so on. Do remember, though, that all these great creations are rather more than a walking marker for a particular human failing. Othello is a great military leader and an apparently irresistible lover. He is a good friend; indeed, a far too trusting one. He is also an outsider. The Venetians are only too happy to take advantage of his prowess in battle, but he remains a "sooty Moor," someone who engages our sympathy precisely because he is held in suspicion by the very people who exploit his talents. One of the reasons he is so vulnerable to Iago's nefarious plotting is because he understands his ambiguous position in Venice itself.

A figure who is all strength, all beauty, all wisdom is, in the end, a god, not a man. That our heroes are also possessed of feet of clay brings them closer to us. If in our projected story we assume that DeWayne decides not to take advantage of Darlene, we should nonetheless see the struggle he goes through to put his love for her before his lust for her. We should feel how tempting her potential seduction is for him. In the end, "doing the right thing" is not very interesting if we are certain from the very first that the character is going to make the "right" choice.

Stainless virtue is pretty dull, though remember as well that if it is carried too far, it can be an intriguing and sometimes destructive vice. Marlowe's Dr. Faustus, "once admired / For wondrous knowledge in our German schools," comes to a hellish end for trying to "practice more than heavenly power permits." This can also work on a more mundane level. John's compassion for Sally is a sign of a caring and concerned human being. That this leads him, years later, to sustain a relationship he wishes to break off is a less than desirable consequence of apparently admirable emotions.

Just as the protagonist of a story engages us more profoundly if he manifests particular human failings, the antagonist of a story is generally more memorable if he is something more complex than a monster of evil. The sly and sinister Fagin in Dickens' *Oliver Twist* sticks with us longer than the novel's rather insipid child hero, and I doubt that most people can name any character from Shakespeare's *The Merchant of Venice* other than its apparent villain, Shylock. In both these instances, the authors take pains to give these figures a touch of dignity, a dash of wit or a streak of unalloyed emotion that allow us some sympathy for them. The single most realized chapter in the Dickens story may well be "Fagin's Last Night Alive," which captures with tremendous intensity the terror of a man the night before he will be hanged. Shylock's grisly demands for his "pound of flesh" are made comprehensible if not justifiable by his own isolation and mistreatment within the Renaissance world.

These days, the lines between hero and villain in literature have grown even less distinct. We have moved away from the rigid codes of behavior that at least theoretically governed people's lives and reactions to particular circumstances one or two hundred years ago. In the novel of the nineteenth century, it was a pretty sure bet a "fallen woman" would come to a bad end. *Oliver Twist*'s Nancy, who attempts to act virtuously in foiling Fagin's burglary plans, dies at the hands of Bill Sykes. Dickens' public anticipated an affirmation of the notion that a young woman's sexual promiscuity would inevitably lead to dire consequences, even if the character attempted to redeem herself.

Compare this to the endless stream of good-hearted prostitutes in twentieth-century novels, or, indeed, to the far vaster number of sexually active women in fiction of the last forty years. You can see how our vision has changed. Certainly, Patrice, possibly pregnant by Luther, is intended to engage our reader's sympathy rather than invite his judgment. The same holds true for Marsha, who, though it is at best only implied in our story, most of us will simply assume in this day and age is sleeping with John.

The social sciences have made us ever more aware of how complex the human animal can be and reminded us that people are odd amalgamations of good and bad. Satisfying though the old-fashioned shoot-'em-up is, gratified though we may feel when the obscenely violent drug lord meets an obscenely gruesome end or the spunky young peasant lass turns out to be a noble lady who can marry the prince, in the back of any reader's mind is a realization that life is not and generally has never been that simple. Life, as most of us know it anyway, is full of contradictions and compromises and complexities that often reduce everything to varying shades of gray. Most individuals we come in contact with—those we like and those we don't—are neither saints nor sinners, but a messy combination of the two. Mother Teresa doubtless lost her temper from time to time, and Mafia dons are capable of peculiar generosity. Human beings, in all but the most extreme of instances, are inconsistent, bundles of selflessness and selfishness whose responses may be viewed as probabilities rather than as certainties.

Ironically, it's often easier to successfully humanize a villain than sully a hero. Evil seems to fascinate us in a way good does not. The German philosopher Hans Jonas went so far as to say that wickedness is "more direct, more *compelling* [emphasis added], less given to differences of opinion" than virtue. Hence, a dash of sentiment or a flicker of wit, when added to our natural interest in a villain, can draw us into his spell. In our era in which everybody, one way or another, seems to be a "victim," childhood trauma or some terrible turn of fate can incline an audience to symphathize with or at least try to understand the most heinous figures. I was quite surprised, a few years ago, to find a student audience defending the actions of my character Jay Skikey in *The Professor of Aesthetics*. Here I thought I had created a real monster of depravity, a man of motiveless malevolence. These readers, however, argued that the horrors of his boyhood and youth made his sadism, if not justifiable, at least comprehensible.

This does not mean that, to give your protagonist a fighting chance against such a villain, she has to be a child molester, alcoholic or adulterous. It implies, however, that she ought to be possessed of some characteristics that do not necessarily jibe with our ideas of virtue. She may be intemperate, self-serving, unscrupulous—somehow ambiguous, capable of being wrong. This is not a wildly new idea. Many of the great nineteenth-century "novels of manners," such as those of Jane Austen or William Makepeace Thackeray, employ in very general terms the kinds of plots we associate with the contemporary romance genre, but avoid hackneyed development by creating protagonists who are profoundly flawed. Austen's matchmaking Emma is shortsighted, snobbish and meddlesome. Thackeray's Becky Sharp, in *Vanity Fair* (tellingly subtitled *A Novel Without a Hero*), is a traditional "poor girl on the make" of staggering ruthlessness. Even such an apparently iconic character as Sherlock Holmes becomes more than that due to his mysterious idiosyncrasies: his violin playing, his use of cocaine, the shadow of melancholia that haunts him always. This added richness makes the grand master of deduction more than an automaton, gives him a vulnerability we would not anticipate and affirms his final human frailty, despite all his uncanny intellectual power.

GROWTH AND REVELATION

If we can no longer assume our protagonist will be a portrait of un-besmirchable goodness nor our villain a dark-hearted bounder, how can we and our readers tell one from the other? The answer may lie in another historical shift of attitude that has been underway for the last few centuries and has accelerated in our own day. I suspect what we look for most consistently in the modern hero is *growth*. Protagonists grow; antagonists don't. If, on the one hand, we've come to think of ourselves as the sum of our instincts and experiences and neuroses, we also live in an age, especially in this country, where we anticipate that people are able to change: We can quit smoking, lose weight, get a better job, achieve happiness. Interestingly, this really isn't so different from the age-old concept of redemption. However, in our time, it is not the salvation of our immortal soul that intrigues us, but the capacity for the individual to learn and so achieve greater consciousness, even if the character herself does not recognize this has occurred.

James Leo Herlihy's Joe Buck, after Ratso Rizzo's death in *Midnight Cowboy*, is "scared to death." Yet, the gloom of this conclusion is ameliorated somewhat, for us if not for him, by the realization that the Joe we leave is not the callow and self-centered Texas stud we met in the first chapter, but rather a figure who has known love, made sacrifices, acquired a new and more profound knowledge of the world that may lead him to a greater knowledge of his own self. This is not unlike what we may hope for our character John. The ending of our little tale is pretty bleak, but in recognizing consciously the source of his inability to act, John has come to a point where, in the future, he may be able to act differently.

So, how do we show characters growing? The most primitive method is the "life-changing event." The heart of the ill-tempered spinster is melted by the plight of the orphan. The whiner and gold-brick distinguishes himself in battle when his buddies are placed in real danger. The earthquake/hurricane/tornado/plane crash/ship-wreck brings out the true heroism and goodness of a cast of conniv-ers/adulterers/thieves/con men/snobs. Before you laugh, remember these last examples, if a bit overboard, have provided the grist for an endless stream of popular novels for the last fifty years.

Certainly, such events *do* occur. A bitter family dispute, a brush with death, the birth of a child can alter an individual's entire view of the world and the way he comports himself in it. In literature, Scrooge is simply the most famous example of a character who suddenly sees the light, while the action of such recent best-sellers as Jacquelyn Mitchard's *The Deep End of the Ocean* finds its engine in the changes wrought in a woman's life upon the sudden disappearance of one of her children.

Nonetheless, most growth and change come about in a more gradual way, and their manifestations are more subtle. There is a *process* involved. To recognize that process, of course, we may have to know something about not only who a character is but where he's coming from. Some years back, I read a student novel involving a young American working in the go-go financial world of 1980s Tokyo. The protagonist and his experience were winningly evoked, and yet, there was something dissatisfying about the book. What the author and I concluded was that, in order for his character to engage us, we had to know a great deal more about who he had been *before* he went to Japan. His actions there and even why he was there in the first place remained obscure.

After a couple years of rewriting, John Burnham Schwartz's *Bicycle Days* was published, with chapters set in the present interspersed with those that provided a picture of his protagonist's childhood and youth. As a consequence, we could see what Japan represented to this particular character, how its foreignness and ritual provided a kind of comfort for him and a page upon which to write himself anew. Without such background, his motivations were often obscure; with it, he emerges as both a powerful and sometimes contradictory figure and one with whom those who will never have the chance to live in Japan or anywhere else so exotic can nonetheless identify.

Schwartz's book, from the beginning, was a bildungsroman—that "novel of growing up" I mentioned early on. What he did was make his hero's maturation more complex and meaningful to us by including action from before the life-changing experience of his move to Japan. A traditional bildungsroman, of course, implies growth in the most literal sense, but this process manifests itself without the author presenting a character's entire life. In my comic novel, *The Book of Marvels,* though details of the heroine's background are larded into the text, most of the action occurs in a single, drought-ridden summer. The sheltered and conventionally religious Lila Mae, recently divorced, is forced to find a job and ends up on the staff of the Quiet Meadows Convalescent Hospital. In caring for her quirky and demanding patients, she works beside an assortment of people of whose lives she sincerely disapproves. Over the course of the book, and over the course of dealing with those facing death itself, Lila Mae discovers that the rigid nostrums she grew up with and that she imbibes week to week on her favorite religious programs are less and less relevant to her. Her doubting-Thomas patient, Mr. Ricks, challenges her to embrace life to the fullest; her sexually active and in some cases homosexual co-workers demonstrate a kind of hands-on devotion and sacrifice the sanctimonious TV preachers seem to lack. Her romantic inclinations toward Wellesley Coe—her imperfect but sincere and tireless suitor who works at Midas Muffler—grow stronger despite Lila Mae's efforts to dismiss his intentions as mere temptations of the flesh.

Lila Mae does not achieve her new understanding of the world in one fell swoop. It comes to her in fits and starts, climaxing only when the televangelist to whom she has been most devoted is revealed as a charlatan. Just as conflict and tension are most effective when modulated, so the development of a character is more interesting (and more realistic) if her growth does not trace a straight and unbroken line toward new awareness.

One way to put over this process is in scenes that *echo* earlier ones. Various times in *The Book of Marvels*, we see Lila Mae before the television with its "inspirational" programming and can recognize in these instances a pattern of increasing skepticism. Her relationships with certain patients and the other aides and orderlies at the hospital shift slowly from self-righteous superiority toward comprehension and sympathy as they reach out to her in attempts to rescue her from the romantic, spiritual and moral muddles in which she finds herself. In the end, Lila Mae does not lose her faith. Rather, it evolves into a more forgiving, more accepting, more humane one that allows her to participate in a more complex and richer world. Her growth as a character occurs as a consequence of her experience.

This final result of growth is related to a concept that James Joyce called epiphany, a moment when "the commonest object . . . seems to us radiant," one that, when experienced, reveals the essence of that moment and, hence, allows he who observes it to view the world through different eyes. To avoid limiting ourselves only to Joyce's terms, let's adopt a more general if equally charged word, *revelation*. In modern fiction, in a very general way, the characters who are most memorable and remain with us most strongly are those who—as a consequence of struggle and experience—attain a new consciousness, a greater wisdom.

This often means they are possessed from the outset by a certain otherness, a sense of their own differences from those around them, some element that sets them apart. It is in the working through of that otherness that they achieve their revelation. This quality can be something as dramatic as the "black Jewish Lesbian," whom comedians are fond of using as the prototype of contemporary diversity, who over time finds her place in the world. However, it can also be something as quiet as our Gloria's widowhood and her own unrecognized yearning that lead her to decide to repaint that kitchen: the subtle sign of her own revised understanding of who she is and what she needs.

Broadly, what this indicates in a character is *integration*; the otherness has been dealt with and become a part of the whole of the individual in question. Contradictions within the protagonists may not have disappeared, but they have reached a balance, and the conflict within the character is resolved. You could argue that traditional villains don't grow, that they are, by definition, integrated personalities, even if this means they are thoroughly wicked. Protagonists are, initially, unintegrated, and what interests us in them is their movement toward wholeness.

Such movement is not always successful. Its consequences are not always desirable ones. The last of García Márquez's Buendía clan realizes in the midst of the apocalypse of Macondo that "races granted one hundred years of solitude do not receive a second opportunity in this world." Even comedies often conclude on a rueful or tentative note. Part and parcel of Lila Mae's serenity at the end of *The Book of Marvels* is a realization that the world is often chaotic and that "you could make terrible, terrible mistakes, ones you could not correct, ones that . . . you would always regret."

In Fitzgerald's *The Great Gatsby*, we can see growth, lack of growth and growth that does *not* lead to revelation. Tom and Daisy do not change at all. They are, finally, villains in the piece. Gatsby himself has grown, but his desire is focused on an unworthy or impossible object, and his life ends violently. Only Nick moves to a new consciousness, a new awareness, though the larger revelation he achieves is of an America whose essence is very close to tragic.

Knowledge, so the commonplace tells us, is power. It is not, however, a guarantor of happiness.

EXERCISES

1. Compose a comic scene that involves at least three flat "stock" characters.

2. Go back to one of your completed stories. Try to identify which characters are flat, angled and rounded. Experiment with altering their "geometries": that is, rework one of the flat characters as more angled and vice versa.

3. Choose a flat or angled character from one of your completed pieces and write a sketch of him as a rounded character.

4. Consider your characters' relationships according to some of the criteria I've mentioned (e.g., combative, contrasting, etc.). Are they somewhat repetitive from piece to piece? Try writing a story that involves a kind of interaction that is different from the ones you've identified in your work so far.

5. Make a list of the protagonists you've created over the last couple years and of their particular traits. How do they resemble and differ from each other, or do they? Do the same with your antagonists. Try writing a story in which your protagonist manifests some of the qualities you've identified in your villains, and an antagonist who manifests some of the qualities of your heroes.

6. In your fictions, do your protagonists achieve some kind of revelation? What are these? Again, is the revelation always the same? How might these be altered?

AFTERWORD

So I've come to the end, and I've barely scratched the surface. There is so much more to be said, so much else to impart, suggest, endorse and warn against. As I noted at the outset, for each example given, there is probably an opposite and equal example. For each assurance, there is one just as legitimate that absolutely contradicts it.

Still, I hope what you have read has been useful. You'll note that, throughout my discussions of a variety of topics, whether talking about language or characterization, certain terms keep cropping up: *otherness, surprise, complexity, appropriateness* and so on. This should not surprise us in our quest to make our fiction more compelling, for it points toward the notion of our stories as a unified whole. The questions we can ask ourselves about the way our plot develops are not all that unlike those we ask about the growth of our characters. Is the line of action—or that movement toward revelation—too straight and unbroken? Is the unexpected but logical shift in our protagonist's attitude paralleled in an unexpected but logical shift in the language she employs?

In the end, few activities are as personal, as idiosyncratic, as artistic creation. Prayer, dreams, what you like to do in bed—these sorts of things come closest. Fiction is not an occupation for the faint of heart, nor for the smug. It is a calling that, in its very essence, implies an investment of self few other endeavors demand.

That word *calling* is not accidental here. Again and again, I have employed a rhetoric that comes from life's most transcendent and miraculous elements—sex and birth and faith and so on. In the present critical climate, this may seem pretentious or merely silly, a holdover from those concepts of art's sacredness as conceived by the Romantics of the nineteenth century. Yet, I continue to believe that most people who undertake the task do approach it with that kind of sincerity and devotion. Fiction is not, as Fanny Brice would put it, chopped liver. Even in a world in which we cannot predict how technology will alter storytelling as we have known it for the last three or more hundred years, those of us who write do feel that what we have to say and how we say it will make some difference, will, at least on some personal level, give joy or consolation or illumination to someone we have never met. At best, it might motivate that note from Oshkosh or Amarillo I spoke of in the prologue, that concrete sign of your connections with your audience.

There are still readers out there willing to collude, willing to be your coconspirators. And you should be one with your fellow writers. We need books to turn us every which way but loose, and then turn us loose as well. We want to be told about ourselves and others, our world and ones we'll never know. Through fiction, we want to be the millionaire, the criminal, the teenager, the widower, the gender we are not. We want to comprehend DeWayne and John and Gloria. We want to see the world through different eyes, feel emotions we have only imagined, understand the human animal in a way we have not before.

One final thought: Writing is a lonely business. When all is said and done, as you go about your work, it is you alone at your keyboard, you and your ghosts. But these shadows of your imagination can give you comfort, and with luck they will guide you through the complexities of plot and language and characterization to the ending, the right ending, for your story. And that ending will be your story's beginning. Not of its creation, but of its own life.

I often describe the climactic scene of the Spanish novel *Niebla*—"*Mist*"—by Miguel de Unamuno. In the story, the protagonist, Agustín, is contemplating suicide. Before he makes a decision, however, he decides to consult the great philosophy professor at the University of Salamanca, who, as it happens, is the self-same Unamuno. So the author confronts his unwitting character and finally can contain himself no longer. He tells Agustín that he will, indeed, kill himself, that the choice has already been made. Unamuno invokes those godlike powers of the writer I have mentioned so many times. He has decided. His character is doomed.

Agustín, needless to say, is devastated by the news—not only that his suicide is a given, but that he himself is simply a figment of Unamuno's imagination. The writer is touched and saddened by the young man's despair. But then, rather suddenly, Agustín recovers himself. It may be true, he says, it may be inevitable that soon he will end his life. But he is a character in a book. Every time somebody picks up that book and reads it, that character will live again. But when Unamuno dies, Augustín reminds the author, "you will die forever."

We write for many reasons—for the pleasure of creation, for the hope of communicating some emotion or truth to our fellows, because we "can't not write," because we want to be rich and famous and so afford that beach house on Maui. Finally, though, we write as a defense against the void, against the unknown that is the other side of death. Writing—any kind of creation—represents a stab at immortality. For most of us, it doesn't work. But it is worth a try.

Now it's your turn.

ABOUT THE AUTHOR

Christopher T. Leland is the author of five novels: *Letting Loose* (Zoland Books, 1997), *The Professor of Aesthetics* (Zoland Books, 1994), *The Book of Marvels* (Scribners, 1990), *Mrs. Randall* (Houghton Mifflin, 1987) and *Mean Time* (Random House, 1982), which was a finalist in the Hemingway Prize competition for best first novel. He has taught at Harvard University, Bennington College, Pomona College and the University of California, San Diego. Leland lives in Detroit, where he is professor of English and head of the creative writing section of the department of English at Wayne State University.

INDEX

Emma, 197
Ending. *See* Conclusion
English
  difficulties with, 60-61
  history of, 61-63
Escape, reading as form of, 7-8
Ethan Frome, 143-144, 160
Every Man for Himself, 50, 130-131
Expecting Someone Taller, 45
Experience
  achieving distance from, before
    writing about, 36-37
  other people's, as source for
    material, 39-40

Fact, vs. fiction, 105-106
Fairy tales, as source for material, 43
Fantasy, 10
Faulkner, William, 40, 44, 53, 65-66,
  90, 127, 180
Faust, 49
Fiction
  adolescent, 5
  escapist, 7-8
  historical, 9, 50-52
  nineteenth century vs. twentieth
    century, 145
  of otherness, 8-11
  vs. fact, 105-106
  See also Fantasy, Horror story,
    Science fiction
Finger, Anne, 143-145
First-person narrator, 112-114
First-person plural narrator, 115
Fitzgerald, F. Scott, 113, 139-140,
  201-202
5 Cs, of plotting, 120-139
Flashback, 154-158
  defined, 155
Flat characters, 187-188
Flaws, in characters, 194-197
Fleming, Ian, 130, 186-187

Focus
  establishing, in beginning, 90-93
  through narrator, 106-108
Folk tales, as source for material, 43
Foreshadowing, 131
Form, and function, 147-149
Forster, E.M., 97, 187
Frame narrative, 159-161
Fuentes, Carlos, 115

García Márquez, Gabriel, 91-92, 131
Gardner, John, 44
Goals, setting, as writer, 25-26
Going After Cacciato, 34
Gordimer, Nadine, 34-35
Grapes of Wrath, The, 73
Gravity's Rainbow, 91-92
Greasy Lake, 67
Great Expectations, 138
Great Gatsby, The, 113, 125, 139-140,
  201-202
Grendel, 44
"Gryphon," 38-39
Guns of August, The, 50

Hamlet, 41, 135-136
Hamlet, The, 90
Hammer, Mike, as icon, 186
"Hell-Bent Men and Their
  Cities," 76
Hemingway, Ernest, 38, 65, 171,
  178, 189
Herlihy, James Leo, 79-80, 198
"Highlights," 74
Historical fiction, 9
History, as source for fiction, 50-52
Holmes, Sherlock, 197
  series, 130
Holt, Tom, 45
Horror story, 8

"I Stand Here Ironing," 146
Icons, characters as, 185-187
Imagining Argentina, 53